ONE WEEK LOAN

D1341266

Gayatri Spivak

Ethics, Subalternity and
the Critique of Postcolonial Reason

Stephen Morton

polity

First published in 2007 by Polity Press

Polity Press
65 Bridge Street
Cambridge CB2 1UR, UK

Polity Press
350 Main Street
Malden, MA 02148, USA

ISBN-10: 0-7456-3284-X
ISBN-13: 978-07456-3284-1
ISBN-10: 0-7456-3285-8 (pb)
ISBN-13: 978-07456-32858 (pb)

A catalogue record for this book is available from the British Library.

Typeset in 10.5 on 12 pt Palatino
by SNP Best-set Typesetter Ltd, Hong Kong
Printed and bound in Great Britain by MPG Books Ltd, Bodmin, Cornwall

The publisher has used its best endeavours to ensure that the URLs for external websites referred to in this book are correct and active at the time of going to press. However, the publisher has no responsibility for the websites and can make no guarantee that a site will remain live or that the content is or will remain appropriate.

Every effort has been made to trace all copyright holders, but if any have been inadvertently overlooked the publishers will be pleased to include any necessary credits in any subsequent reprint or edition.

For further information on Polity, visit our website: www.polity.co.uk

Contents

For Patricia Gwen Morton 1943–2005

Acknowledgements

I wish to thank the anonymous readers of this book for their astute and insightful comments on the manuscript. Thanks also to colleagues in English at the University of Southampton (past and present), especially Stephen Bygrave, Bryan Cheyette, David Glover, Lucy Hartley, Cora Kaplan, Peter Middleton, Nicky Marsh, Herman Rapaport and Sujala Singh; to Ellen McKinlay and John Thompson at Polity for their help and patience in the preparation of this manuscript. Finally, thanks to Susan Kelly for her constant intellectual insight, careful reading, love and friendship.

I am grateful to the following publishers for permission to cite from the following sources: Oxford University Press, India, for permission to cite from: Sumit Sarkar 'The Conditions and Nature of Subaltern Militancy: Bengal from Swadeshi to Non-Co-operation, c. 1905–22', in *Subaltern Studies III: Writings on South Asian History and Society*, ed. Ranajit Guha (New Delhi: Oxford University Press, 1984), pp. 271–320; Gayatri Chakravorty Spivak 'Subaltern Studies: Deconstructing Historiography', in Ranajit Guha, ed., *Subaltern Studies IV* (New Delhi: Oxford University Press, 1985), pp. 330–63; and Gayatri Chakravorty Spivak, 'A Literary Representation of the Subaltern: Mahashweta Devi's "Stanadayini"', in Ranajit Guha, ed., *Subaltern Studies V: Writings on South Asian History and Society* (New Delhi: Oxford University Press, 1987), pp. 91–134; University of Oregon for permission to cite from: Corinne Scheiner, '*Teleiopoesis, Telepoesis*, and the Practice of Comparative Literature', *Comparative Literature* 57 (3), Summer 2005, pp. 239–45; Duke University Press for permission to cite from: Gayatri Chakravorty Spivak 'Responsibility', *boundary 2*, 21 (3) (Autumn 1994), pp. 19–64, and Gayatri Chakravorty Spivak, 'Terror: A Speech After 9–11', *boundary 2*, 31 (2) (Summer 2004), pp. 81–111; The Johns Hopkins University Press for permission to cite from: Gayatri Chakravorty Spivak's essay 'Theory in the Margin: Coetzee's *Foe* Reading Defoe's *Crusoe/Roxanna*', in Jonathan Arac and Barbara Johnson, eds, *Consequences of Theory: Selected Papers of the English Institute, 1987–88* (Baltimore: Johns Hopkins University Press, 1991), pp. 154–80, Gayatri Chakravorty Spivak, 'Translator's Preface' to Jacques Derrida, *Of Grammatology* [1967] (Baltimore: Johns Hopkins University Press, 1976); Routledge for permission to cite from Gayatri Chakravorty Spivak, 'French Feminism Revisited: Ethics and Politics' in Feminists Theorize the Political ed. judith Butler and Joan W. Scott. (London: Routledge, 1992) and Gayatri Chakravorty Spivak, 'Limits and Openings of Marx in Derrida', *Outside in the Teaching Machine* (New York: Routledge 1994).

Every effort has been made to seek permission to cite from sources where appropriate, and any permissions outstanding at the time that this book goes to press will be acknowledged in future editions of the book.

Abbreviations

Many of Spivak's essays are reprinted in *CPR, IOW* and *OTM*. See also the list of her writings on p. 184 below.

ANNI   'A Note on the New International', *parallax*, 7 (3) (2001):12–16

CPR   *A Critique of Postcolonial Reason: Towards a History of the Vanishing Present* (Cambridge, Mass.: Harvard University Press, 1999)

CSS   'Can the Subaltern Speak?', in *Marxism and the Interpretation of Culture*, ed. Cary Nelson and Larry Grossberg (Urbana: University of Illinois Press, 1988), 271–313

CT   'Claiming Transformation', in *Transformation: Thinking Through Feminism*, ed. Sara Ahmed, Jane Kilby, Celia Lury, Maureen McNeil and Beverley Skeggs (London: Routledge, 2000), 119–30

DD   *Death of a Discipline: Lectures in Critical Theory* (New York: Columbia University Press, 2003)

GW   'Ghostwriting', *diacritics*, 25(2) (summer 1995): 65–84

IM   Preface to Mahasweta Devi, and commentaries on *Imaginary Maps: Three Stories*, trans. Gayatri Chakravorty Spivak (New York and London: Routledge, 1995)

IOW   *In Other Worlds: Essays in Cultural Politics* (London: Methven, 1987)

IP   'International Public Hearing on Crimes Related to Population Policies', *Re/productions*, 1 [no date]; see *http://www.hsph.Harvard.edu/grhf-asia/repro/gcspivak.html*

ISD	'Imperialism and Sexual Difference', *Oxford Literary Review*, 7 (1–2) (1986): 225–40
OTM	*Outside in the Teaching Machine* (New York and London: Routledge, 1993)
PCC	*The Postcolonial Critic: Interviews, Strategies, Dialogues*, ed. Sarah Harasym (London: Routledge, 1990)
PH	'Public Hearing on Crimes against Women', *Women against Fundamentalisms*, 7 (1995); see http://www.af.gn.apc.org/journal7p3.htm
R	'Responsibility', *boundary 2*, 21 (3) (1994): 19–64
RM	'Revolutions that as yet have no Model: Derrida's *Limited Inc.*', *diacritics*, 10 (4) (winter 1980): 29–49
RW	'Righting Wrongs', in *Human Rights, Human Wrongs: The Oxford Amnesty Lectures, 2001*, ed. Nicholas Owen (Oxford: Oxford University Press, 2003), 164–227
SM	'Supplementing Marxism', in *Whither Marxism?*, ed. Steven Cullenberg and Bernd Magnus (New York: Routledge, 1995), 109–19
SP	'Schmitt and Poststructuralism: A Response', *Cardozo Law Review*, 21 (5–6) (2001): 1723–37
SR	*The Spivak Reader*, ed. Donna Landry and Gerald Maclean (London: Routledge, 1996)
SSSP	'Scattered Speculations on the Subaltern and the Popular', *Postcolonial Studies*, 8 (4) (2005): 475–86
T	'Terror: A Speech after 9–11', *boundary 2*, 31 (2) (2004): 81–111
TD	'Touched by Deconstruction', *Grey Room*, 20 (2005): 95–104
TM	'Theory in the Margin: Coetzee's *Foe* Reading Defoe's *Crusoe/Roxana*,' in *Consequences of Theory: Selected Papers of the English Institute, 1987–88*, ed. Jonathan Arac and Barbara Johnson (Baltimore: Johns Hopkins University Press, 1991), 154–80
TP	'Translator's Preface' to Jacques Derrida, *Of Grammatology* [1967] (Baltimore: Johns Hopkins University Press, 1976)
TT	'Teaching for the Times', in *Decolonizing the Imagination*, ed. Jan Nederveen Pieterse (London: Zed Press, 1995), 177–202
TWT	'Three Women's Texts and a Critique of Imperialism', *Critical Inquiry*, 12 (1) (1985): 243–61

Introduction

Gayatri Chakravorty Spivak is best known for her formative contribution to and ongoing critique of what is generally known as postcolonial studies. Although there is some truth to this popular characterization of Spivak's intellectual enterprise, this description is also rather reductive. Spivak's critical corpus is certainly informed by the philosophical, cultural, political and economic legacies of European colonialism in former colonial societies; however, the scope and influence of her work is by no means restricted to the effects of colonialism. Her critical work also includes numerous articles, books, interviews and translations on a wide range of topics: from poststructuralist thought and literary criticism; continental philosophy, psychoanalysis, feminist theory, Marxism and post-Marxism; through the position of disempowered 'subaltern' peoples who are excluded from political representation in postcolonial nation-states such as India and Bangladesh, the international division of labour, the limitations of universal human rights discourses and international development policies; to readings and translations of nineteenth- and twentieth-century literature. What is more, Spivak's intellectual activity is informed and supplemented by her work in rural teacher-training schools in Bangladesh and India.

Spivak's reputation as a leading postcolonial intellectual is due in part to her persistent criticism of European literary and philosophical texts for providing ideological support for European colonialism. This overtly political criticism of European culture, literature and philosophy from the standpoint of an educated, middle-class woman who migrated from India to work in the United States academy in the late 1950s may have contributed to her impromptu appointment as an unofficial intellectual spokesperson for the postcolonial world in the public sphere of Anglo-American literary and cultural studies during the 1980s and 1990s. Yet, Spivak has been critical of such a position throughout her career, and has been careful to situate her position in relation to a broader community of postcolonial intellectuals, including Chandra Talpade Mohanty, Sara Suleri, Aiwah Ong, Ketu Katrak and Deniz Kandiyoti.

What is more, Spivak has rejected the label 'postcolonial' in her recent theoretical writing. One of the main reasons for this shift in Spivak's critical position is an increasing recognition (along with such intellectuals as Aijaz Ahmad, Arif Dirlik, Michael Hardt and Antonio Negri) that postcolonial theory focuses too much on past forms of colonial domination, and is therefore inadequate to criticize the impact of contemporary global economic domination and the structural adjustment policies of the International Monetary Fund and the World Bank on the economies and societies of the global South.

Despite this shift in emphasis, Spivak's earlier intellectual production is at least in part bound up with the intellectual history of postcolonial theory and cultural criticism. Along with Edward Said and Homi Bhabha, Spivak is widely acknowledged as a substantial figure in the field of postcolonial studies. Her readings of nineteenth- and twentieth-century English literary texts; her translations of the Bengali-language writer Mahasweta Devi; and her historiographic research with the Subaltern Studies historians have had a major influence in shaping the field. Essays such as 'Three Women's Texts and a Critique of Imperialism' (1985) and 'Can the Subaltern Speak?' (1988) are widely anthologized and frequently cited as exemplary texts of postcolonial theory.

These diverse elements of Spivak's thought cannot be presented as a coherent system or neatly divided into separate phases. As Spivak has repeatedly emphasized in interviews, her work draws on a range of different theoretical methodologies, such as Marxism, feminism and deconstruction, which are often incommensurate if not mutually antagonistic. Rather than attempting to reconcile these different approaches, however, Spivak has emphasized the importance of preserving the discontinuities between Marxism, feminism and deconstruction (*PCC*, 15). Spivak has modestly compared this practice to one of a 'theoretical gadfly' or a 'bricoleur' who uses 'what comes to hand' (*PCC*, 55). However, this self-characterization runs the risk of trivializing the significance of Spivak's intellectual practice. As one commentator has observed, what Spivak's preservation of the discontinuities between Marxism, feminism and deconstruction offers readers is 'a rigorous form of rule breaking'.[1] Rather than strictly adhering to the protocols and vocabularies of any one particular theoretical paradigm or philosophical system, Spivak frequently employs a rigorous rhetorical strategy of interruption and supplementation, which questions the authority and truth claims of different theoretical methodologies.

But this is not to suggest that the rhetorical strategy of interruption is an end in itself. For Spivak, the persistent interruption and supplementation of any one theoretical argument is informed by her engagement with urgent political questions about disempowered individuals and groups whom Spivak sometimes designates as subaltern. Such groups include the colonized, women in colonial and postcolonial societies, tribal groups, and the rural peasantry in South Asia. In this respect, Spivak's work could be seen to disrupt the disciplinary codes and specialized vocabulary of western academic philosophy and critical theory in order to render the voices, histories and experiences of the disempowered and the disenfranchised intelligible to her readers. Yet this critical and political endeavour is not as simple as it might sound. Indeed, Spivak's ongoing commitment to find a theoretical language and method that can do justice to the subaltern groups she seeks to engage with necessarily demands a complex, sophisticated and provisional style that is constantly in process and open to revision.

Life and context

Like the work of other leading 'postcolonial intellectuals', including Homi Bhabha and Edward Said, Spivak's thought is self-consciously marked by her diasporic location and cultural background. As some commentators have observed, Spivak's work often draws on autobiographical information to illustrate and clarify her arguments.[2] Others have argued that this self-conscious focus on autobiography stands in for an engagement with the more urgent political concerns she frequently invokes, such as the plight of disenfranchised, 'subaltern' groups living in the global South.[3] Yet such an argument overlooks the significance of Spivak's intellectual biography to an understanding of her own writing and theoretical affiliations.

Gayatri Chakravorty was born in Calcutta on 24 February 1942, the year of the artificial famine in India and five years before India gained independence from British colonial rule. The artificial famine was created by the British military in India as a ruse to feed the allied forces in the Pacific during the Second World War. Although it was illegal to protest against the famine, a group of Indian radicals had found a way to actively demonstrate against British rule through performance and street theatre. By forming a group known as the Indian People's Theatre Association (IPTA), these non-professional actors and directors used theatre as a medium through which to promote nationalist sentiment.[4] It was this political context in pre-independence Calcutta that shaped Spivak's earliest childhood experience: as she states in an interview with Alfred Arteaga, her earliest childhood memories are of the songs and plays performed by the IPTA (*SR*, 16). Spivak came from a middle-class Hindu family, and attended a missionary school in Calcutta, where she was taught by tribal Christians, who were 'lower than middle class by origin, neither Hindus nor Muslims, not even Hindu untouchables, but tribals – so called aboriginals – who had been converted by missionaries' (*SR*, 17). As I suggest in later chapters, this early experience of being taught by women 'who were absolutely underprivileged, but who had dehegemonized Christianity in order to occupy a social space where they could teach their social superiors' (*SR*, 16) has continued to mark the trajectory of Spivak's work.

Spivak graduated from Presidency College of the University of Calcutta in 1959 with a first-class honours degree in English, including gold medals for English and Bengali literature. The teaching of the English literary canon in Indian universities could be seen to continue the ideological legacy of British colonial education policies which were intended to instruct and enlighten the Indian middle class in the morally and politically superior culture of the British.[5] Indeed, during the 1950s degree requirements at the University of Calcutta 'amounted to a comprehensive first-hand reading knowledge of all literature in "English" from just before Chaucer up to the mid-twentieth century, with a special focus on Shakespeare' (*SR*, 1). Yet although Presidency College was well known for its academic excellence and traditional curriculum, the social demography of its students was mixed. The influence of the college's politically active intellectual Left can be seen to mark the trajectory of Spivak's published work from the early 1980s to the present.

After taking a master's degree in English at Cornell University, Ithaca, New York State, and a year's fellowship at Girton College,

Cambridge, Spivak took up an instructor's position at the University of Iowa. While at Iowa she completed her doctoral dissertation on the work of William Butler Yeats, which was supervised by the literary critic Paul de Man at Cornell. This was subsequently developed into a book entitled *Myself I Must Remake: The Life and Poetry of W. B. Yeats* (1974). At first glance, this book offers a fairly conventional reading of the Irish writer's life, poetry and his reinvention of Celtic mythology. Yet *Myself I Must Remake* also situates Yeats's work in terms of the history of British colonialism in Ireland. In this respect, Spivak's early text could be seen to anticipate the rise of postcolonial literary criticism, and the influence of Yeats's work on other anti-colonial writers such as the Nigerian Chinua Achebe and the West Indian Derek Walcott.

Spivak and postcolonial theory

Spivak's experience of following a traditional degree programme in English literary history at the University of Calcutta and her subsequent move to the United States in the early 1960s offers one possible explanation for how she came to be such a significant figure in the critical elaboration of postcolonial theory in Anglo-American university departments of literature during the 1980s and early 1990s. Indeed, some of Spivak's best-known essays, such as 'Three Women's Texts and a Critique of Imperialism' (1985) and 'Theory in the Margin: Coetzee's *Foe* Reading Defoe's *Crusoe/Roxana*' (1991), offer critical readings that overtly challenge the ideology of colonialism embedded in classic English literary texts, notably Charlotte Brontë's *Jane Eyre* (1847) and Daniel Defoe's *Robinson Crusoe* (1719). In this respect, Spivak's critical work appears to challenge the legacy of British colonial policies for educating the middle- and upper-class elite in India, which she had experienced first hand as an undergraduate at the University of Calcutta.

What is more, both 'Three Women's Texts' and 'Theory in the Margin' focus on twentieth-century Anglophone literary texts such as Jean Rhys's *Wide Sargasso Sea* (1966) and J. M. Coetzee's *Foe* (1986), which counter the cultural authority of English classic literary texts by re-writing them from the point of view of marginal characters such as the Creole character Bertha Mason in *Jane Eyre* or the character of Friday in *Robinson Crusoe*. Such a critical focus on texts that counter the dominant narratives of colonial authority by asserting the voices of figures who had previously been marginalized and silenced by such narratives contributed to the efforts of many other postcolonial writers and critics seeking to find a vocabulary for reading and valuing literary texts produced in former European colonies.

For the literary critic Bart Moore-Gilbert, the early reception of Anglophone postcolonial texts such as Achebe's *Things Fall Apart* (1958) tended to compare individual writers to 'the British tradition' rather than defining a distinctive Nigerian national literature.[6] The need for more situated critical approaches, such as Spivak's, which can engage with and value the location, style and histories of postcolonial texts is therefore crucial.

As I go on to argue, Spivak's engagement with the Franco-Maghrebian philosopher Jacques Derrida and his critique of western metaphysics has certainly helped to generate a more sophisticated critical framework and vocabulary that can account for the singular histories, locations and practices of different postcolonial texts without recourse to the imperial paradigm that Moore Gilbert describes.

Yet this is not to suggest that Spivak's work uncritically celebrates postcolonial literary and cultural texts simply by virtue of the fact that they represent postcolonial societies. Indeed, many postcolonial texts such as Salman Rushdie's *Midnight's Children* (1981) and Ngugi wa Thiongo'o's *A Grain of Wheat* (1967) are critical of the emancipatory promises of postcolonial nationalism. Like Rushdie and Ngugi, much of Spivak's work is overtly critical of postcolonial nationalism in general. One of the main reasons for this critical stance is because the political independence of many former European colonies in the mid-twentieth century failed to lead to the social liberation of many disempowered subaltern groups such as women, the poor, the rural peasantry or the illiterate. Instead, postcolonial nationalism often seemed to benefit a small elite group, who were, as Spivak puts it, 'instrumental in changing the geopolitical conjuncture from territorial imperialism to neocolonialism' (*IOW*, 245).

Rather than focusing on a particular national literature, Spivak has tended to concentrate on literary, historical, cultural and economic texts that attempt to articulate the lives of socially and economically disempowered subaltern groups who are often ignored in postcolonial texts that focus on the dominant national narratives from the standpoint of the elite. Indeed, Spivak's ongoing commentaries on and translations of the short stories and novels by Mahasweta Devi are an exemplary case in point. As I argue in chapter 1, Spivak's commentaries on Devi's work offer a crucial and situated counterpoint to the exaggerated political claims that are sometimes made on behalf of postcolonial writing.[7]

Deconstruction

Like the postcolonial intellectuals Edward Said and Homi Bhabha, Spivak has often been criticized for drawing on the western poststructuralist theory of Jacques Derrida, Michel Foucault and Jacques Lacan. Such charges are based on the assumption that poststructuralist theory is a product of European philosophy and culture, and is therefore inadequate to criticize the cultural, social and economic legacies of European colonialism. In an interview with three scholars at Delhi University, however, Spivak justifies her use of western poststructuralist theory, arguing that, 'I cannot understand what indigenous theory there might be that can ignore the realities of nineteenth-century colonialism' (*PCC*, 69). For Spivak, the very idea of an indigenous theory uncontaminated by the legacy of nineteenth-century colonialism is anachronistic because it assumes a romanticized, prelapsarian ideal of a coherent national culture outside history.

The poststructuralist theories of Derrida, Foucault and Lacan do not simply represent a new form of intellectual imperialism for Spivak. Rather, poststructuralist theory has provided Spivak with a conceptual apparatus that enables her to question the cultural and philosophical foundations of western imperialism. One consequence of this political investment in poststructuralist theory is that Spivak does not always adhere strictly to the rigorous codes and disciplinary conventions of a particular theoretical paradigm.

Yet, this is not to suggest that her work is lacking in coherence or theoretical rigour. Alongside Rachel Bowlby, Barbara Johnson and Geoffrey Bennington, Spivak is one of the leading commentators on and translators of Derrida. Her 'Translator's Preface' (1976) to his *Of Grammatology* (French original 1967) provided a rigorous and accessible introduction to Derrida's work, situating his thought in relation to the philosophy of Hegel, Husserl and Heidegger, the structural linguistics of Ferdinand de Saussure, the psychoanalysis of Freud and Lacan, the archaeology of Foucault, the structural anthropology of Claude Lévi-Strauss, and the literary criticism of Roland Barthes.

Spivak's strategy of interrupting deconstruction may seem to depart from more orthodox philosophical interpretations of Derrida. Rather than simply discrediting Spivak's readings as errant or non-rigorous, however, it is perhaps more productive to approach Spivak's inventive use of Derrida's thought as an exemplary case of deconstruction's significance beyond the terms of academic philosophy. For instance, Spivak's call for a 'setting-to-work' of deconstruction in the context of globalization and development is exemplified by a series of critical interventions, which expand and develop the political implications of deconstruction. In 'Responsibility' (1994), for example, Spivak combines a careful reading of Derrida's critique of Heidegger's complicity with National Socialism in *Of Spirit* with an account of the contemporary western intellectual's responsibility towards the World Bank's Flood Action Plan in Bangladesh. Similarly, in *A Critique of Postcolonial Reason* (1999) Spivak uses a deconstructive politics of reading to track the exclusion of the poorest women in the global South from discussions of contemporary postmodern culture. For Spivak, one of the most difficult challenges that deconstruction poses to politically orientated forms of criticism such as Marxism, feminism or postcolonialism is its insistence that resistance and opposition are bound in a relation of complicity with the thing that is being criticized. As Derrida puts it in *Of Spirit* (French original 1987), 'Even if all forms of complicity are not equivalent, they are *irreducible*. The question of knowing which is the least grave of these forms of complicity is always there – its urgency and its seriousness – but it will never dissolve the irreducibility of this fact'.[8] In saying that all forms of complicity are irreducible, Derrida is not suggesting that all forms of political criticism are ultimately bound to fail because they are complicit with their object of critique; rather, Derrida is saying that the recognition of complicity is what enables criticism to become ethically responsible to its object of critique.[9]

Another important influence on the development of Spivak's thought is the work of Paul de Man, who, as mentioned above, had supervised her doctoral dissertation on Yeats at Cornell during the 1960s. Yet it is de Man's later writings that have most clearly informed the development of Spivak's thought. In 'Imperialism and Sexual Difference' (1986), for instance, Spivak draws on de Man's suggestion in *Allegories of Reading* (1979) that 'the basis of a truth claim is no more than a trope' to make the argument that feminism is 'engaged in a tropological deconstruction' (ISD, 225). As I argue below, Spivak's deconstructive approach to feminism is not simply intended to undermine or weaken the legitimacy of its political claims. Rather, Spivak's employment of de Man's tropological deconstruction works to counter feminism's unacknowledged complicity with imperialism.

And in her more recent works – *A Critique of Postcolonial Reason* (1999), for example – Spivak has continued to draw on de Man: his later writings on allegory, irony and parabasis have developed her ethical reading strategy, a strategy that questions the global division of labour; this separates her implied readership of humanities students and intellectuals in the universities of the global North and disempowered 'subaltern' constituencies in rural areas of the global South.[10]

Marxism and the subaltern

Spivak's political concern with socially and economically disempowered subaltern constituencies in the global South may seem to be at odds with Derrida's deconstruction of political programmes such as Marxism. Spivak has frequently emphasized the ethical importance of deconstruction's persistent questioning of rational political programmes such as socialism, feminism or anti-colonial nationalism, and political identities such as the proletariat, woman or the colonized (*PCC*, 104). For some critics, Spivak's commitment to the theoretical rigour and vocabulary of deconstruction works to impede her political commitment to such groups.[11]

Yet Spivak's essays and interventions also tend to interrupt the theoretical protocols of deconstructive reading with political discussions of subaltern women in the global South. Such an interruption of deconstruction from a more materialist standpoint may suggest a prioritization of Marxism over deconstruction in Spivak's work. Indeed Spivak has frequently criticized Derrida for failing to understand Marx's theory of industrial capitalism as described in the second volume of his *Capital* (German original 1885). Such a defence of a correct reading of Marx's economic theory against Derrida's deconstructive reading of Marx might suggest that Spivak is more of an orthodox Marxist than a deconstructive theorist. For the literary critic Robert J. C. Young, however, Spivak's critical negotiation of Marxism and deconstruction is perhaps better understood if it is situated within a broader intellectual history of decolonization, and the attempts of various anti-colonial intellectuals – among them M. N. Roy, C. L. R. James, Frantz Fanon, Kwame Nkrumah,

Mahatma Gandhi and Samir Amin – to revise and adapt the concepts and arguments of European Marxist thought in order to make them relevant to the specific conditions of the postcolonial world.[12]

Spivak's critical engagement with the Subaltern Studies historians is an exemplary case of this critical revision and reconstruction of Marxism in a postcolonial framework. Along with South Asian historians such as Partha Chatterjee, Dipesh Chakrabarty, Shahid Amin, Gyan Pandey, David Arnold and David Hardiman, Spivak has emphasized the failure of India's national independence to bring about a social revolution for women, the working class and the rural peasantry. In a discussion of the suicide of Bhubaneswari Bhaduri, a woman who was subsequently discovered to have been involved in one of the armed nationalist groups in colonial Bengal, for instance, Spivak has argued that the gendered subaltern cannot speak. This statement has often been taken out of context to mean that socially and economically subordinate groups cannot act or speak because they are excluded from cultural and political representation. As argued below, such readings ignore how Spivak's statement that the subaltern cannot speak is a performative statement, which signifies the failure of Bhubaneswari Bhaduri's suicide to register as a sovereign speech act. Instead of simply repeating the exclusion of economically and socially subordinate groups from dominant nationalist history, Spivak has used the critical tools of deconstruction to trace the inscriptions of subaltern resistance and agency in the dominant historical archives.

Feminism

Spivak's engagement with literary texts and theoretical paradigms such as Marxism and deconstruction has always been concerned with the silencing and exclusion of non-western women's voices and agencies from cultural and political representation. Writing and teaching as a South Asian diasporic intellectual in a US academic department of English literary studies in the 1980s, when key feminist texts such as Luce Irigaray's *This Sex Which Is Not One* and *Speculum of the Other Woman*, Julia Kristeva's *About Chinese Women* and Hélène Cixous' and Catherine Clément's *The Newly Born Woman* were first translated into English, Spivak approached western feminist theory as one of the most appropriate and sophisticated methodologies for reading literary texts. Yet, at the same time, Spivak has been persistently critical of the universalist claims of some western feminist thought to represent *all* women, rather than acknowledging its culturally partial and relatively privileged position. Indeed, this can be seen in Spivak's critique of *About Chinese Women* in 'French Feminism in an International Frame', as well as her more recent criticisms of World Bank policies that target women in the global South as objects of benevolence.

Overview

This study builds on the insights of my introductory textbook on Spivak's work[13] to offer a more advanced and sustained analysis of Spivak's thought. In particular, it traces the ethical dimension manifest in her persistent critique of Marxism, feminism, deconstruction and postcolonial studies. The book thus seeks to argue that what underpins Spivak's essays and interventions is a political commitment to achieve what she calls a relation of ethical singularity with the subaltern.

Starting with an evaluation of Spivak's analysis of the ideological function of English literature in the civilizing mission of colonialism, chapter 1 assesses how Spivak's essay 'Three Women's Texts and a Critique of Imperialism' expands and develops the insights of colonial discourse studies through an inventive re-reading of Immanuel Kant's concept of the categorical imperative. The chapter goes on to examine how Spivak's postcolonial criticism interrogates the political claims of postcoloniality. Focusing on Spivak's readings of Jean Rhys, J. M. Coetzee and Mahasweta Devi, I argue that Spivak's approach to reading literary texts has a pedagogical imperative to encourage readers to engage with the knowledge and experience of the subaltern, which cannot be accounted for by dominant systems of knowledge and representation.

Chapter 2 examines Spivak's critical engagement with deconstruction, beginning with her 'Translator's Preface' to *Of Grammatology*. Here I argue that the preface not only provides a rigorous and systematic introduction to the philosophical questions that Derrida's work seeks to address, but also spells out the implications of Derrida's critique of ethnocentrism in the work of Jean-Jacques Rousseau and Claude Lévi-Strauss for postcolonial theory. Following a discussion of Spivak's reading of Paul de Man, the chapter then explores the way in which her engagement with the work of Derrida and de Man has enabled her to develop an ethics of reading, which is responsible to the singularity of the subaltern.

Chapter 3 examines Spivak's critique of Marxist political economy. A reading of Spivak's critique of Marx's account of the Asiatic mode of production is followed by a discussion of Spivak's deconstructive reading of Marx's labour theory of value. Some critics have argued that Spivak's reading of Marx after Derrida is politically suspect precisely because Spivak's use of Derrida undermines the theoretical foundations of Marxist thought, while others have argued that Spivak's recuperative reading of Marx's labour theory of value is incommensurate with her deconstruction of Marx's positivism in essays such as 'Can the Subaltern Speak?'.[14] In my reading, Spivak's engagement with Marx after Derrida is secondary to her argument that the value form is a shifting site of ethical and political contestation. With reference to the work of Dipesh Chakrabarty, this chapter concludes by arguing that Spivak offers a translational theory of reading heterogeneous forms of subaltern labour, which interrupts the global flow of capital and commodities.

Chapter 4 situates Spivak's theoretical writings on the subaltern in relation to the work of the Subaltern Studies collective. By comparing Spivak's writings on the subaltern to the work of other Subaltern Studies historians, including Partha Chatterjee, Ranajit Guha, Dipesh Chakravarty and Gyanendra Pandey, this chapter argues that what is at stake in Spivak's challenge to the positivism of the Subaltern Studies collective is an ethical demand to invent a new critical idiom that can do justice to the singular histories and practices of the gendered subaltern.

Continuing this concern with the gendered subaltern, chapter 5 examines Spivak's contribution to feminist thought. Focusing on her theory of strategic essentialism and her reading of Hélène Cixous and Marie-Aimée Hélie Lucas, I consider how Spivak's thought has negotiated the tensions between feminism and decolonization. The chapter concludes that Spivak's recent critique of global development policies targeting women in the global South re-defines the political and ethical horizons of transnational feminist thought.

Chapter 6 traces a shift in Spivak's thought from a postcolonial critique of western reason to a critique of postcolonial reason. Starting with Spivak's reading of Kant's *Critique of Judgement* in *A Critique of Postcolonial Reason*, I then consider how Spivak extends her critique of Kantian aesthetics to the contemporary rhetoric and politics of the anti-sweatshop movement. Against what Spivak terms the foreclosure of the native informant in Kantian aesthetics and contemporary global development policies, the chapter argues that Spivak's account of the female freedom fighter and the woman of the global South gradually transforms the non-relational space of ethical singularity into a space of political decision and responsibility.

The Conclusion examines Spivak's recent work on transnational literacy and subaltern rights. Focusing on Spivak's vision of comparative literature as a discipline that can train the imagination to learn to listen to the voice of the other, I argue that what Spivak means by the training of the imagination is part of a complex ethical commitment to a singular pedagogical approach which underpins much of her critical writing: to learn to learn from the subaltern.

1

Postcolonial Criticism and Beyond

Gayatri Spivak's reputation as a leading postcolonial critic is partly a consequence of her critique of eighteenth- and nineteenth-century English literature, and its relationship to the maintenance of colonial power. Yet Spivak has also made an important contribution to the development of a critical vocabulary and theoretical framework through which to read postcolonial texts by a range of writers including Jean Rhys, Hanif Kureishi, Salman Rushdie, Mahasweta Devi and J. M. Coetzee.

This is not to suggest, however, that Spivak's critical corpus can be easily reduced to the term postcolonial. Indeed, her critical work is extremely difficult to define simply because Spivak constantly revises her arguments in order to effectively refuse identification by any single category or label such as 'postcolonial', 'feminist' or 'Marxist'. Such a resistance to interpretation is exemplified by comparing two of her book titles: *The Postcolonial Critic* (1990) and *A Critique of Postcolonial Reason* (1999). If the first signifies an affiliation to postcolonial studies, the second indicates a clear critical distancing from the 'postcolonial' label. Such a shift in focus is not merely a symptom of changing intellectual trends, but a political commitment to re-thinking and revising theoretical concepts and approaches in response to social, economic and political changes in the contemporary world order.

In order to grasp the social and political significance of Spivak's shifting intellectual position *vis-à-vis* postcolonial studies, it is important to situate the development of Spivak's thought in relation to the history of postcolonial theory and criticism. In essays such as 'Three Women's Texts and a Critique of Imperialism' (1985) and 'Theory in the Margin: Coetzee's *Foe* Reading Defoe's *Crusoe/Roxana*' (1991) Spivak offers an important critical challenge to English literary and cultural texts by emphasizing how the study of such works as *Robinson Crusoe* or *Jane Eyre* served the interests of colonial power by representing English national culture as inherently more civilized than non-European nations, and therefore provided the cultural justification for colonialism.

In this respect, Spivak's work could be seen to develop Edward Said's argument in *Orientalism* (1978) that colonial power was maintained in and through different discourses. Such a view is, however, complicated by the fact that Spivak asserted in the early 1990s that 'her work is not really on colonial discourse' but is rather concerned with 'the contemporary cultural politics of neocolonialism in the US' (*PCC*, 164). Despite this distancing of her own intellectual project from that of Said, the critical reception of Spivak's work during the 1980s and early 1990s, in particular essays such as 'Three Women's Texts and a Critique of Imperialism', 'The Rani of Sirmur' and 'Theory in the Margin', has often tended to associate Spivak's work with Said's intellectual and critical formation.

In broad terms, there may seem to be superficial resemblances between Said's analysis of Orientalism and Spivak's reading of nineteenth-century British literary texts as a political tool that represented the superiority of British culture. For Said, rather than being 'representative and expressive of some nefarious "Western" imperialist plot to hold down the "Oriental" world', Orientalism is 'a *distribution* of geopolitical awareness into aesthetic, scholarly, economic, sociological, historical and philological texts [. . . ;] it is, above all a discourse that is by no means in direct corresponding relationship with political power in the raw, but rather is produced and exists in an uneven relationship with various kinds of power'.[1]

Spivak's critique of nineteenth-century English literature as a political tool that represented the superiority of British culture to its colonized subjects can certainly be seen to develop Said's argument in *Orientalism* that colonial power was maintained and reproduced through different disciplines, discourses and texts. Indeed, Spivak's reading of such novels as *Jane Eyre* and Mary Shelley's *Frankenstein* (1818) may seem generally commensurate with Said's model of colonial discourse. However, as argued below, Spivak is also critical of Said's use of Foucault's model of discourse and power to formulate a theory of colonial discourse on the grounds that Foucault's analysis of power and knowledge forecloses a consideration of the postcolonial world, and it is on this point that Spivak parts company with Said.

Spivak's readings of postcolonial texts by writers such as Jean Rhys, Assia Djebar, Salman Rushdie, Maryse Condé and Mahasweta Devi also appear to challenge the cultural authority of classic European literary texts. For this reason, Spivak may seem to provide a critical vocabulary that is able to counter what Chinua Achebe described as colonialist criticism, or texts that evaluate post-colonial texts according to the norms and criteria of European literature. Yet, as Spivak has recently suggested, the celebration of postcolonial literary texts as inherently radical simply by virtue of their representation of postcolonial societies is also problematic: it can tend to ignore the historical failure of many anti-colonial national independence movements to achieve economic independence from former colonial powers, or to emancipate socially and economically subordinate groups such as women, the rural peasantry or indigenous groups.

What is more, postcolonial intellectuals such as Edward Said and Homi Bhabha, as well as Gayatri Spivak in the Anglo-American academy, rose to prominence at a time when global economic organizations such as the World Bank and the International Monetary Fund were re-colonizing the national economies of many former European colonies through a system of economic dependency and rigid trade restrictions. This has led some critics such as Arif Dirlik to argue that postcolonial theory aids and abets this process of global capitalist restructuring.[2] Such an argument may seem to undermine the political claims of postcolonial theory, but it also ignores how Spivak's materialist engagement with postcolonial theory has always made connections between the international division of labour and development policies on the one hand and the cultural analysis of texts on the other. I examine this important debate in more detail in chapter 3, but I now go on to assess the way in which Spivak's essays have been taken up in colonial discourse studies.

English literature and the axiomatics of imperialism

Spivak's argument that the teaching of English literature is bound up with the civilizing mission of British colonialism is reflected in her assertion, made in 1985, that it 'should not be possible to read nineteenth-century British literature without remembering that imperialism, understood as England's social mission, was a crucial part of the cultural representation of England to the English' (TWT, 262). This statement frames Spivak's essay on Charlotte Brontë's *Jane Eyre*, Jean Rhys's *Wide Sargasso Sea* and Mary Shelley's *Frankenstein*; it also evokes a speech made in 1835 by Thomas Babington Macaulay, a 'Minute on Indian Education'. Macaulay, in his capacity as a member of the Supreme Council of India, emphasized the importance of English literature as an instrument for disseminating the moral values of British culture to the Indian middle class, who were, at that time, subjected to the policies of the British East India Company. Furthermore, Macaulay argued that it was necessary to educate an elite class in Indian society who could act as interpreters between the English and the non-English speaking Indian population: 'a class of persons, Indian in blood and colour, but English in taste, in opinions, in morals and in dialect'.[3]

The social mission of English studies in India during the period of British colonial rule thus forms the geopolitical and historical context against which Spivak's criticism of English literary studies takes place. The literary historian Gauri Viswanathan has further developed this argument in her book *Masks of Conquest* (1990). In Viswanathan's account:

> [T]he discipline of English came into its own in an age of colonialism
> [. . .] no serious account of its growth and development can afford to
> ignore the imperial mission of educating and civilizing and colonial
> subjects in the literature and thought of England, a mission that in
> the long run served to strengthen Western cultural hegemony in
> enormously complex ways.[4]

Like Viswanathan, Spivak emphasizes how English studies played an important role in reinforcing the political authority of the British Empire by persuading the Indian middle class that there was a moral and intellectual purpose behind colonialism. As I argue next, this colonial rhetoric is particularly apparent for Spivak in the figurative language and geographical metaphors of such nineteenth-century British novels as *Jane Eyre*.

Jane Eyre *and the axiomatics of imperialism*

For many literary critics *Jane Eyre* (1847) seems to advocate women's agency and self-determination in a rigidly patriarchal Victorian society. It may thus seem like an unlikely text to identify as a target for postcolonial criticism. As Spivak argues, however, it is precisely the narrative of female individualism in *Jane Eyre* that is bound to the narrative of imperialism: 'The broad strokes of my presuppositions are that what is at stake for female individualism in the age of imperialism, is precisely the making of human beings, the constitution and "interpellation" of the subject not only as individual, but as "individualist"' (TWT, 263). Whereas many feminist critics of *Jane Eyre* had tended to focus on Jane's struggle for self-determination within the constraints of the nineteenth-century bourgeois domestic sphere, Spivak argues that this constitution of the British female self as an individualist is predicated on the exclusion of the white Jamaican Creole female character, Bertha Mason, from the category of the human. By refusing to recognize Bertha as a human, in other words, Spivak suggests that Brontë refuses to allow readers to feel sympathy for Bertha; as a consequence, Jane's narrative of social mobility and economic independence (which Spivak calls female individualism) is placed beyond moral criticism.

Spivak begins her reading of *Jane Eyre* with a discussion of Jane's marginalization within the domestic sphere of the Reed family home at Gateshead before analysing the 'family/counter-family' parallelism that structures the narrative:

> In the novel, we encounter, first, the Reeds as the legal family and Jane, the late Mr. Reed's sister's daughter as the representative of a near incestuous counter-family; second, the Brocklehursts, who run the school Jane is sent to, as the legal family and Jane, Mrs. Temple, and Helen Burns as a counter-family that falls short because it is only a community of women; third, Rochester and the mad Mrs. Rochester as the legal family and Jane and Rochester as the illicit counter-family. Other items may be added to the thematic chain in this sequence: Rochester and Celine Varens as structurally functional counter-family; Rochester and Blanche Ingram as dissimulation of legality – and so on. (TWT, 266)

For Spivak the crucial point in Jane Eyre's narrative of self-determination is her movement from the counter-family to the family-in-law. This movement from a subordinate position in the Reed household to an equal position in the Rivers household is facilitated by the 'ideology of imperialist axiomatics' (TWT, 267).

What Spivak means by this phrase is clarified in a subsequent discussion of Immanuel Kant's concept of the categorical imperative. For Kant the categorical imperative refers to a transcendent moral law prior to empirical knowledge that regulates human behaviour. As such, the categorical imperative is a 'moving displacement of Christian ethics from religion to philosophy' (TWT, 267). In this process of displacement, Spivak argues that the transcendent laws regulating appropriate moral conduct can serve the interests of state power, when these transcendent codes are taken to provide a programme for moral education: 'The dangerous transformative power of philosophy [. . .] is that its formal subtlety can be travestied in the service of the state' (TWT, 267). In the political context of the British Empire's civilizing mission, the 'formal subtlety' of the categorical imperative can be travestied to make the 'native "subject"' the 'object of what might be termed the terrorism of the categorical imperative' (TWT, 267). Put differently, the civilizing mission of colonialism is presented as a progressive and modernizing programme to 'the native "subject"', however this rhetoric effaces the violence of colonial power and knowledge, which treat 'the native "subject"' as an object to be controlled. Spivak describes the civilizing mission as a form of terrorism because it conceals the violence of colonialism within a transcendent moral law. Such terrorism is foregrounded in Spivak's rephrasing of the categorical imperative: '*make* the heathen into a human so that he can be treated as an end in himself' (TWT, 267). It is this violent act of making the heathen into a human through the civilizing mission of colonialism that Spivak calls terroristic. In so doing, Spivak defines the ideology of imperialist axiomatics as the use of transcendent concepts like morality or culture to justify colonialism as a civilizing mission and to conceal colonialism's economic imperative and its violent methods.

Spivak transposes this reading of Kant's categorical imperative onto *Jane Eyre* in two ways. Firstly she contends that Brontë's rendering of Bertha Mason as non-human, as well as Jane's acceptance of Rochester's account of the 'field of colonial conquest' as a 'hell' that he was instructed to leave by 'a divine injunction rather than human motive' (TWT, 266), exemplifies how Jane's narrative of female individualism and appropriate moral conduct is predicated on 'an unquestioned ideology of imperialist axiomatics' (TWT, 267). Secondly Spivak argues that the 'tangent narrative' of St John Rivers's missionary work in British India is a further travesty of moral law by a colonial state. Citing a passage from the novel, Spivak observes how Rivers's rhetorical justification for his mission is structured by a series of oppositions, including: knowledge and ignorance; peace and war; freedom and bondage; religion and superstition; and heaven and hell (TWT, 268). Reading Rivers's speech against the grain, Spivak argues that these dichotomies are not transcendent moral categories prior to state control and imperial power. Instead, 'Imperialism and its territorial and subject-constituting project are a violent deconstruction of these oppositions' (TWT, 268).

Spivak's analysis of 'the unquestioned ideology of imperialist axiomatics' (TWT, 267) that underpins Jane's narrative of social mobility and moral conduct in *Jane Eyre* contrasts strikingly with previous Marxist and feminist readings of the novel. For Marxist critics such as Terry Eagleton, 'Jane's move from the counter-family set to the set of the family in law' is read 'in terms of the ambiguous *class* position of the governess' (TWT, 267). And for the feminist critics Sandra Gilbert and Susan Gubar, Bertha Mason was read 'only in psychological terms as Jane's dark double' (TWT, 267).

Yet Spivak's reading of *Jane Eyre* has also been criticized by Susan Meyer, in ' "Indian Ink": Colonialism and the Figurative Strategy of *Jane Eyre*' (1996) for ignoring Brontë's ambivalence about colonialism. In Meyer's argument, Spivak shows feminism 'to be inevitably complicitous with imperialism' by a 'sleight of hand'.[5] While Meyer agrees with Spivak's 'broad critique of an individualistic strain of feminism' in *Jane Eyre*, she takes issue with the description of Bertha's racial identity as both a white Creole and a native: 'Bertha is either native or not native to suit Spivak's critique'.[6] Against this 'sleight of hand', Meyer examines the ambiguous representation of Bertha Mason's racial identity in the text, and situates this in relation to nineteenth-century discourses of race in the colonial West Indies. In doing so, Meyer suggests that Brontë makes a 'serious and public, although implicit critique of British slavery and British imperialism in the West Indies'.[7]

What is at stake in Meyer's reading of *Jane Eyre* is the significance of Brontë's use of figurative language from the British colonies rather than a straightforward defence of Brontë's position. Significantly, Meyer also expands on Spivak's argument that Jane's narrative of female individualism is predicated on the construction of Bertha as a non-human Other. In Meyer's account, Brontë uses the discourse of slavery 'to represent class and gender inequality in England'.[8] While Brontë's figurative strategy does at times foreground the economic relationship between Rochester's private property and colonial slavery, Meyer argues that in Bertha Mason 'Brontë creates a character of the non-white races to use as the vividly embodied signifier of oppression in the novel, and then has this sign, by the explosive instability of the situation it embodies, destroy itself'.[9] Like Spivak, Meyer emphasizes how a discourse of colonial oppression is ultimately subordinated to Jane's narrative of female individualism. However Meyer also contends that the economic independence Jane achieves at the end of the text has its source in the profits of colonial slavery:

> [Jane's wealth] comes from her uncle in Madeira, who is an agent for a Jamaican wine manufacturer, Bertha's brother. The location of Jane's uncle John in Madeira, off Morocco, on the West African coast, where Richard Mason stops on his way home from England, also indirectly suggests, through Mason's itinerary, the triangular route of the British slave traders, and suggests that John Eyre's wealth is implicated in the slave trade. The resonant details of the scene in which Brontë has Jane acquire her fortune mark Jane's financial and literary implication in colonialism as well.[10]

The difference between Meyer's argument and Spivak's turns on the degree to which Brontë opposed the discourses of slavery and colonial oppression that provide a figurative language for class and gender oppression in the Victorian domestic sphere of *Jane Eyre*. Certainly, Meyer's reading of Jane Eyre's financial implication in colonialism adds an important materialist dimension to Spivak's argument that Jane's narrative of female individualism is achieved at the expense of Bertha Mason, who is relegated to the position of an inarticulate and non-human other in the novel. Yet, Spivak's observation that colonial discourse constructs 'a self-immolating colonial subject for the glorification of the self-immolation of the colonizer' (TWT, 270) complicates Meyer's reading of Bertha's suicide in the text as an example of what she calls 'the great act of cleaning in the novel, which burns away Rochester's oppressive colonial wealth and diminishes the power of his gender'.[11] In Meyer's account Bertha is a 'vividly embodied sign of oppression in the novel',[12] who destroys herself in an act of purification. For Spivak, however, this act of purification in the novel is an act of self-immolation, a phrase that recalls her analysis of the practice of *sati*-suicide, an exceptional and situated practice of Hindu widow sacrifice, in the essay 'Can the Subaltern Speak?'. Spivak's reading of Hindu widow sacrifice is examined in chapter 4. For the purposes of this chapter, however, it is worth noting that Spivak's description of Bertha's suicide as *self*-immolation attributes political agency and resistance to an act that is encrypted in Brontë's novel as an act of purification. Yet such a reading of Bertha's role is beyond both Brontë's and Meyer's critical frame of reference, which is itself bound within the terms of colonialism's figurative language; and it is precisely this figurative language that Spivak seeks to question. I therefore now proceed to examine Spivak's analysis of Jean Rhys's re-writing of this passage from the postcolonial standpoint of Antoinette/Bertha in *Wide Sargasso Sea* since it is in this novel that the question of Bertha's agency is developed.

Postcolonial re-writing

Jean Rhys's Wide Sargasso Sea

Spivak's reading of *Jane Eyre* in 'Three Women's Texts and a Critique of Imperialism' has made an important and influential contribution to the study of colonial discourse. Yet in contrast to postcolonial critics such as Edward Said, who tends to focus on classic European literary texts that represent the contradictions of imperialism, Spivak has also focused on postcolonial texts that work to challenge or complicate dominant narratives of colonial authority in European literature and culture by re-writing these narratives from a different historical and cultural point of view.

Spivak's reading of *Wide Sargasso Sea* is an exemplary case in point. Published in 1966 by the Dominica-born British novelist Jean Rhys, this novel has been read as a prequel to *Jane Eyre* because its first and third sections re-write the classic fictional inter-text from the point of view of Bertha/Antoinette. For this reason *Wide Sargasso Sea* has often been read as an exemplary postcolonial text, which challenges the colonial narrative underpinning *Jane Eyre*.

On a first reading, Spivak seems to contribute to this reading of *Wide Sargasso Sea* by emphasizing that Rhys 'keeps Bertha's humanity, indeed her sanity as critic of imperialism intact' (TWT, 268). Spivak compares a passage from each novel to develop this point. In Brontë's version, Jane ' "hears a snarling, snatching sound, almost like a dog quarrelling" and then encounters a bleeding Richard Mason' (TWT, 268), while in Rhys's narrative Grace Poole recounts how Bertha 'flew' at Richard Mason when he said ' "I cannot interfere legally between yourself and your husband" ' (TWT, 269). Whereas Brontë represents Bertha Mason as a figure whose function is 'to render indeterminate the boundary between human and animal' (TWT, 268), in 'Rhys' retelling, it is the dissimulation that Bertha discerns in the word "legally" [. . .] that prompts her violent *reaction'* (TWT, 269). In other words, Rhys draws attention to the legal definition of Bertha as Rochester's private property in the patriarchal terms of English common law.

What is more, in *Wide Sargasso Sea* the white Creole character Antoinette is renamed Bertha by the unnamed male narrator (whom we are encouraged to identify as Rochester). He does so when he discovers that Antoinette resembles the first name of her mother, Annette, who is incarcerated in a mental asylum. Antoinette's sense of her cultural and personal identity is already fragile prior to this act of renaming since 'as a white Creole child growing up at the time of emancipation in Jamaica, [she] is caught between the English imperialist and the black native' (TWT, 269). For this reason, Spivak contends that Rochester's act of renaming is violent because it effectively denies her any sense of personal or cultural identity, and thereby adumbrates her subjection to the discourse of imperialism in the third part of the novel.

Rather than simply repeating this tragic narrative of the colonial subject as victim, however, Spivak proceeds to explore Antoinette's narrative of identity formation with reference to the Narcissus myth in Ovid's *Metamorphoses*. By tracing the repetition of mirror imagery in the text, Spivak suggests that Antoinette seeks a more secure sense of self in her friendship with Tia, the black servant girl (TWT, 269). After the Emancipation Act, however, passed in Jamaica in 1833, this friendship – between a white Creole and a black ex-slave – becomes fraught. Rhys registers Tia's racial and class antagonism towards Antoinette as a white Creole child of the old planter class by having Tia throw a 'jagged stone' at Antoinette and making her head bleed (TWT, 269). Immediately after Tia throws the stone, Antoinette describes how the two girls 'stared at each other, blood on my face, tears on hers. It was as if I saw myself. Like in a looking glass' (TWT, 269). In Spivak's account, this passage instantiates a sequence of mirror images in the text, which symbolize Antoinette's search for a secure sense of self. Comparing Antoinette's search for identity with Narcissus' recognition of his reflected mirror image as his self in Ovid's *Metamorphoses*, Spivak argues that the repetition of Antoinette's identification with Tia in a later dream sequence is fractured by imperialism: 'Here the dream sequence ends, with an invocation of none other than Tia, the Other that could not be selved, because the fracture of imperialism rather than the Ovidian pool intervened' (TWT, 269).

Such a fracture refers to the transformation of Antoinette into Bertha Mason 'so that Jane Eyre can become the feminist individualist heroine of British fiction' (TWT, 270). Indeed, Spivak reads Antoinette's fractured identity as an 'allegory of the general epistemic violence of imperialism, the construction of a self-immolating subject for the glorification of the social mission of the colonizer' (TWT, 270).

What Spivak implies but does not explicitly state in her reading of *Wide Sargasso Sea* is that the novel does not offer a postcolonial re-writing of *Jane Eyre* in any straightforward sense. While Bertha is constructed as a colonial other in *Jane Eyre*, in *Wide Sargasso Sea* Antoinette is also a member of the white colonial elite. Such a view is developed by the literary critic Peter Hulme, who argues that *Wide Sargasso Sea* is 'a novel which deals with issues of race and slavery, yet is fundamentally sympathetic to the planter class ruined by emancipation'.[13] As a member of the ex-colonial planter class, Antoinette may seem like an unlikely protagonist for a postcolonial text. For this reason, Spivak turns her readers' attention to Christophine, Antoinette's black maid from Martinique, as an example of a woman who understands the cultural specificity of practices such as obeah, as well as challenging the authority of the unnamed male narrator in the second part of the book.

Although Christophine is tangential to the main narrative of the book, Spivak suggests that she functions as disruptive excess, 'who cannot be contained by a novel which rewrites a canonical English text within the European novelistic tradition in the interest of the white Creole rather than the native' (TWT, 272). Such a reading may serve to counter-balance Rhys's privileging of Antoinette as a tragic postcolonial heroine. However, in the Caribbean setting of the text, the opposition between Creole and native which Spivak invokes is complicated by the absence of an authentic native subject. As Peter Hulme notes: 'in the West Indies the "native" is either for the most part absent – if what is meant is indigenous – or "creole" – if what is meant is "born in the West Indies"'.[14] For Hulme, the absence of an indigenous subject in the West Indies signifies the buried history of the colonial violence perpetrated against the Caribs and Arawaks, which is codified in *Wide Sargasso Sea* through the amnesiac condition of the novels' protagonists. During their honeymoon at the town of Massacre, for instance, Rochester asks Antoinette about the origins of that name: '"Who was massacred here?", Rochester asks, "Slaves?" "Oh no", Antoinette replies, "Not slaves. Something must have happened a long time ago. Nobody remembers now"'.[15] For Hulme, the massacre in this extract refers to 'the killing in 1674 of Indian Warner, the half-Carib son of one of the foremost English colonists in the West Indies, Sir Thomas Warner'.[16] Against Spivak's claim that Christophine is a figure of disruptive excess in the novel, Hulme proceeds to argue that 'the really troubling figures "in the margins" of *Wide Sargasso Sea* are the coloured Cosways, Daniel and Alexander'.[17] For Hulme these figures are troubling because they disclose a history of European conquest, genocide and anti-colonial struggle in Dominica, and allow readers to question the ways in which *Wide Sargasso Sea* negotiates the nineteenth-century materials of Dominican history rather than accepting its aesthetic representation of Caribbean history at face value.[18]

Spivak's suggestion that Christophine is a representative native figure in the text because she was born in Martinique may seem to elide the absence of indigeneity and the history of colonial violence and anti-colonial resistance in Dominica, which Hulme invokes. Yet this elision also points towards a more sophisticated reading of the text. While Hulme seeks to restore a detailed historical account of European conquest, violence and anti-colonial struggle in Dominica to our understanding of *Wide Sargasso Sea*, Spivak's reading points to the impossibility of such a historicist interpretation. For the colonial history of African slave labour and miscegenation has precisely prevented the straightforward recovery of a Dominican history from the perspective of the Dominican people in the same way that the colonial history of genocide has prevented the recovery of an authentic indigenous Dominican subject. By concentrating on Christophine as a marginal figure in the text, Spivak's reading is more concerned with the way in which Christophine stands as a figure of textual resistance, who counters the colonial rhetoric of characters such as Rochester, than with Christophine's authenticity as a native.

Spivak's reading of Christophine as a disruptive figure in the text also complicates Hulme's suggestion that Antoinette's social status as a member of an ex-planter family undermines her credibility as a figure of anti-colonial resistance. For despite her privileged social position, Antoinette's identification with Tia and Christophine could be read as a symbol of political identification with the plight of African slaves. As Mary Lou Emery argues in *Jean Rhys at World's End* (1990), when the planter class lost its social and economic status in Jamaica after the Emancipation Act of 1833, Antoinette's mother (Annette) declared that they are 'marooned', suggesting that 'her family [had] been wrecked and abandoned to their fate on the island'.[19] However, in Antoinette's imagination, Emery contends that the word maroon also connotes the 'African [. . .] slaves who escaped from the plantations to hidden and nearly inaccessible parts of the islands'.[20] As a consequence, Annette inadvertently suggests to her daughter 'an alliance' with the 'Africans brought to the islands, and Afro-Creoles born on the islands, all of whom became identified as Maroons through their desire for freedom, strategies of flight, and tactics of guerrilla warfare'.[21]

Antoinette's identification with Tia and Christophine is not only a search for a non-essentialist cultural and political identity, but also for political agency. As Spivak points out, it is the return of Tia in Antoinette's dream at the end of the text that prompts her to burn down Thornfield Hall in both *Jane Eyre* and *Wide Sargasso Sea*. Rather than reading this dream as a repetition of Tia's traumatic rejection of Antoinette as a member of the white colonial elite in the aftermath of the Emancipation Act and the torching of her family home at Coulibri by black anti-colonial insurgents, Emery suggests that Antoinette's dream work is a strategy of political identification with former slaves that enables her to learn 'traditional means of resistance' from 'the history of the blacks on the island'.[22] Such a reading is further borne out when Antoinette subsequently awakens, and realizes what she must do to resist her incarceration at Thornfield Hall. In a reading that seems to depart from Spivak's argument, Emery argues that Antoinette's death is not a passive resignation to colonial authority, or an 'act of suicide, but of flight, *marronage*'.[23] In Emery's account, Antoinette's self-immolation and her torching of Thornfield Hall can be read as an active decision to rebel against colonial power, which is informed by the oral tradition of the blacks on the island and the obeah of Christophine.

Emery's reading of Antoinette's fate in *Wide Sargasso Sea* as an act of anti-colonial resistance both complements and complicates Spivak's reading of Antoinette's death as an act of self-immolation. By situating Antoinette's death in the fire at Thornfield Hall in relation to the history of black Jamaican anti-colonial insurgency, Emery attributes agency and meaning to Antoinette's flight. In a re-written version of 'Three Women's Texts and a Critique of Imperialism', published as part of a chapter on literature in *A Critique of Postcolonial Reason*, Spivak concedes that Emery's suggestion 'that the textual practices of *Wide Sargasso Sea* borrow from the techniques of the obeah – complicates [her] conviction that the other cannot be fully selved' (*CPR*, 132). Yet in a cryptic footnote on Emery's essay, Spivak emphasizes that she cannot be ' "responsible" within Christophine's text' in the same way that she is 'with Bhubaneswari Bhaduri' in her essay 'Can the Subaltern Speak?' (*CPR*, 131 n. 30). By drawing a parallel between her readings of Christophine and Bhubaneswari Bhaduri, Spivak suggests that what might seem to be a sign of women's oppression and disempowerment could actually be a sign of clandestine agency and resistance. As argued in chapter 4, Spivak's reading of Bhubaneswari Bhaduri's suicide examines her attempt to hide her involvement in a violent anti-colonial nationalist movement in India during the 1920s. In Spivak's account, Bhubaneswari had been assigned to an assassination mission, which she was unable to carry out. Bhubaneswari attempted to efface her involvement with the anti-colonial resistance movement by disguising the circumstances of her death as an act that resembled the practice of Hindu widow sacrifice. As a clandestine act of resistance, which is recorded as suicide, Bhubaneswari's death can thus be seen to resemble Antoinette's resistance in *Wide Sargasso Sea*. Spivak acknowledges that her reading of Antoinette's death in *Wide Sargasso Sea* is less locationist than that of Emery, which I take to mean less located in the history of anti-colonial insurgency and resistance in the Caribbean. Yet, at the same time, by drawing a parallel between her reading of Bhubaneswari's death and Emery's reading of Antoinette's death as an act of *marronage*, Spivak attributes agency and resistance to what might otherwise be interpreted as Antoinette/Bertha's tragic ending.

J. M. Coetzee's Foe *and the curious guardian at the margin*

Towards the end of her revised analysis of *Wide Sargasso Sea* in *A Critique of Postcolonial Reason*, Spivak compares her reading of the departure of Christophine in the text and the 'case of Friday in *Foe*' as 'a move to guard the margin' (*CPR*, 132). Such a reading emphasizes how postcolonial texts written in English or the European languages do not simply challenge the authority of colonial discourse by transparently representing the voices of the colonized, but rather guard the margin by withholding the voices of the colonized from representation. This reading strategy questions the political efficacy of national culture to decolonize the minds of postcolonial subjects and offers a conceptual space within which the vulnerability of the oppressed can be addressed.

In 'Theory in the Margin: Coetzee's *Foe* Reading Defoe's *Crusoe/Roxana*' (1991) Spivak argues that postcolonial texts are becoming commodified as cultural objects for a western readership: 'works in poor English translation or works written in English or the European languages in the recently decolonized areas of the globe or written by people of so-called ethnic origin in First World space are beginning to constitute something called "Third World literature"' (TM, 154). Mindful of her own participation in the commodification of postcolonial texts for an Anglo-American reader, Spivak adds that 'the upwardly mobile exmarginal [. . .] can help commodify marginality' (TM, 154). To counter this problem, Spivak invokes a discussion of marginality in the work of Derrida and Jean-Paul Sartre. Such a move may seem oddly incommensurate with the discussion of the postcolonial intellectual's participation in the commodification of the margins; yet for Spivak, Derrida's concern with the unknowability of the margins provides a vocabulary to distinguish between her position as a postcolonial intellectual and the marginality of the characters she speaks about later in her essay. Whereas Sartre's radical humanist subject betrays a Eurocentric arrogance, which 'consolididate[s] it*self* by imagining the other' (TM, 155), Spivak argues that deconstruction undoes this Eurocentrism by performing a double gesture. She formulates such a double gesture as follows: 'Begin where you are; but, when in search of absolute justification, remember that the margin is wholly other' (TM, 155). In the terms of Derrida's argument, the margin is what defines the philosopher's search for absolute knowledge, yet it cannot be grasped as a positive conceptual thing; this ill-named thing always escapes comprehension and is therefore 'wholly other'. For Spivak, Derrida's argument also has important consequences for postcolonial reading because it emphasizes that the non-European other is wholly unknowable by the western humanist self. Yet this marginal position where the other is unknowable does not simply mean that the other does not continue to act and live. Rather, Spivak argues that people designated 'other' occupy the position of curious guardians, who marginalize and withhold their culture from the systematic terms of dominant representation and knowledge. By marking the position of the curious guardian at the margin, Spivak identifies a rhetorical strategy for resisting the commodification of marginality.

Spivak goes on to clarify her argument about the marginalized non-western Other by focusing on J. M. Coetzee's *Foe* (1986), a fictional re-writing of Defoe's *Life and Adventures of Robinson Crusoe* (1719) and *Roxana* (1724). Spivak follows her prefatory discussion of Marx's reading of *Robinson Crusoe* in *Capital* (Vol. I) by countering the common assumption that the novel is 'about capitalism' (TWT, 160). In Spivak's view, many commentators overlook the specific *pre*-capitalist context in which Marx mentions *Robinson Crusoe* to illustrate how the use value of labour time is abstracted from the material body that produces it: 'The concrete individual is inherently predicated by the possibility of abstraction, and Marx's first great example of this is Robinson' (TM, 160). That is to say, Marx referred to the figure of Robinson Crusoe in order to make a point about the way in which the fruits of human labour become abstracted from the specific body that produced them, and not about the exchange of money.

Spivak makes this digression as a contrastive point, which underlines how Coetzee's *Foe* interrupts the European narrative of history and labour presented in *Robinson Crusoe*: '*Foe* is more about spacing and displacement than the timing of history and labor' (TW, 161). Whereas Defoe's Robinson Crusoe is the 'normative man in nature', who is committed to the productive administration of the island's natural resources for mercantile capitalism, *Foe's* Crusoe has no interest in documenting time or producing an inventory of tools from the shipwreck: 'Although produced by merchant capitalism, Crusoe has no interest in being its agent, not even to the extent of saving tools' (TM, 161).

As Spivak goes on to argue, *Foe* is more concerned with 'gender and empire [. . .] than the story of capital' (TM, 161). Whereas Defoe's text 'had no room for women' (TM, 161), Coetzee has a female narrator: Susan Barton writes a manuscript entitled *The Female Castaway*, as well as a letter and a memoir that frame 'the story of her discovery of Crusoe and Friday, Crusoe's death on board ship on the trip back to England and her arrival in England with Friday' (TM, 162). Such a narrative is supplementary to a straightforward reversal of the dichotomy between the colonizer and the colonized (or Crusoe and Friday) in Defoe's original. As Spivak observes, Coetzee interrupts the colonial inter-text by referring to a different Defoe novel: 'Coetzee makes the final episode of [. . .] *Roxana* flow into this citation of *Robinson Crusoe*' (TM, 163). The reason why Coetzee does so is to transform 'the bourgeois individualist woman' into an 'agent of *other*-directed ethics' (TW, 164). Whereas Defoe's heroine in *Roxana* is a self-interested individualist who 'cannot utter her passion for woman's freedom except as a ruse for her real desire to own, control, and manage money' (TM, 165), Coetzee's Susan Barton counters this patriarchal representation of female individualism and dismisses it as one of 'Mr Foe's ideas of a woman's dilemma, as merely "father born"' (TM, 165).

In Coetzee's re-writing of *Robinson Crusoe* the colonial narrative of Friday and Crusoe is paralleled by a mother-daughter plot, which

Susan Barton attempts to rescue from its patriarchal value coding. However, Barton's attempt to define a mother-daughter plot outside patriarchal value coding is frustrated by (what Susan Barton assumes to be) 'Foe's fabrication' (TM, 165). It is for this reason that Susan Barton 'cannot recognize' the 'woman who claims to be her daughter [and who] haunts her footsteps' (TM, 165). Indeed Barton's narrative quest for her daughter is ultimately subordinated to her desire to 'construct Friday as a subject' (TM, 168). In Spivak's reading, Coetzee's failure to maintain these two narratives simultaneously in 'a continuous narrative space' marks a significant aporia, which highlights the 'impossibility of a political program founded on overdetermination' (TM, 166). In other words, Coetzee's novel highlights the limitations of an alliance politics between anti-colonialism and feminism on the grounds that there are always antagonisms between and among different social and political movements. Such an argument echoes the point made by Ernesto Laclau and Chantal Mouffe in *Hegemony and Socialist Strategy* (1985), that there is no essential or necessary ground for political affiliation and alliance between different oppressed groups.

Similarly in 'Theory in the Margins' it is the lack of a necessary alliance between feminism and anti-colonialism that leads Spivak to conclude that feminism and anti-colonialism 'cannot occupy the same narrative space' (TM, 168). Susan Barton attempts to cross the aporia between feminism and anti-colonialism by 'broaching the real margin that has been haunting the text since its first page' (TM, 168): the figure of the colonized subject, Friday.

Comparing Defoe's representation of Friday with that of Coetzee, Spivak emphasizes that Coetzee does not simply give voice to Friday. Whereas Defoe keeps 'Friday's language acquisition skills at a fairly low level' (TM, 169), Coetzee refuses the benevolent anti-imperialist impulse to simply give Friday a voice. Such a refusal is exemplified in 'the last scene of Friday in Susan's narrative' (TM, 170), wherein Susan attempts to teach Friday how to write. In this writing lesson, one of the words that Barton attempts to teach Friday is 'Africa'. For Spivak this scene is particularly significant because it highlights the limitations of decolonization, and the impossibility of recovering a national identity uncontaminated by the legacy of colonialism. For Spivak, Susan Barton, as a representative 'metropolitan anti-imperialist', fails to teach Friday 'the proper name of his nation or continent' (TM, 170). This failure is significant because it demonstrates how the critical and political agenda of decolonization is founded on a catachresis, or a name without an adequate referent: *'Africa*, a Roman

name for what the Greeks called "Libya," itself perhaps a latiniza-
tion of the name of the Berber tribe Aourigha (perhaps pronounced
"Afarika")' (TM, 170). By invoking the etymology of Africa, Spivak
emphasizes that the project of national liberation can 'only ever be a
crucial political agenda against oppression' and that it 'cannot
provide the absolute guarantee of identity' (TM, 170).

Spivak's reading of *Foe* not only exemplifies the limitations of
nationalism as an emancipatory programme, but also upsets the
correlation of postcolonial literature and Third-world national liberation movements advocated by critics such as Barbara Harlow in
Resistance Literature (1987) and Bill Ashcroft and others in *The Empire
Writes Back* (1989). Friday's inability to enunciate the minimal pho-
nemic units of English could be taken as a sign that he is symboli-
cally silenced by the dominant discourse of Susan Barton's nationalist
pedagogy, as well as being physically silenced by slaveholders when
they cut out his tongue. Yet this is not to suggest that Friday has no
agency or voice outside western representation. In another scene,
Friday draws an image on a slate of 'open eyes, each set upon a foot'
(cited in TM, 171), which he erases as soon as Susan Barton demands
to see the slate. Spivak identifies this scene as a significant example
of Friday as the 'guardian of the margin' (TM, 171). By erasing his
drawing and withholding its meaning from both Susan and Foe,
Friday also withholds the possibility of his agency and cultural
sovereignty. While Susan asks 'How can Friday know what freedom
means when he barely knows his name?' (TM, 171), Spivak suggests
that Friday's knowledge of freedom cannot be accounted for in the
systematic terms of western knowledge and representation; instead,
Friday's cultural sovereignty is encrypted in the rows of 'walking
eyes'. As a consequence of this cryptic inscription, it is impossible
to determine whether the 'walking eyes' are 'rebuses, hieroglyphs,
[or] ideograms' or whether their secret is that 'they hold no secret
at all' (TM, 171). For Spivak, Friday is 'an unemphatic agent of withholding in the text' (TM, 172). Against Susan Barton's attempt to
construct the colonized subject as a victim who must be represented
in order to be saved, Friday 'withdraws to a space that may not be
a secret but cannot be unlocked' (TM, 172).

For Spivak the ambivalence of this withheld space places the
'native subject' in a position of agent rather than victim. As discussed in later chapters, Spivak has developed this strategy of withholding a voice from dominant discourse and representation in
'Can the Subaltern Speak?' and in *A Critique of Postcolonial Reason*.
It is worth noting here, however, that withholding is a recurrent

rhetorical and political concept-metaphor in Spivak's work: it often signifies a refusal to be represented in the dominant terms of a colonial authority or elite nationalist formation. Following the logic of Spivak's argument, since the representation of subaltern constituencies effectively means silencing their voice and demands, the refusal of representation offers a provisional strategy of resistance. What is more, the walking eyes that Friday inscribes and erases in *Foe* also leave a cryptic trace of a situated cultural practice and subaltern history, which cannot be translated and accommodated into a dominant system of representation.

Such a subversive form of subaltern writing parallels the cave painting in Mahasweta Devi's 'Pterodactyl, Puran Sahay and Pirtha', one of three stories translated by Spivak in the publication entitled *Imaginary Maps* (1995). In this story, a tribal boy named Bikhia draws a pterodactyl on the wall of a cave in the fictional Indian village of Nagesia; this cave drawing takes on a life of its own in the consciousness of the tribal community as that community starts to die from starvation, water pollution and poverty. For the protagonist Puran Sahay, an educated, middle-class, left-wing journalist who visits the village to write a report on the oppression of the aboriginal community in India, the plight of the tribal community is caused by state corruption, caste oppression, dispossession and famine. Yet, as Puran gradually realizes through a non-verbal exchange with Bikhia about the pterodactyl cave drawing, '[t]here are no words in [the tribals'] language to explain the daily experience of the tribal in India'.[24] This silent message involves a face-to-face encounter between Puran and Bikhia in which Puran tries to interpret Bikhia's eyes: 'What do the eyes want to tell Puran? [. . .] There is no communication between eyes. Only a dusky waiting without end'.[25] Despite Puran's attempts to decipher Bikhia's meaning, he ultimately realizes that he cannot do this. For Bikhia's drawing of the pterodactyl stands as an unrepresentable sign of the way in which the tribal community understands its own history, its relationship to the land and its precarious future. And since this subaltern knowledge is encrypted in the cave drawing of the pterodactyl it cannot be translated in the secular terms of India's postcolonial narrative. Like Friday in Coetzee's *Foe*, Bikhia stands as a guardian of the margin who protects the meaning of his culture by withholding it: 'Having drawn that stone tablet Bikhia is the guardian of the new *myth*. He will protect it'.[26]

Spivak's reading of Coetzee's *Foe* makes three important points. Firstly, her observation that anti-colonialism and feminism cannot occupy the same narrative space highlights the limitations of western feminism to account for the plight of colonial subjects. Secondly, Spivak's reading of the writing lesson draws attention to the limitations of nationalism as a political programme that claims to represent and emancipate the whole population. Thirdly, Spivak's discussion of withholding emphasizes the limitations of postcolonial critical approaches that interpret speech and self-representation as an unequivocal sign of agency and emancipation.

Indeed it is significant that in 'Theory in the Margin' Spivak's last word is a critical response to Benita Parry's critique of postcolonial theory in an article entitled 'Problems in Current Theories of Colonial Discourse' (1987). In Parry's account, the postcolonial theory of Homi Bhabha, Abdul J. Jan Mohammed and Gayatri Spivak effectively silences the voice and agency of postcolonial subjects because they are overly dependent on western poststructuralist critiques of representation, which define agency and subjectivity as an effect of language. Spivak's rebuttal to Parry's critique starts with a curious autobiographical and identity-based claim that Bhabha, Jan Mohammed and Spivak 'are natives too' (TM, 172). Such an assertion may seem to sit uneasily with the poststructuralist critique of identity and representation that Spivak frequently advocates elsewhere. What is crucial, however, is Spivak's epistemological and ethical counter-claim that the margins cannot be known, recovered or transparently represented in the straightforward way that Parry suggests: 'my particular word to Parry is that her efforts (to give voice to the native) as well as mine (to give warning of the attendant problems) are judged by those strange margins of which Friday with his withholding slate is only a mark' (TM, 173).

Mahasweta Devi and the limits of decolonization

Spivak's critical response to Benita Parry in 'Theory in the Margin' is part of a broader debate about the limitations of nationalism as an emancipatory programme in the postcolonial world. For critics such as Benita Parry, Aijaz Ahmad, Neil Lazarus and Ranajit Guha (among others), national liberation was a crucial part of decolonization, which often succeeded in mobilizing the people in a collective struggle against European colonial rule. While these critics acknowledge the limitations of postcolonial nationalisms, which privilege the interests of dominant or elite groups in particular postcolonial societies, they also stress the importance of distinguishing between elite forms of anti-colonial resistance and popular forms of resistance, such as organized peasant insurgency, strike action or the participation of women in anti-colonial resistance movements. Furthermore, they suggest that rearticulating the nation as a progressive political form from the standpoint of the subaltern rather than the elite is a crucial strategy for postcolonial theory because it is capable of producing a counter-narrative of liberation in the context of the capitalist world system.

For theorists such as Robert Young, Gayatri Spivak and Homi Bhabha, however, the nation-state as a regulative political concept is inadequate to describe anti-colonial liberation struggles partly because of its provenance in eighteenth-century bourgeois European society and philosophy. As Spivak observes in her essay 'More on Power/Knowledge': '[i]n the historical frame of [. . .] decolonization – what is being effectively reclaimed is a series of regulative political concepts, the supposedly authoritative narrative of which was written elsewhere in the social formations of western Europe' (*OTM*, 48). Moreover, Spivak proceeds to question the automatic assumption that political independence is 'an unexamined good that operates a reversal' between colonialism and decolonization (*OTM*, 48).

It is not only nationalism's European provenance that prompts poststructuralist theorists such as Spivak, Young and Bhabha to question its political efficacy in the postcolonial world. Another explanation for the questioning of national independence relates more specifically to the historical conditions of national independence in India, which have been persistently criticized by the Subaltern Studies historians. As Robert Young observes in *Postcolonialism: An Historical Introduction* (2001):

> Originating from a country which achieved political independence without a social revolution, the Subaltern Studies historians have sought to reconfigure the struggles of ordinary people who had customarily fallen outside historical narratives, been characterised in general terms as the masses, whose resistance has been continuous and who have yet to achieve emancipation or social equality.[27]

I examine Spivak's critical engagement with the Subaltern Studies historians in more detail in chapter 4. The crucial point that I want to underline here is that Spivak's critique of postcolonial nationalism makes more sense if it is situated in relation to the specific social and historical circumstances of Indian independence.

Such a critique is most clearly articulated in Spivak's prefaces to and commentaries on the writing of Mahasweta Devi, who has persistently addressed the plight of socially and politically marginalized groups in India in her fiction and journalism. In 'A Literary Representation of the Subaltern', for instance, Spivak offers a commentary on Devi's short story 'Stanadayini' (which Spivak translates as 'Breast Giver'). In Devi's own commentary, the story 'is a parable of India after decolonization' (cited in *IOW*, 204). It concerns the plight of Jashoda, a lower-caste woman who has been a wet nurse to several children in a wealthy, upper-middle-class Brahmin household and dies from breast cancer as a result.

In Spivak's reading of 'Breast Giver', the story does not merely offer 'a parable of India after decolonization', but also highlights the failure of nationalism to transform the lives of subaltern women. Spivak questions the 'emancipatory possibilities' of nationalism 'within the imperialist theater' and suggests that postcolonial nationalism in India has often worked to suppress the 'innumerable examples of resistance throughout the imperialist and pre-imperialist centuries' (*IOW*, 245). Furthermore, such forces of nationalism have been 'instrumental in changing the geo-political conjuncture from territorial imperialism to neo-colonialism' (*IOW* 245).

Spivak's concern with examples of subaltern resistance is also exemplified in her critique of the Subaltern Studies historians (see chapter 4 below). Yet her general point that elite nationalism has failed to change the social and economic circumstances of subaltern constituencies such as women, the rural peasantry and tribal communities is also relevant to 'Breast Giver'. By carefully distinguishing between the histories and practices of subaltern groups on the one hand and the history of elite nationalism and its complicity with neocolonialism on the other, Spivak refutes Devi's authorial interpretation of 'Breast Giver' as a parable of the postcolonial nation on the grounds that this reproduces the gendered terms of dominant nationalist rhetoric:

> [T]he ideological construct 'India' is too deeply informed by the goddess-infested reverse sexism of the Hindu majority. As long as there is this hegemonic cultural self-representation of India as goddess-mother (dissimulating the possibility that this mother is a slave), she will collapse under the burden of the immense expectations that such a self-representation permits (*IOW*, 204).

Spivak takes issue with Devi's interpretation of the story as a parable on the grounds that it ignores the embodied experiences and history of the subaltern protagonist Jashoda; instead, it contributes to the 'reverse sexism' of patriarchal Hindu nationalist mythology. Devi herself implies that Jashoda's cancerous body stands as a vehicle for the tenor of the postcolonial nation. Such a reading erases the materiality of the mother's body. As Sandhya Shetty notes in a related article on the Mother India trope, '(Dis) figuring the Nation' (1995): 'If Jashoda as gendered subaltern is only a sign-vehicle that transports the burden of a "greater meaning" (nation as exploited and abused mother/slave), then she fails fully to be a representation or signifier of subalternity as such'.[28] Spivak suggests that Devi's interpretation overlooks a crucial dimension of her story: 'how the narratives of nationalism have been and remain irrelevant to the life of the subordinate' (*IOW*, 245).

In Spivak's reading, Jashoda's position 'invokes the singularity of the gendered subaltern' (*IOW*, 252). In other words, Jashoda's social location cannot be known or represented *as such*: 'the subaltern's own idiom did not allow [her] to *know* [her] struggle so that [she] could articulate himself as its subject' (*IOW*, 253). Instead, the social consciousness of the subaltern can be grasped only through dominant or 'elite' critical approaches. Spivak therefore evaluates a series of different 'elite approaches' to Devi's story and considers the various ways in which the singularity of Jashoda's position interrupts the epistemological claims of different critical methodologies including Marxist feminism, liberal feminism and feminist theory informed by Lacanian psychoanalysis.

Spivak's critical engagement with Marxist feminism is broadly sympathetic to the many Marxist-feminist theorists who argue that women's domestic labour is conventionally excluded from European Marxist thought, which is exclusively concerned with the wage labour of the masculine, working-class subject. However, such an argument does not account for the reproductive labour of subaltern women like Jashoda. Citing a 'representative generalization' from the Marxist-feminist theory of Lise Vogel – that it is men's role as subsistence providers during the childbearing period that forms the material basis of women's oppression – Spivak argues that 'Stanadayini' reverses this generalization (*IOW*, 247). In Spivak's view, it is the income generated by Jashoda's 'repeated gestation and lactation' during her employment as a wet nurse to a wealthy Brahmin family that allows her to support her husband and her family. Indeed the 'sale of Jashoda's labour power' shifts the focus of Marxist feminist theory from the family as the subject of reproduction to the mothering female (*IOW*, 248). From the gendered standpont of the subaltern woman, this challenges the masculine-centred logic underpinning the labour theory of value in the work of materialist thinkers such as Marx.

Further, Spivak's 'account of the deployment of some Marxist-feminist "themes" introduces a stutter in the presupposition that women's work is typically non-productive of value' (*IOW*, 249). This 'stutter' signifies an interruption in the universalizing critical narrative of western Marxist feminism by the reproductive body of the gendered subaltern (*IOW*, 250). Yet this is not to suggest that such a singular example of women's reproductive labour should be taken as the basis for a radical rethinking of Marxist feminism. Spivak's more subtle and modest claim is that it is 'the body's susceptibility to the production of value which makes it vulnerable to idealization and therefore to insertion into the economic' (*IOW*, 252).

Spivak's criticism of liberal feminist readings takes issue with the tendency of non-Marxist anti-racist feminism in Anglo-America to overlook class antagonisms between the elite and the subaltern in Third-world literature. Citing Devi's representation of the elite male character Haldarkarta, Spivak argues that the story 'dramatizes indigenous class formation under imperialism and its connection to the movement towards women's social emancipation' (*IOW*, 254). Although this patriarchal figure in Devi's story might seem an unlikely figure to enable women's social emancipation, it is Haldarkarta's political and economic power as a 'comprador capitalist' that allows 'the Haldar women to move into a species of reproductive emancipation seemingly outside of patriarchal control' (*IOW*, 255). In Spivak's account, a liberal feminist approach to this story would concentrate on the Haldar women's reproductive emancipation and ignore the fact that this emancipation is also enabled by the reproductive labour of 'the gendered subaltern (Jashoda)' (*IOW*, 256).

One of the questions raised by Spivak's critique of liberal feminism is whether women's 'reproductive rights' should be a universal political goal for global feminism (Spivak's contribution to debates about reproductive rights is discussed further in chapter 5 below). In the context of this analysis of Spivak's commentary on 'Breast Giver', however, note the following tantalizing observation: 'The solution to Jashoda's problem cannot be mere reproductive rights but productive rights as well [. . .;] these rights are denied her not just by men but by elite women as well. This is the underlying paradox of population control in the Third World (*IOW*, 258). What Spivak implies but does not state here is that western liberal feminism's privileging of 'reproductive rights' as a universal political goal can inadvertently serve to oppress subaltern women in the global South if it is translated into the rhetoric of population control by elite women in India. Since Spivak does not elaborate on the politics of population control in 'A Literary Representation of the Subaltern', I will not discuss it further here. Suffice it to say that such a concern prefigures an important theme in Spivak's later contributions to feminist scholarship (see chapter 5). To conclude this chapter, I consider how Spivak criticizes the claims of French feminist theory.

Spivak's critical engagement with feminist theory starts with a brief discussion of the valorization of 'woman's orgasmic pleasure [. . .] in excess of copulation or reproduction' (*IOW*, 258) in the French feminist theory of Luce Irigaray and Monique Wittig. Rather than elaborating on the arguments of a particular French feminist thinker, however, Spivak turns to an essay by the psychoanalyst Jacques Lacan,' 'A Love Letter', first published in French in 1975. The explanation given for this detour is that Lacan's text constitutes 'a man's text about women's silence' and that this will help to clarify a claim by an unnamed Bengali woman writer that ' "Mahasweta Devi writes like a man" ' (*IOW*, 258). Spivak's discussion of Lacan's text may seem to shift away from Spivak's critique of feminist theory. However, as I now suggest, Spivak's reading of Lacan also helps to clarify some of the limitations of western feminist theory.

Spivak argues that the Lacanian definition of *jouissance* cannot be reduced to woman's orgasmic pleasure, even though it is a marker of gendered subjectivity: 'Thought, as *jouissance*, is not orgasmic pleasure genitally defined, but the excess of being that escapes the circle of the reproduction of the subject. It is the mark of the Other in the subject' (*IOW*, 259). This general philosophical sense of *jouissance* as an excess that cannot be known or grasped as a positive presence is often interpreted as inherently radical by western feminist theorists such as Luce Irigaray or Monique Wittig because it refuses the logic of masculine intelligibility. However, as Spivak points out, this radical understanding of *jouissance* cannot be universally applied to the social and political position of subaltern women such as Jashoda, whose body is 'the place where the sinister knowledge of decolonization as failure of foster-mothering is figured forth produces cancer' (*IOW*, 260). If, as Spivak suggests, Devi's figuration of Jashoda's cancerous breast as a monstrous part-object that mocks her reproductive body is an example of *jouissance*, it is 'very far from the singularity of the clitoral orgasm', which is often

taken to exemplify women's *jouissance* in western feminist theory
(*IOW*, 260).

Towards the end of 'Breast Giver', the narrator describes how 'the
sores on [Jashoda's] breast kept mocking her with a hundred mouths,
a hundred eyes' (*IOW*, 260). In this passage, Jashoda's breast stands
as a metonym for her reproductive maternal body. By transforming
this metonym into a monstrous figure with mouths and eyes and
other human features, Devi foregrounds the continued exploitation
of the subaltern female body after decolonization. In Spivak's
reading, Devi's employment of anthropomorphism is further regis-
tered by the original Bengali phrase *Byango korte thaklo*, which
Spivak translates as 'kept mocking' (*IOW*, 260). Recalling the Sanskrit source (*vyangya*) of the modern Bengali word for mock (*byango*),
Spivak argues that 'the sores on Jashoda's breast' do not only "mock
her" as the English translation suggests, but they also mock the
process of signification (*IOW*, 260).

Spivak's reading of Devi's use of figurative language to register
the materiality of Jashoda's cancerous body reveals '(a race-and-
class-specific) gendering at work in Lacanian theory' (*IOW*, 261). For
this reason, Spivak supplements her critique of Lacanian feminist
theory with a commentary on the tragic ending of 'Breast Giver',
where Jashoda is described as both a 'Hindu female' and 'God
manifest' after a painful death from breast cancer, yet is cremated
by an untouchable in a burning ghat (*IOW*, 240). Spivak suggests
that there may seem to be a conceptual resemblance between the
equation of Jashoda's death and the divine in 'Breast Giver' and
Lacan's correlation of woman's *jouissance* and the idea of God in his
Seminar XX. For just as Lacan contends that '[i]t is in so far as her
jouissance is radically Other that the woman has a relation to God',[29]
so Jashoda is described as divine.

Yet for Spivak the superficial resemblance, which she identifies,
between the ending of 'Breast Giver' and Lacan's seminar on female
sexuality ignores the dynamics of caste and religion that frame the
representation of Jashoda's death. The naming of Jashoda as a
'Hindu female' stands in ironic contrast to her subordinate status
in the Haldar household. As Sandhya Shetty observes, 'this com-
mandeering of the urban subproletariat woman as allegorical sign
is ironic given the historical emergence of "Mother India" as a
bourgeois ideological construct'.[30] Furthermore, Spivak notes a shift
in the religious register used in Devi's closing description of Jashoda
from a 'satiric indexing of the ideological use of goddesses' to a
'discourse of philosophical monotheism' (*IOW*, 262).

Spivak tries to account for this shift in register by reading it as a failure of the subaltern subject (the fictional character Jashoda) to translate the discourse of religion into the discourse of militancy. In doing so, she seems to overlook the irony implicit in Devi's description of Jashoda as 'God manifest'. Spivak is not unaware of this difficulty, however, and attempts to rectify it by distinguishing between the story (*énoncé*) and the text as statement (*énonciation*). This distinction enables Spivak to clarify the difference between the protagonist's ideological subjection to the bourgeois nationalist myth of Mother India as a subaltern woman and the implied author's ironic use of elite religious discourse to criticize the disenfranchisement and exploitation of subaltern women.

Taken together, Spivak's readings of Mahasweta Devi's 'Breast Giver' work to interrupt the critical paradigms of Marxist feminism, liberal feminism and Lacanian feminist theory. This strategy of critical interruption exemplifies how Devi's writing has, at least in part, provided Spivak with a vocabulary to articulate the experience and knowledge of the subaltern woman. In this respect, the practice of reading for Spivak is a social, political and ethical act which involves learning to learn from the subaltern.

2

Deconstruction

The previous chapter focuses on Spivak's important contribution to postcolonial literary studies. Yet this is not to suggest that the scope and influence of her thought is confined to the discipline of literary studies. For Spivak's career-long engagement with Derrida and deconstruction has also involved critical interventions in social and political studies, development studies, women's studies, philosophy, geography and history. As I argue in this chapter, Spivak's readings of Derrida, including her 'Translator's Preface' (1976) to *Of Grammatology* and writings such as 'Responsibility' (1994) and *A Critique of Postcolonial Reason* (1999), have demonstrated the social and political relevance of Derrida's work; they also provide a rigorous introduction to some of the most significant philosophers to have influenced Derrida. In so doing, Spivak has defended Derrida's thought against erroneous and reductive readings, which sought to equate deconstruction with relativism and the denial of a referential world outside language and textuality.

Deconstruction and textuality

As Derrida frequently pointed out, deconstruction refuses straight-forward definition: 'All sentences of the type "deconstruction is X" or "deconstruction is not X" *a priori* miss the point'.[1] For Derrida, 'deconstruction is not a doctrine; it's not a method, nor is it a set of rules or tools'.[2] Rather, deconstruction is concerned to trace the blindspots and aporias that underpin systems of philosophical truth, yet cannot be accounted for in the positive terms of philosophy's propositional logic.

One of the most repeatedly misunderstood phrases that has been invoked to exemplify Derrida's theoretical position is '[t]here is nothing outside of the text' (*il n'y a pas de hors texte*).[3] For some critics and commentators this phrase epitomizes Derrida's denial of a 'real world' outside the text.[4] Such readings, however, overlook Derrida's argument that writing or 'the text' constitutes the so-called 'real world'. Further, these readings miss the specific theoretical genealogy of the word 'text' in Derrida's thought. As the cultural historian John Mowitt has argued in his book *Text* (1992), the very word in Derrida's theoretical vocabulary denotes an object which produces 'the complex institutional structure of knowing'.[5] In this definition 'the text is an ambivalent object or field' which 'is simultaneously shared by several disciplines, while also exposing those disciplines not merely to the borders they share, but to their limits as formations of disciplinary power'.[6] For Mowitt, 'it is not just because anything *could* be read as a text' in Derrida's thought 'that nothing is outside the text'.[7] Rather, it is precisely because reading is a subjective or 'psychical activity', which 'necessarily textualizes whatever it reads, that nothing can present itself within the psyche without doing so on the textual register'.[8]

It is important to note that much of Derrida's thought is concerned to trace the textual structures that underpin disciplinary philosophy. In this sense, the text is an '(anti)disciplinary pivot between literature and philosophy'.[9] This is not to suggest that Derrida is concerned with the meaning of literary texts as such. Indeed for more orthodox philosophical commentators on Derrida's work, for example Rodolphe Gasché, attempts to characterize or appropriate Derrida's thought as a form of literary theory ignore the rigorous engagements with western philosophy that much of his work undertakes. Nevertheless, it is fair to say that Derrida's reading of philosophical texts from Plato to Heidegger exposes the textual or rhetorical structures that frame those texts.

Spivak's 'Translator's Preface' to *Of Grammatology*

It is precisely this deconstructive approach to reading philosophical texts that Spivak addresses in her 'Translator's Preface' (1976) to Derrida's *Of Grammatology* (French original 1967). Indeed, many reviewers at the time of publication praised Spivak's preface for making the complexity and subtlety of Derrida's thought accessible to Anglophone readers. Hugh M. Davidson, for instance, stated that Spivak's 'sympathetic 87-page "Translator's Preface" [. . .] makes a heroic and largely successful effort to bring us to the point of entry into Derrida's text'.[10] Others, such as Roland A. Champagne, were critical of the 'uneven quality' of Spivak's translation, arguing that her 'glossing method', used to recover 'the polyvalence of the original text', 'prevents the reader from following [Derrida's text] step by step'; however, Champagne also praised Spivak's sensitivity to the many implications of Derrida's polyvalent language as well as the explanatory value of her preface.[11] In a similar vein, the literary critic Denis Donoghue asserted in The *New Republic* (1977) that 'Spivak's long introductory essay is nearly as difficult as the text it precedes, but it is extremely perceptive and helpful'.[12] What is more, Donoghue claimed that Spivak's translation of Derrida is 'deliberately literal' in its attempt to render the philosophical nuances of Derrida's thought: '[Spivak] is determined that if we encounter [Derrida] at all we will earn the right to do so by coping with his recalcitrance'.[13] In defence of Spivak's complex rendering of Derrida, Donoghue concluded that '[a]n easy translation' of Derrida's *Grammatology* 'would be a bad translation'.[14]

In an article entitled 'Touched by Deconstruction' (2005), Spivak reflects on the influence that Derrida has had on her work, and in particular the profound impact that translating *Of Grammatology* had on her intellectual development. Significantly, Spivak admits that 'no one taught [her] deconstruction' (TD, 95), and that her encounter with Derrida's thought was not informed by a formal philosophical training. This is not to suggest, however, that a degree in western philosophy is a necessary prerequisite for reading Derrida. Indeed, Spivak proceeds to ask what it means 'to be correct about deconstruction' (TD, 96). As an English honours graduate from Calcutta University, Spivak suggests that her singular engagement with Derrida's thought is as legitimate a reading as any other philosophical interpretation.

Moreover, as I now suggest, Spivak's preface clearly situates Derrida's thought in relation to the western philosophical tradition. Rather than assess the merits of her translation, I now examine the contribution that it made to the critical understanding and reception of Derrida's thought and then consider how *Of Grammatology* shaped the trajectory of Spivak's thought.

Much of Spivak's preface is concerned to trace the philosophical sources and debates with which Derrida engages. Citing Friedrich

Nietzsche's essay 'On Truth and Falsity in their Ultramoral Sense' (1873–4), for instance, Spivak observes how the nineteenth-century German philosopher influenced Derrida's deconstructive approach through disclosing the metaphorical basis of philosophical truth. For Nietzsche, truth is a 'mobile army of metaphors, metonymies, anthropomorphisms'; 'truths are illusions of which one has forgotten that they *are* illusions' (cited in TP, xxii). In a similar vein, for Spivak, Derrida uncovers the textual basis of philosophical truth by exposing textuality as the unacknowledged ground upon which philosophical truth claims are made.

One strategy that Derrida employs in this process is to cross out particular words or concepts in philosophical texts, a strategy that Derrida calls placing 'under erasure'. As Spivak observes, in his *Question of Being* (German original 1955) Martin Heidegger argued that we always assume that something exists 'in order for the nature of anything in particular to be defined as an entity' (TP, xiv). As a consequence, the answer to the question of Being, or 'what is?', is always anterior to thinking and language, and thus can 'never be formulated as an answer to the question "what is . . ." ' (TP, xiv). In order to present this unrepresentable question, which is prior to thought and language, 'Heidegger crosses out the word "Being", and lets both deletion and word stand' (TP, xv).

Yet, as Spivak goes on to argue, Heidegger's claim that 'Being' is prior to language and thought 'sets up Being as what Derrida calls the "transcendental signified" ' (TP, xvi). That is to say, the answer to the question of Being is transcendental because it transcends language and signification, and it is the final signified because all concepts and ideas refer back to the unanswerable question of Being. In this respect, Heidegger seeks to recover a lost presence. By contrast, Spivak argues that 'Derrida seems to show no nostalgia for a lost presence' (TP, xvi). Instead he 'suggests that what opens the possibility of thought is not merely the question of being, but also the never-annulled difference from "the completely other' " (TP, xvii). In other words, Derrida holds that the condition of possibility for thought is not the unrepresentable answer to the question of Being, but a 'mark of the absence of a presence, an always already absent present, of the lack at the origin' (TP, xvii).

In Spivak's account, the crucial difference between Derrida's position and that of Heidegger is that Heidegger seems to hold a residual belief in the referential power of language as a transparent signifying system to convey meaning. For Derrida, by contrast, language is 'a structure of difference' (TP, xvii). Drawing on

Ferdinand de Saussure's *Course in General Linguistics* (French original 1922), according to which 'in language there are only differences, and no positive terms',[15] Derrida emphasizes that the structure of language is nothing other than a series of marks or traces, which denote an always-absent presence. For Derrida a thing is not defined by what it is, but rather in relation to what it is not. Whereas Heidegger placed the word 'Being' under erasure in the hope that its final meaning might be restored, Derrida rejects the possibility of such a transcendent meaning. It is for this reason that Derrida places the word 'sign' under erasure in *Of Grammatology* (TP, xvii).

For Derrida, the structure of differences that constitutes the relationship between linguistic signs is simultaneously a structure of infinite deferral because the systematic play of linguistic signs never reaches a fixed relation of identity with the referents they claim to denote. In an essay of 1968 Derrida invents the term *différance*, which means to differ and to defer, in order to convey the double movement of signification in space and time. As Spivak explains, Derrida's argument is indebted to Saussure's thesis in *The Course in General Linguistics* that the process by which meaning is constructed through language is based on a system of differences, or binary oppositions, in which the meaning of a word is defined in relation to what it is not.

In the philosophical terms of Derrida's argument, concepts such as truth, presence, knowledge and meaning are similarly defined by what they are not: in plain terms, truth is defined by falsity, presence by absence, knowledge by non-knowledge, and meaning by nonsense. What is more, the coherence of concepts such as truth, presence, knowledge and meaning are constituted by the exclusion of the opposite term. This constitutive exclusion of the opposite term in a binary opposition makes it appear as if a given concept such as truth, presence, knowledge or meaning is self-identical. Yet, for Derrida, the task of the deconstructive thinker is to disclose how the coherence of a particular concept is predicated on the exclusion of its opposite term through a persistent process of reversal and displacement. In Derrida's argument, a binary opposition cannot be simply overcome through the reversal of the two terms that structure that opposition, since to do so would be to remain caught within the terms of that opposition. Instead, Derrida elaborates a reading strategy that traces the simultaneous overturning of a binary opposition, which brings low what was high, and, at the same time, marks the interval between this reversal and the 'irruptive emergence of a new "concept"'.[16] For Derrida, this interval is undecidable, and as such it refuses the resolution of a contradiction between two terms in a binary opposition.

In her 'Translator's Preface' to *Of Grammatology* Spivak emphasizes that European thinkers from Hegel to Freud anticipated Derrida's double sense of *différance* even if they did not articulate the concept in the same terms. In the *Science of Logic* (German original 1816), for instance, Hegel employed the word different to account for the comprehension of the presence of time through a relation of difference.[17] Such a differential notion of time was developed further by Nietzsche and Freud in their accounts of the unconscious. As Derrida contends, when both Nietzsche and Freud 'put consciousness into question in its assured certainty of itself [. . .] they did so on the basis of *différance*'.[18] For Nietzsche the unconscious is 'that vast arena of the mind of which the so-called "subject" knows nothing' (TP, xxv). Put differently, consciousness is the effect of a play of differential forces of which the subject is largely unconscious.[19]

Freud expands on Nietzsche's concept of the unconscious in order to account for the structure of human memory and consciousness in *The Interpretation of Dreams* (German original 1900) and 'A Note upon the "Mystic Writing Pad"' (1923). In so doing, Freud also anticipates Derrida's deconstruction of metaphysics. As Spivak points out, '[w]hether he acknowledges it or not, Freud implies that the psyche is a sign-structure "sous rature," [under erasure] for like the sign, it is inhabited by a radical alterity, what is totally other' (TP, xxxviii). The analogy between the structure of the sign and that of the psyche recalls Derrida's argument in 'Freud and the Scene of Writing' (1967) that the psyche is structured like a text. As mentioned earlier, Derrida emphasizes that the psyche can make sense of the world only through the textual structure of language. More specifically, by invoking Freud's idea of deferred action (*Nachträglichkeit*), Derrida suggests that the process of signification or making meaning is indefinitely postponed or deferred through a trace-structure. Just as Freud argued in *The Interpretation of Dreams* that repressed memories cannot be represented as such, but are retrospectively revealed through a process of sublimation and deferred action, so for Derrida writing is a process of deferral.

Besides examining some of the key thinkers and concepts that have influenced the development of Derrida's thought in her preface to *Of Grammatology*, Spivak also stresses that Derrida problematizes the relationship between literature and philosophy by revealing how textuality inhabits both of these disciplines (TP, lxxii). As mentioned above, subsequent philosophical commentators on Derrida's work, for example Rodolphe Gasché, Irene Harvey and John Llewelyn, have argued that readings of Derrida that try to align his work with literature run the risk of falsely equating deconstruction with anti-foundationalism or relativism. In so doing, such readings ignore the significance of Derrida's careful engagement with the rational codes and conventions of western philosophical discourse.[20]

In his *Tain of the Mirror* (1986) Gasché situates Derrida's concern with writing and textuality in relation to Hegel. Referring to *The Phenomenology of Spirit* (1807), Gasché describes how Hegel sought to resolve the irreducible antinomy between the thinking subject and the object of cognition in Kant's work by developing a speculative theory of reflection that would transcend the dichotomies of subject and object.[21] To achieve this goal, Hegel elaborated a theory of the speculative proposition that would 'alter radically the relation between subject and predicate in predicative sentences or empirical propositions'.[22] Since the ordinary proposition isolates and separates the subject and the predicate it 'seems an inappropriate form of expression for speculative content', because the content of speculative thought seeks to transcend differences between the subject and object of cognition.[23] In Gasché's argument, Derrida radically develops Hegel's speculative thought via Nietzsche, Husserl and Heidegger in order to account for the (non)representable ground or supplementary condition of possibility, which underpins philosophical truth claims, yet cannot be resolved in the dialectical terms of speculative reason.

Like Gasché, Spivak is aware of the dangers of readings of Derrida's thought which pass over his careful engagement with philosophical texts, and signals this as follows:

> [Derrida's thought] might seem an attractively truant world of relativism. But the fearful pleasure of a truant world is the sense of an authority being defied. That absolute ground of authority Derrida would deny. It would be a spurious pleasure for the literary critic to feel that this is a more literary idiom than the austere propositional logic we habitually associate with philosophy proper. Textuality inhabits both and the distinction between them remains to be deconstructed. (TP, lxxii)

While Spivak does not simply equate Derrida's thought with anti-foundationalism or relativism, her reading of Derrida does not define his thought as 'pure' philosophy either. In this respect, Spivak anticipates Geoffrey Bennington's criticism of orthodox philosophical readings of Derrida (such as Gasché's), which attempt to situate his thought in relation to the history of western philosophy. Since Derrida is primarily concerned to trace the constitutive aporias that are *excluded* from western philosophical discourse in order to maintain the coherence and closure of philosophical truth, Bennington contends that philosophical commentaries on Derrida are not philosophical enough precisely because they attempt to account for Derrida's thought by framing it within the very western philosophical tradition that Derrida seeks to destabilize.[24]

What is more, such readings ignore how philosophy itself is impure because it often borrows words and metaphors from other discourses and disciplines in order to bypass aporia and to present its concepts as logical and systematic. In the 'Critique of Teleological Judgement' (1790), for instance, Kant turned to anthropological metaphors to bridge the gap between the empirical knowledge of nature on the one hand and the cognition of a transcendent universal law behind nature on the other. As Spivak argues in *A Critique of Postcolonial Reason*, the anthropological metaphor that Kant drew on to close the gap between empirical knowledge and the transcendent universal law is the bourgeois, masculine subject of western reason ('man').[25] By positing 'man' as the cause of transcendent reason, in other words, Kant tried to circumvent the antithesis between empirical knowledge and transcendent reason.

As I go on to argue, Spivak's reading of Kant's use of anthropological metaphors in *A Critique of Postcolonial Reason* exemplifies what she calls the foreclosure of the native informant and the privileging of the bourgeois, masculine subject as the universal subject of reason in European thought. At this point, however, I turn to another significant influence on the development of Spivak's engagement with deconstruction: the work of Paul de Man.

Paul de Man and the rhetoric and politics of reading

As mentioned above, Paul de Man was Spivak's doctoral supervisor at Cornell University in the early 1960s, and subsequently became known as one of the leading advocates of deconstructive criticism in the United States.[26] It was partly de Man who encouraged Spivak to translate *Of Grammatology* before he himself had read Derrida (TD, 97). Significantly, Spivak's translation was published in 1976, a year before de Man's deconstructive reading of Derrida's reading of Rousseau's 'Essay on the Origins of Language' in *Of Grammatology*. It is to de Man's critical reading of Derrida's reading of Rousseau that I now turn.

For Derrida, Rousseau's essay appears to foreground what Derrida calls phonocentrism, or the repression of writing outside full speech, which has provided the foundation for western metaphysics. Yet at the same time, Derrida questions whether Rousseau fully intended to foreground the privileging of speech and the debasement of writing in this essay. Indeed, Derrida suggests that the ambivalence of Rousseau's language in the 'Essay on the Origins of Language' undermines the very idea that there is a coherent self named Rousseau who is fully present and in control of his own writing. Moreover since Rousseau never openly declares 'the disappearance [of full presence] in the word itself, in the illusion of immediacy',[27] Derrida concludes that Rousseau is unable to account for the radical insights of his own text. For this reason, Derrida contends that Rousseau's essay repeats the phonocentric fallacy that Derrida attributes to many other philosophers of the western metaphysical tradition.

For de Man, however, Derrida's reading of Rousseau does not go far enough. While de Man praises the story that Derrida tells of Rousseau 'getting [. . .] a glimpse of the truth, but then going about erasing, conjuring this vision out of existence, while also surreptitiously giving in to it and smuggling it within the precinct he was assigned to protect', he also argues that Derrida's terminology cannot account for 'the exact epistemological status of the ambivalence that lies at the heart of Rousseau's language'.[28] In de Man's argument the 'epistemological status' of this ambivalence in Rousseau's text lies in the language of the text rather than the subject.

By focusing on the language of Rousseau's text, de Man posits a more generous and sophisticated reading of Rousseau's essay, in which he argues that the ambivalence of Rousseau's text is inherent in its rhetorical organization. By 'accounting for the rhetoricity of its own mode', de Man proceeds to emphasize that the essay 'postulates the necessity of its own misunderstanding'.[29] In de Man's reading, the story that Rousseau tells about the origin of languages and the 'degradation of melody into harmony, of language into painting, of the language of passion into the language of need, [and] of metaphor into literal meaning' is 'an allegory of the text's misunderstanding'.[30] Put more simply, de Man argues that Rousseau's 'Essay on the Origin of Languages' (1781) implies something other than that which it literally states. Yet this alternative meaning cannot be known or understood. For de Man, what Rousseau's text exemplifies is that all reading is misreading and all understanding misunderstanding.

As Rodolphe Gasché has persuasively argued in *The Wild Card of Reading: On Paul de Man* (1998), the crucial difference between the deconstructive approaches of Derrida and de Man is that Derrida 'questions understanding [only] to the extent that it shows understanding to depend for its possibility on the medium of [the] undecideability of writing'; de Man's theory of reading by contrast 'questions the very possibility of understanding altogether'.[31]

As a theorist who is influenced by both Derrida and de Man, Spivak may seem to be unconcerned with the differences between the philosophical positions of these two thinkers. Nevertheless, there are significant instances in Spivak's early work where she seems to criticize the work of de Man. In an essay titled 'Revolutions that as yet have no Model' (1980), for example, Spivak criticizes what she calls 'American deconstructivism' for rehearsing a self-transcendent trope of Romantic irony. Citing a passage from de Man's essay on Rousseau's *Confessions* (1764–70), Spivak argues that de Man's speculations on the allegory of irony, which stage the systematic undoing of all tropological cognitions and the possibility of understanding, are a repetition of a rhetorical solipsism that de Man inherited from such Romanticist thinkers as Friedrich Schlegel. In Spivak's account, one of the limitations with de Man's rhetorical mode of reading is that it forestalls an engagement with the political.

Such a concern is further elaborated in an essay titled 'Imperialism and Sexual Difference' (1986), in which Spivak draws on de Man's claim that the 'basis of a truth claim is no more than a trope' to articulate the race-blindness of some feminist literary theory. The critical implications of Spivak's reading strategy in this essay are spelled out in an interview with Sarah Harasym, editor of *The Postcolonial Critic* (1990). In response to Spivak's use of de Man in 'Imperialism and Sexual Difference', Harasym observes that Spivak 'borrows and shows the limits of borrowing uncritically a strategy of reading articulated by Paul de Man' (*PCC*, 107). Such a critical strategy prompts Harasym to ask Spivak whether the crucial difference between de Man and Spivak is that 'de Man's readings tend to stop at various aporia', whereas Spivak's readings 'stress the necessity of thinking beyond the aporia as they focus on the situational specific forces of the opposition in order to find a place of

practice' (*PCC*, 107). While Spivak seems to be in general agreement
with Harasym's reading, she also conjectures whether de Man's
later work on the movement 'from the description of tropological
and performative deconstruction to a definition of the act' might
offer a new politics of reading (*PCC*, 107–8).

Spivak's speculative gesture towards de Man's politics of reading
in this interview signals a shift in her critical position *vis-à-vis* de
Man's rhetorical mode of reading, which is developed in her *Critique
of Postcolonial Reason* (1999). In particular, Spivak's reading of Kant's
use of anthropological metaphors serves to exemplify how de Man's
rhetorical reading of Kant's thought has influenced Spivak (*CPR*,
15–20). In this reading, Spivak draws on de Man's lecture 'Kant and
Schiller', which was first presented in 1983, the year of his death,
but was not published until 1996. Here, de Man argues that Kant's
use of anthropological metaphors to describe the strictly epistemological problem of understanding nature is a rhetorical strategy. In
other words, when Kant described the impossibility of knowledge
of nature in subjective and empirical terms, this recourse to a subjective and empirical register was an analogy, which 'had nothing
to do with the pragma of the relationship between human beings'.[32]
Yet, as de Man proceeds to argue, critics of Kant from Schiller
onwards have misread Kant's use of anthropological tropes as if it
were a literal truth claim about the capacity of the human subject
to achieve knowledge of nature through an awesome and terrifying
encounter with the sublime.[33] Such a misreading has also served to
justify Romanticist programmes for the aesthetic education of the
European bourgeois individual. Rather than simply correcting what
de Man calls Schiller's aberrant reading of Kant by avoiding Kant's
use of anthropological tropes, Spivak proposes to ' "situate" [. . .] the
anthropological moment in Kant' (*CPR*, 16). In so doing, Spivak
attempts to account for the 'dissimulated history and geography of
the subject in Kant's text' (*CPR*, 16).

I examine this 'dissimulated history and geography of the subject'
in more detail in chapter 6. Suffice it to say at this point that Spivak's
reading of Kant draws on de Man's rhetorical mode of reading to
situate the geopolitical determinants of the Kantian subject and
to track the foreclosure of the native informant in Kant's work.

Spivak, however, does not simply privilege the deconstructive
thought of de Man over that of Derrida in her later work. While de
Man's late work allows her to track the geopolitical determinants of
the Kantian subject in *A Critique of Postcolonial Reason*, it is Derrida's
reading of Rousseau and Lévi-Strauss in *Of Grammatology* that

provided Spivak with the conceptual tools to criticize the cultural and philosophical authority of the West. In her preface to *Of Grammatology*, Spivak notes a 'geographical pattern' in Derrida's argument, whereby a relationship between logocentrism and ethnocentrism is 'indirectly invoked' (TP, lxxxii). Such an indirect link may not seem sufficient grounds for an articulation of postcolonial theory. Indeed for critics such as Tobin Siebers, Derrida's critique of logocentrism in the work of Rousseau and Lévi-Strauss seems to foreclose the possibility of an ethical dialogue between the anthropologist and her interlocutors.[34] This criticism of Derrida is more forcefully articulated by the postcolonial theorist Homi Bhabha in his essay 'The Commitment to Theory' (1989), published in *The Location of Culture* (1994). In Bhabha's account, Derrida's theoretical presentation of the Nambikwara Indians in his critique of Lévi-Strauss's anthropology is part of a 'strategy of containment where the Other text is forever the exegetical horizon of difference, never the active agent of articulation'.[35]

What Derrida calls the impossibility of an egalitarian, ethical relation between the anthropologist and his interlocutors in the work of Rousseau and Lévi-Strauss resurfaces in Spivak's own reflections on the impossibility of achieving an ethical relation with the singularity of the subaltern in her later work. I examine this aporetic non-relationship in more detail below, but first outline some of Spivak's key statements on the benefits and limitations of deconstruction for postcolonial theory.

Deconstruction and postcolonial theory

In the preface to *Of Grammatology*, Spivak acknowledges that 'the *East* is never seriously studied in the Derridean text' (TP, lxxxii). Yet she does suggest that Derrida's polemical critique of Lévi-Strauss's representation of the Nambikwara as a people without writing demonstrates the usefulness of Derrida's deconstruction of logocentrism for postcolonial theory. The importance of deconstruction for postcolonial theory is further borne out by Spivak's observation in an interview with Elizabeth Grosz that there is a parallel between Derrida's deconstruction of the western philosophical tradition and Spivak's interrogation of the legacy of the colonial education system in India, which taught students to regard the western humanist subject as a universal standard of enlightenment to which non-European subjects should aspire (*PCC*, 7). In a different, but related discussion in 'Can the Subaltern Speak?' Spivak invokes Derrida's critique of the western science of writing to account for the British colonial law's transformation of the fragmentary archive of Hindu scriptures into an authoritative source for the production of Hindu civil law in the late eighteenth century. Similarly, in 'Responsibility', Spivak discusses the responsibility of contemporary western intellectuals to development policies such as the World Bank's Flood Action Plan in Bangladesh, exemplifying the relevance of Derrida's account of the intellectual's responsibility in *Of Spirit* (1987) beyond the disciplinary framework of institutional philosophy (within which Derrida's account takes place).

What these examples suggest is that Spivak's persistent engagement with deconstructive thought is part of a broader attempt to articulate theoretical rigour with an ethico-political commitment to the singularity of the subaltern. For this reason the differences between the theoretical positions of thinkers such as Derrida and de Man often seems secondary to the ethico-political agenda of Spivak's theoretical interventions. In an interview with Sarah Harasym, for instance, Spivak has emphasized that '[d]econstruction cannot found a political program of any kind' (*PCC*, 104). The use of deconstruction lies rather in its potential to act as a safeguard against rational political programmes that claim to speak in the name of minority groups such as the worker, the woman or the colonized (*PCC*, 104).

The setting to work of deconstruction

The appendix to *A Critique of Postcolonial Reason*, entitled 'The Setting to Work of Deconstruction', provides one of the most explicit statements to date on how deconstruction informs Spivak's own thought. As one of the leading commentators on deconstruction, Spivak is clearly aware that it is not a coherent method with a fixed set of transcendent rules and scientific principles that can be simply applied to a given object, text or political event in advance. Yet Spivak also emphasizes that deconstruction is limited by its framing within 'the descriptive and/or formalizing practices of the academic or disciplinary calculus' (*CPR*, 429). Against this institutional or disciplinary limit, Spivak posits what she calls the 'setting to work' of deconstruction.

What Spivak means by this phrase is not simply an application of deconstruction, but an operation that is faithful to the strict sense in which Derrida uses the word 'work': 'for Derrida what the word "work" marks is outside and discontinuous with the formulations of philosophy as an end in itself, with a logical systematicity that is mere calculus' (*CPR*, 428). Significantly, Spivak invokes Derrida's rhetorical and thematic use of exergue and parergon to exemplify what she means by the 'setting to work of deconstruction'. The exergue or parergon are those elements of a text that are outside the main body of the work, whether in prefaces, afterwords or appendices; such marginal elements are invoked here to designate the ways in which the critical work of deconstruction exceeds the disciplinary frame of institutional philosophy.

Like Derrida, Spivak has also used the exergue and the parergon as rhetorical devices to foreground the significance of deconstruction beyond the disciplinary framework of institutional philosophy. Indeed, Spivak's preface to *Of Grammatology* and appendix *A Critique of Postcolonial Reason* are both examples of such a device.

What crucially distinguishes Spivak's setting to work of deconstruction from Derrida's attempt to address questions and topics that are beyond the remit of disciplinary philosophy are the areas in which Spivak sets deconstruction to work. As Spivak notes in 'The Setting to Work of Deconstruction', the non-philosophical topics and questions that Derrida addressed in his work include literature, poetry, law and justice. Such questions may complicate the philosophical frame of reference in which Rodolphe Gasché, Irene Harvey and others have read Derrida's work. Yet as Spivak points out, these questions and topics do not actually challenge the 'formalizing calculus specific to the academic institution' (*CPR*, 430), which rationalizes knowledge as an end in itself. Even on those occasions when Derrida does broach more explicitly political topics such as European immigration, socialism, apartheid, Zionism or the rogue state, Spivak emphasizes that these topics are never addressed in a way that is identical with what she calls 'the setting to work of deconstruction outside the formalizing calculus specific to the academic institution' (*CPR*, 431).

By contrast to Derrida, the anti-disciplinary object of deconstruction that Spivak posits in 'The Setting to Work of Deconstruction' is 'counterglobalist or development activism' (*CPR*, 429). Although her appendix, a condensed overview of deconstructive thought, does not elaborate on this point or give specific examples of 'counterglobalist or development activism', Spivak's use of deconstructive language to describe such forms of activism serves to illustrate what she means by 'the setting to work of deconstruction'. She describes the paradoxical non-relationship between Non-Governmental

Organizations on the one side and subaltern constituencies in the global South on the other in the deconstructive terms of the aporia of exemplarity. Such a deconstructive example confounds the very logic of exemplarity.

Aporias of exemplarity in Spivak and Derrida

What Spivak means by the aporia of exemplarity is an example that cannot be verified according to the rational principles of philosophical logic. In philosophical logic, the example often serves to exemplify an abstract universal claim. Yet as Derrida suggested in 'Violence and Metaphysics' there are singular examples that cannot be empirically verified to support such universal claims. In a discussion of transcendental knowledge claims, for instance, Derrida invokes God as an exemplary case of an example that cannot be verified to support universal claims about transcendental knowledge: 'The Thought of Being is what permits us to say, without naiveté, reduction, or blasphemy, "God, for example"'.[36] Such an example is aporetic because it confounds the logical passage of thought from a universal truth claim to a particular example. As Gasché puts it, God is 'an example of the unthought Being and of unthought thought'.[37]

Spivak's invocation of counter-globalist resistance movements might seem to be a bad example because it does not support a general philosophical principle. Yet it is precisely because Spivak's example confounds the philosophical logic of exemplarity that it is a good deconstructive example. By invoking the paradoxical non-relationship between western Non-Governmental Organizations who often claim to represent subaltern constituencies in the global South and those subaltern constituencies themselves, Spivak certainly complicates the conventional relationship between the universal truth claim and the particular example. Since Spivak's example of contemporary counter-globalist resistance movements cannot be accounted for by the non-philosophical vocabulary that Derrida often uses, Spivak supplements her description of this aporetic relationship with Paul de Man's definition of irony in his late theoretical writings. That Spivak strains to account for this deconstructive example in the deconstructive language of Derrida's thought is significant because it identifies the limitations of Derrida's thought for thinking the political in a global context, as well as clarifying what Spivak means by the 'setting to work' of deconstruction.

De Man, reading otherwise and the setting to work of deconstruction

Spivak's recourse to de Man's definition of irony at the very moment that Derrida's words seem to fail her might render what she means by the 'setting to work of deconstruction' rather opaque. Spivak tries to evoke the subaltern figure of the native informant through a strategy of reading that attends to the 'source relating "otherwise" [. . .] to the continuous unfolding of the main system of meaning' (*CPR*, 430). While this 'source' cannot be represented or understood in the positive terms of the 'main system of meaning', its non-presence is evoked through a process of reading otherwise. To clarify what she means by this process of reading otherwise, Spivak refers to a passage in de Man's *Allegories of Reading* (1979), in which allegory is re-thought as irony.

The passage occurs in a chapter titled 'Excuses': de Man notes how the 'figural line' in Rousseau's *Confessions* refuses a stable relationship between the literal narrative and its allegorical significance. As a result, there is a discontinuity between what de Man calls the rhetorical codes of performative rhetoric and cognitive rhetoric, which constitute the allegory in the *Confessions*.[38] The extension of this discontinuity between different modes of rhetoric throughout Rousseau's text becomes what de Man calls the permanent parabasis or sustained interruption of allegory. In de Man's argument, this interruption shares an affinity with irony because it undermines all attempts at reading and understanding through metaphor or analogy.

Spivak invokes de Man's re-thinking of irony 'as a sustained interruption from a source relating "otherwise" [. . .] to the continuous unfolding of the main system of meaning' (*CPR*, 430) in order to emphasize the way in which subaltern constituencies in the global South can interrupt the logic of global development. In so doing, Spivak implies that the practices and agencies of subaltern constituencies cannot be known or represented in the terms of the main system of meaning (the logic of global development). What is more, the persistence of this non-systematic, subaltern interruption within the logic of global development suggests that Spivak's reading strategy resists the temptation to simply represent the disempowered or the oppressed, and to propose the establishment of an alternative economic system, such as socialism or communism.

Indeed Spivak distinguishes this persistent strategy of reading otherwise – which she also names 'the setting to work of deconstruction without reserve' – from 'the failures of establishing an alternative system' (*CPR*, 430). Read in isolation, such a proposition would undoubtedly be anathema to many Marxist intellectuals. However, as I argue in chapter 3 below, Spivak does not simply jettison socialism as a political and economic idea. Rather, by invoking Derrida's concept of *différance*, Spivak re-conceptualizes socialism as 'a constant pushing away – a differing and a deferral – of the *capital*ist harnessing of the *social* productivity of capital' (*CPR*, 430). Spivak thus complicates the evolutionary narrative that underpins socialism as it is classically understood in Marx's theory of historical materialism (as a progression from feudalism to capitalism to socialism), and points towards a different way of understanding the temporal relationship between capitalism and socialism.

Spivak's rethinking of de Man's allegory of reading to describe counter-globalist development action may seem to render the singular agency, knowledge and practices of disenfranchised, subaltern groups inaccessible to knowledge and representation. As a consequence, the theory of reading posited by de Man might appear to be incommensurate with the urgent political considerations that Spivak frequently invokes in her essays. For such a deconstructive theory of reading may call into question the very foundations of rational political thought and action.

Yet, it is precisely this 'ungrounding' of the foundations of rational political thought that allows a political decision to be reached. As Thomas Keenan has cogently argued in his *Fables of Responsibility* (1997), a related discussion of the political implications of de Man's theory of reading:

> Reading, in [de Man's] sense, is what happens when we cannot apply the rules. This means that reading is an experience of responsibility, but that responsibility is not a moment of security or of cognitive certainty. Quite the contrary: the only responsibility worthy of the name comes with the removal of grounds, the withdrawal of the rules or the knowledge on which we might rely to make our decisions for us. No grounds means no alibis, no elsewhere to which we might refer the instance of our decision. If responsibility has always been thought in the Western ethical, political and literary traditions as a matter of articulating what is known with what is done, we propose resituating it as an asymmetry or an interruption between the orders of cognition and action.[39]

As Keenan suggests, what is crucial for de Man is that allegorical reading or reading otherwise interrupts the 'orders of cognition and action'. Spivak develops this reading strategy further in 'The Setting to Work of Deconstruction'. By applying de Man's theory of reading otherwise to the global justice movement, Spivak questions the rational foundations of political action in order to re-imagine a politics that is responsible to the singularity of the other.

One example of such an allegory of responsibility is Vikram Seth's short story 'The Elephant and the Tragopan', which was published in a collection titled *Beastly Tales from Here and There* (1993). In this story, Seth employs the fabular convention of an animal tale written in rhyming couplets to evoke the building of a dam in the fictional valley of Bingle. Against the plans to build the dam, the elephant and the tragopan mount a campaign to save the valley and its animal inhabitants from eviction and the destruction of their home. Through coded references to Bangladesh (which Seth renames Bingledesh), Seth encourages readers to interpret the animals' fight to save their home as an allegory for the struggle of the rural peasantry to oppose the forced dispossession and displacement that may result from the World Bank's Flood Action Plan. Seth's refusal to follow the convention of ending his fable with a moral is significant because it places the responsibility for the animals' fate on the shoulders of the reader rather than the implied author: 'The resolution of their plight/Is for the world, not me, to write.[40] 'The Elephant and the Tragopan' thus operates as a fable of responsibility, which questions the certainty of rational political programmes that try to determine the political future. Moreover, in placing the responsibility for the 'resolution' of the animals' plight on the shoulders of 'the world', Seth implies that 'the world' is also complicit in 'the plight' of the animals.

Spivak and responsibility

In her essay 'Responsibility' (1994) Spivak interrupts a reading of responsibility in Derrida's *Of Spirit* with a seemingly discontinuous account of a conference on the World Bank's Flood Action Plan in Bangladesh. For Spivak, Derrida's reading of Heidegger offers a reflection on the responsibility of the contemporary intellectual. Spivak draws an analogy between deconstruction's attempt to account for Heidegger's responsibility to the concept of spirit underpinning National Socialism and the contemporary Euro-American intellectual's relationship to dominant capitalism and development (R, 35).

Clearly Spivak is not suggesting that there is a straightforward parallel between National Socialism and the World Bank's development policies and debt programmes. What she is arguing is that Derrida's reading of spirit in Heidegger provides a reading strategy that can help western intellectuals address the limitations of dominant structures of responsibility and representation, which silence subaltern voices. One example of this silencing is the presentation and mistranslation of a speech by Abdus Sattar Khan, 'an aging leader of the peasant movement', who delivered a speech on the flood management technique of the Bangladeshi peasantry at the conference on the World Bank's Flood Action Plan in the European Parliament, Strasbourg (R, 60–2). Like the elephant and the tragopan in Vikram Seth's story, this elderly gentleman could be seen to act as a political representative for the cause of the Bangladeshi peasantry, whose way of life is so obviously threatened by the World Bank's policies. Yet, as Spivak emphasizes, the man 'was staged as a slice of the authentic, a piece of the real Bangladesh', whose speech was poorly translated and who was forced to deliver his speech within the allotted time of twenty minutes. Consequently 'there was such a great gulf fixed between [Sattar Khan's] own perception of how to play his role in a theater of responsibility and the structure into which he was inserted that there was no hope for a felicitous performance from the very start' (R, 61).

Spivak's analysis of Sattar Khan's silencing is significant because it demonstrates how there is no rhetorical space from which disempowered, subaltern subjects from the global South can speak in the European 'theater of responsibility', where decisions are made that affect the life and environment of the people of the global South. In so doing, Spivak offers an allegory of responsibility, in which the structures of political representation that underpin the European Parliament paradoxically work to silence and foreclose the voice of the subaltern.

Anthropology and ethics

Against this silencing and foreclosure of the subaltern, Spivak's deconstructive reflections on responsibility and ethical dialogue work towards imagining the conditions of possibility for an ethical dialogue to take place. In her 'Translator's Preface' to Mahasweta Devi's short story collection *Imaginary Maps*, for instance, Spivak rejects the persistence of the anthropological paradigm of field-work, which underpins many attempts by western Non-

Governmental Organizations and development activists to establish an ethical dialogue with their subaltern constituencies: 'no amount of raised consciousness field-work can ever approach the painstaking labor to establish ethical singularity with the subaltern' (*IM*, xxiv). This criticism of the anthropological paradigm recalls Derrida's criticism of Rousseau in *Of Grammatology*, and his recognition that ethics, or the responsibility of the self to the other, cannot exist apart from the violence of writing. In this anthropological paradigm, the structure of ethics and responsibility that binds the western anthropologist and their non-western interlocutors is also bound in a structure of violence.[41]

The anthropological context in which Derrida elaborates this relationship between violence and ethics is significant also because it demonstrates the affinities between deconstruction and Spivak's thought. Derrida's critique of anthropology in *Of Grammatology* is concerned with the way in which western anthropology often represents its object of knowledge – so-called primitive societies – as societies without culture or writing. This representation is violent because it denies the complex system of writing that already exists in non-western societies. Like Derrida, Spivak is also concerned with the conceptual violence that shapes the relationship between the self and the other. What is more, the anthropological context circumscribing Derrida's discussion of conceptual violence in *Of Grammatology* is important for Spivak because it helps to situate Derrida's reflections on ethics and violence in terms of the history of European colonialism, of which the discipline of anthropology is a part.

Yet it is Derrida's critical engagement with Emmanuel Levinas that provides Spivak with the tools to deconstruct the colonial legacy of the anthropological paradigm and to formulate the conditions of possibility for an ethical dialogue with the subaltern. In her preface to Devi's *Imaginary Maps*, for instance, Spivak speaks of the attempt to establish ethical singularity with the subaltern as a secret encounter (*IM*, xxv). This notion of 'ethical singularity' seems to resonate with Levinas's arguments in 'The Trace of the Other' and *Otherwise than Being* (1974). For Levinas, the ethical relation between the self and the other is not simply a conscious decision made by a rational, ethical subject to be responsible to the other. The responsibility for the other comes rather from the call of the other that is prior to the self's knowledge and understanding. What is more, it is the call of the other which constitutes both the subjectivity and responsibility of the self. As Alphonso Lingis explains in the 'Translator's Introduction' to *Otherwise than Being*:

One is answerable before the other, for the other. One is thrown back upon itself in being called upon to answer in the place of another. These two movements, being thrown back upon oneself, being backed up against oneself, and being put in the place of another are inseparable. The being under accusation by the other, the being afflicted by the other, converts at once into a supporting of the other, a being put in the place of the other.[42]

For Levinas the self is singularized as a consequence of the call of the other to respond, and to be responsible to the other. Yet, in Levinas's argument the self does not relate to the other as another self since the other is beyond cognition and comprehension. As Spivak has suggested, Levinas makes a crucial distinction between the French word *autre*, which is used to describe another person, and the plural form *autrui*, which is used in the context of moral acts of respect or generosity towards others.[43] For Levinas, however, the self cannot commit an act of moral responsibility towards a knowable other because the other is anterior to the self. Thus, the phrase responsibility to the other in Levinas does not denote a conscious act of responsibility to a knowable other.

Spivak's use of this language of responsibility and ethical relation may bear some resemblance to Levinas's re-thinking of ethics; however, it does not operate in precisely the same way. By arguing that 'no amount of raised consciousness field-work can ever approach the painstaking labor to establish ethical singularity with the subaltern' (*IM*, xxiv), Spivak suggests that ethical singularity is something that can be consciously achieved through 'painstaking labor'. Such a model of ethical singularity is clearly different from Levinas's argument that ethics and responsibility transcend the individual agency of the self. Indeed, Spivak's claim that an ethical encounter with the singularity of the subaltern is an experience of the impossible could also be read as a comment on the social, linguistic and cultural division between the poles of subalternity and hegemony. Yet, at the same time, Spivak defines the experience of ethical singularity as an experience of the impossible. As Spivak puts it in her preface to *Imaginary Maps*, 'it is impossible for all leaders (subaltern or otherwise) to engage every subaltern in this way [i.e. via a singular ethical encounter], especially across the gender divide. This is why ethics is the experience of the impossible' (*IM*, xxv). Spivak is careful to explain in the next sentence that she is not saying that 'ethics are impossible'; but rather that 'ethics is an experience of the impossible' (*IM*, xxv). In so doing Spivak alludes to the critical engagements both of Derrida and Maurice Blanchot with the ethical thought of Levinas.

In *Totality and Infinity* (1961) Levinas argued that the ethical relation between the self and the other is constituted through a face-to-face encounter and dialogue between the self and the other. Yet this ethical dialogue simultaneously involves the invention of a new kind of language that would do without the verb 'to be'. Such a language would prevent the other from being constituted as an object of knowledge for the self. For Levinas it is imperative to resist this impulse to constitute the other as an object of knowledge since this would be an act of violence towards the other. Yet as Derrida argues in 'Violence and Metaphysics', it is impossible to have a language without predication or an ethical relation without violence: 'there is no phrase which is indeterminate, that is, which does not pass through the violence of the concept. Violence appears with articulation'.[44] In Derrida's reading, Levinas's account of an ethical dialogue without violence between the self and the other would thus seem to be impossible. It is this sense of impossibility in Levinas's account of an ethical relation and dialogue between the self and the other in *Totality and Infinity* that underpins Spivak's insistence that an understanding of the impossibility of ethical engagement is crucial for collective political action.

Ethics and singularity

For critics such as Peter Hallward, however, Spivak's engagement with the ethical dimension of deconstruction seems to conform to the 'familiar strictures of negative theology'.[45] Hallward does not define what he means by negative theology, though he is presumably referring to the idea that the existence of God is confirmed by the fact that God transcends human knowledge and representation. As the theologian Merold Westphal explains in *Transcendence and Self-Transcendence* (2004): '[Negative theology] operates on the assumption that God is real, indeed as superessential, more real than the most exalted creature'. What is more, negative theology 'makes the paradoxical claim that it knows enough about God to know that God is unknowable, that no image of the human senses or concept of the human intellect (whether its origin is reason or revelation) is adequate to the divine reality'.[46] According to advocates of negative theology such as the early Christian neo-Platonist Pseudo-Dionysius the Areopagite, God or the divine is beyond representation and rational cognition: the 'inscrutable One is out of the reach of every rational process. Nor can any words come up to the inexpressible Good, this One, this source of all unity, this supra-existent Being. Mind beyond mind, word beyond speech, it is gathered up by no discourse, by no intuition, by no name'.[47]

Some commentators have attempted to align Derrida's thought with negative theology. However, Derrida has rigorously resisted that alignment on the grounds that negative theology assumes the presence of a supreme being precisely by virtue of its transcendence of human understanding and representation.[48] This position has perhaps been most forcefully articulated in Derrida's essay 'Différance', in which he argues that negative theology is always concerned with 'disengaging a superessentiality beyond the categories of essence and existence, that is, of presence, and always hastening to recall that God is refused the predicate of existence, only in order to acknowledge his superior, inconceivable and ineffable mode of being'. By contrast, *différance* 'derives from no category of being, whether present or absent' because it is the 'very opening of the space in which ontotheology – philosophy – produces its system and its history'.[49]

This distinction between *différance* and negative theology goes some way towards clarifying what Spivak means by ethical singularity as an experience of the impossible. However, Spivak's concept of ethical singularity can be further elucidated by considering Blanchot's *Infinite Conversation* (1969), which includes a critique of Levinas. Although Spivak does not explicitly refer to Blanchot in her account of ethical singularity, her elaboration of an ethical mode of thought certainly merits a comparison with Blanchot's rethinking of Levinasian ethics.

Blanchot's main objection to *Totality and Infinity* is Levinas's persistent recourse to the name of God in describing the ethical relation between the self and the other.[50] In other words, Blanchot argues, when Levinas writes about the Other (*Autrui*), or the other who is beyond being, subjectivity and pronominal reference, he means a transcendent being that is closer to God than to the self. This conception of the Other is consistent with Levinas's engagement with the belief, which is prevalent in Jewish theology, that the proper name of God signifies a divine entity that is beyond being and language. Against Levinas's recourse to the proper name of God, Blanchot stresses the importance of locating the transcendent relation between the self and the other in the social field rather than in the realm of theology: 'it may be that everything that may be affirmed of the relation to transcendence – the relation of God to his creature – ought primarily (for my part, I would say exclusively) to be applied to the social relation'.[51] By dislocating Levinas's ethical relation from a theological framework and applying it to the social relation, I would suggest that Blanchot provides a critical framework through which to read Spivak's use of Levinasian ethics to account for the ethical relation between the postcolonial intellectual and the subaltern in strictly non-theological terms.

Hallward's critique of Spivak seems to be premised on the view that her account of subalternity operates as a form of negative theology because it constructs the subaltern as an absent presence with a singular ontological essence that cannot be grasped as such. As he put it in *Absolutely Postcolonial* (2002), Spivak relegates the subaltern to a quasi-transcendental space that is 'inaccessible to relations of nomination, situation and evaluation'. For Hallward, the subaltern 'is the theoretically *untouchable*, the altogether-beyond-relation: the attempt to "relate" to the subaltern defines what Spivak will quite appropriately name an "impossible ethical singularity"'.[52]

Since Spivak's discussion of the impossible ethical relation and the aporia of exemplarity corresponds with the quasi-transcendental thought of Derrida, Levinas and (as I have suggested) Blanchot, her account of subaltern agency and the limitations of global justice movements might, at times, seem to highlight precisely the problem that Hallward identifies. In other words, Spivak's articulation of urgent political issues in a theoretical language that may seem to verge on the transcendental could appear to undermine the political force of her interventions. Certainly, Spivak oscillates between the use of the term subalternity to denote a non-relational concept that is not unlike Derrida's *différance* on the one hand; and its use as a concrete category to denote the social composition of subordinate groups in South Asia on the other. This oscillation might seem to bear a resemblance to what Hallward calls the 'familiar strictures of negative theology' in Spivak's work.

Yet this superficial resemblance ignores the subtle but important difference between the ontotheological basis of negative theology on the one hand, and the trace structure of *différance* on the other. Unlike negative theology, which presupposes a divine presence that cannot be known or represented at the origin of being, the trace structure of *différance* assumes that difference is at the origin of being and truth. Furthermore, Blanchot's attempt to secularize the ethical relation between the self and the other by placing it in the social sphere clearly recuperates what Levinas calls an ethical relation from negative theology. Similarly, Spivak's formulation of an

ethical relation, in which the subaltern remains inaccessible 'to relations of nomination, situation and evaluation',[53] is clearly different
from the transcendental presence of God in negative theology.
For while the subaltern cannot be defined as a positive category
of thought, the subaltern's withdrawal from dominant systems of
knowledge and representation is nonetheless marked by the trace
of her social, cultural and historical being. It is this trace that
distinguishes Spivak's discussion of subalternity from negative
theology.

   This is not to question Hallward's critique of Spivak on merely
philosophical or even theological grounds. For what is at stake in
Hallward's account is a more general concern, namely that Spivak's
argument – that the subaltern is 'theoretically *untouchable*' and
'altogether-beyond-relation' – hampers the possibility of collective
political action. According to Hallward, the irreducible singularity
of the subaltern in Spivak's work refuses the possibility of an alliance with a broader political movement that can work in solidarity
with groups designated as subaltern to improve their social and
economic conditions.[54] What he overlooks, however, is the fact that
the subaltern *qua* subaltern is, as Spivak explains in 'Scattered Speculations on the Subaltern and the Popular' (2005), removed from 'all
lines of social mobility' (SSSP, 475). Indeed, it is this lack of access
to mobility that Spivak calls 'a version of singularity' (SSSP, 475).
If the singularity of the subaltern is defined by its lack of access
to mobility, the possibility of a broader political movement that
includes the subaltern needs to take the singular social position of
the subaltern into account rather than simply co-opting the subaltern into its hegemonic struggle. As argued below, Spivak's formulation of an impossible ethical relation between the intellectual and
the subaltern is precisely concerned with the possibility of a collective political action responsible to the singularity of the subaltern.

   In a separate but related critique of Spivak's use of Levinas,
Hallward concludes his discussion by saying that her notion of
impossibility is 'non-situational' and suggests that her understanding of singularity is ahistorical.[55] Such a reading ignores the precise
social, historical and political determinants that underpin Spivak's
attempt to theorize an ethical relationship with the subaltern. For
Hallward what constitutes an event is that which marks a 'pure
beginning, the inaugural or uncountable zero of a new time'.[56] For
Spivak, however, the event of India's independence in 1947 excluded
the involvement of the subaltern classes and did not lead to a transformation of the class structure of Indian society. As a consequence,

national independence in India would not qualify as an event in Hallward's definition because it does not mark a break with the social inequalities of Indian society. If Spivak's attempt to theorize an ethical dialogue with the subaltern seems ahistorical and non-situational, this is because the subaltern has been historically excluded from the dominant narrative of India's national independence and not because of Spivak's 'a priori condemnation of disciplined political intervention'.[57]

Spivak's engagement with the ethical dimension of deconstruction is precisely concerned with the ethical limitations of rational political programmes, such as nationalism or Marxism, which have at times failed to do justice to the singularity of subaltern constituencies by subsuming those constituencies within the hegemonic logic of these rational political programmes. As Spivak has put it: 'Subalternity cannot be generalised according to hegemonic logic. That is what makes it subaltern' (SSSP, 475). As I now go on to argue, the experience of the untouchable character Velutha in Arundahti Roy's novel *The God of Small Things* (1997) provides a good example of how Spivak's call for an ethical responsibility to the singularity of the subaltern is not simply opposed to the demand for collective political action (as Hallward suggests), but rather reinforces the necessity for collective political action.

In Roy's novel, Velutha seeks emancipation from the caste system in the South Indian state of Kerala through his work with the Indian communist party, but he is ultimately betrayed by the leader of the local communist party, Comrade Pillai, whose promises of solidarity with the poor and the oppressed does not extend in practice to the plight of untouchable characters such as Velutha. In Comrade Pillai's account, although Velutha 'may be very well okay as a person [. . .] other workers are not happy with him', since from the local viewpoint of Kerala in the late 1960s 'caste issues are very deep rooted'.[58] Furthermore, despite Comrade Pillai's claims that ' "Class is caste, comrades" ',[59] Pillai's refusal to protect Velutha from a murderous police assault for transgressing caste boundaries by having a sexual relationship with Ammu, a caste Hindu woman, is described as 'pharisaic'.[60]

For critics such as Aijaz Ahmad, Roy's representation of Pillai's betrayal of Velutha is typical of the 'hostility towards the communist movement [that] is now fairly common among radical sections of the cosmopolitan intelligentsia, in India and abroad',[61] and ignores the ways in which Marxism was adapted and translated by subaltern insurgents. As Ahmad puts it, 'it is quite implausible that a

Communist trade union leader would actively conspire in a murderous assault on a well-respected member of his own union so as to uphold caste purity'.[62] Ahmad raises some pertinent questions about the limitations of Roy's historical understanding of communism in India, but in doing so he downplays the significance of Roy's attempt to evoke an ethical engagement with the singular position of the untouchable Velutha. By contrast, Spivak's insistence that an understanding of ethics as 'the experience of the impossible' can sharpen the sense of the crucial and continuing need for collective political action (*IM*, xxv) provides a more nuanced critical vocabulary for reading the significance of Velutha's betrayal in *The God of Small Things*. Such a reading would consider how Comrade Pillai, and the communist party he represents, cannot account for Velutha's sexual transgression of caste boundaries within the collective political terms of the workers' movement; and how, because of his apparent refusal to see questions of caste and sexuality as legitimate political questions, Pillai defines Velutha's transgression as 'workers indiscipline in their private life'.[63] Moreover, a reading of Roy's representation of Comrade Pillai in *The God of Small Things* informed by Spivak's deconstructive rethinking of ethics and politics would not simply read the story of Pillai's treatment of Velutha as a transparent sign of Roy's hostility to communism. Instead, such a reading would argue that Comrade Pillai's reprehensible treatment of Velutha marks the ethical limitations of the communist party and the workers' movement *vis-à-vis* the singular position of the subaltern, while also affirming that such an unethical moment marks the continuing necessity for a collective political struggle that includes caste and gender politics in its definition of the political.[64]

Indeed, Spivak's ethical criticism of collective political movements is not simply opposed to collective political movements as Hallward claims in *Absolutely Postcolonial*; rather, as Spivak insists, such an ethical criticism 'sharpens the sense of the crucial and continuing need for collective political struggle' (*IM*, xxv). Further, the reason why Spivak turns to the deconstructive language of responsibility is to *supplement* the failures of political movements to do justice to the plight of oppressed, subaltern constituencies such as untouchables or tribal peoples and without simply rejecting the necessity for collective political struggle altogether. This language of responsibility may not seem to offer a very meaningful sense of collective solidarity, and it may leave one with little more than the vague evocation of 'an impossible social justice glimpsed through secret encounters with singular figures'.[65] However, as Spivak asserts, without this ethical engagement, most political movements 'fail in the long run' (*IM*, xxv).

As suggested in this chapter, Spivak's ongoing engagement with deconstruction has not only enabled her to produce a theoretical vocabulary with which to criticize the cultural, political and economic legacy of colonialism, but it has also allowed her to develop an ethic that is sensitive to the singular position of the subaltern. Such an ethical vocabulary does not provide a blueprint for political transformation. However, it can at least guard against the violence of political programmes, which ignore the singularity of the subaltern.

3

Marxism and Post-Marxism

As suggested in the previous chapter, the work of Karl Marx has had an important influence on the development of Spivak's thought. The distinctive achievement of Spivak's critical engagement with Marx's thought lies in the rethinking of his labour theory of value and the Asiatic Mode of Production (AMP). Spivak's readings of Marx are informed by deconstructive concepts such as *différance*, aporia and the pharmakon.

Spivak's view of Marx as a deconstructive thinker might at first seem to be incompatible with Marx's social and political thought. For deconstruction's emphasis on indeterminacy, deferral, the suspension of the referent and ethical responsibility might appear to be opposed to the concerns with material reality, the demystification of bourgeois ideology, the capitalist exploitation of labour power, and direct political action that many intellectuals and activists associate with Marxist thought.[1] For Paul de Man, however, this dichotomy overlooks the common ground of Marxism and deconstruction. In response to the charge made by Marxist ideology critics that deconstruction denies the existence of a material reality outside language and representation, de Man argues that:

> What we call ideology is precisely the confusion of linguistic with natural reality, of reference with phenomenalism. It follows that, more than any other mode of inquiry, including economics, the lin-guistics of literariness is a powerful and indispensable tool in the unmasking of ideological aberrations, as well as a determining factor

in accounting for their occurrence. Those who reproach literary theory for being oblivious to social and historical (that is to say ideological) reality are merely stating their fear at having their own ideological mystifications exposed by the tool they are seeking to discredit. They are, in short, very poor readers of Marx's *German Ideology*.[2]

Rather than simply discrediting Marx's thought, de Man emphasizes the importance of reading Marx carefully in order to avoid the confusion of linguistic and natural reality. In this respect, deconstruction is not simply opposed to Marxism, but rather traces the non-originary origins or aporias that underpin Marx's thought.

In a similar vein, Spivak has underlined the importance of re-thinking the dichotomy between Marxism/deconstruction through a modified translation of Marx's Eleventh Thesis on Feuerbach (1845). Since this thesis is often invoked to exemplify Marx's unequivocal position as a social and political thinker who is opposed to the apolitical activity of philosophical interpretation, Spivak's modified translation of Marx serves to complicate the dichotomy. The original German of the thesis reads 'Die Philosophen haben die Welt nur verschieden interpretiert, es kömmt drauf an, sie zu verändern',[3] and is conventionally translated as follows: 'The philosophers have only interpreted the world in various ways; the point is to change it'.[4] Whereas translations of Marx usually interpret *verändern* as 'to change', Spivak argues that this is neither the most common nor the most forceful word for change and 'means strictly speaking, to make other' (*IOW*, 208). By juxtaposing the present participle *haben interpretiert* ('have interpreted') and the infinitive *zu verändern* ('to make other'), Spivak suggests that Marx attempts to connect the different activities of critical interpretation and social transformation instead of simply opposing them. What is more, the phrase 'to make other' suggests a less determinate temporality than 'to change it' and gestures towards a more open-ended model of the political future.

Significantly, Spivak's translational reading of the 'Eleventh Thesis on Feuerbach' is further borne out in a related discussion of Marx's text by Thomas Kemple:

Marx does not wish to indicate a division between two separate realities, as between the connection of thought and the activity of changing the world. Rather, he attempts to negotiate the potential and actual connections between interpreting the world (*interpriet- eren*) and changing it or rendering it other (*ver-ändern*). The silent pause marked by the comma interrupting the eleventh thesis on Feuerbach is literally a place between 'what is' and 'what ought to be', or between 'what is not' and 'what may yet be'.[5]

Kemple adds that Marx's 'sense of the relation between interpreta- tion and change is also conveyed, but less perfectly expressed in the phrase *"es kommt drauf"*, which may designate both the idea of "coming upon" something from the past and or at some time in the future, and the act of "coming at" something from here or some- where else'.[6]

In Spivak's translation of the Eleventh Thesis, Marx's imperfect phrase, which is usually translated 'the point is', is 'rethought as the future anterior' (*OTM*, 97–8). In deconstructive terms, the future anterior denotes the deferred effects of a past event or trace, which become intelligible only from a retrospective position in the future. This deconstructive re-thinking of Marx's phrase thus combines the two senses identified by Kemple to describe what 'the point *will have been*'. In this reading, Marx embeds a future-oriented address to his implied readers (the European industrial proletariat), which is as much an imperative to read the world otherwise through a critical engagement with Marx's thought, as it is a call for immediate social transformation.[7]

This deconstructive rethinking of Marx's Eleventh Thesis is cer- tainly characteristic of Spivak's engagement with Marx. This is not to suggest, however, that deconstruction operates as a master dis- course in Spivak's reading of Marx. For her deconstructive reading of Marx also interrupts and complicates her engagement with Derrida. Indeed, Spivak has questioned the accuracy of Derrida's *Spectres of Marx* (1993). In 'Limits and Openings of Marx in Derrida', Spivak argues that Derrida 'seems not to know Marx's main argu- ment'; that he 'confuses industrial with commercial capital, even usury; and surplus value with interest produced by speculation' (*OTM*, 97). Similarly in 'Ghostwriting' (1995), Spivak argues that Derrida presents a caricature of Marx's labour theory of value in *Spectres of Marx*, which defines use value as good and exchange value as bad (GW, 74). Derrida has responded to Spivak's critique of Marx by arguing that her reading of *Spectres of Marx* is a misread- ing, which reproduces Spivak's rhetorical stance as a critic who is, by her own admission, too proprietorial about Marx's thought.[8]

What is significant about Derrida's response to Spivak's critique is that Derrida takes issue with the rhetoric of Spivak's argument rather than the specific claim that Derrida overlooks Marx's theory of industrial capital or the ambivalence of use value in Marx's labour theory of value.

Indeed, what is at stake in Spivak's questioning of Derrida's reading of Marx is not merely a disagreement about the nuances of Marx's theoretical argument. Spivak is rather more concerned to re-articulate Marxism and deconstruction in such a way that Marxism can account for the contemporary international division of labour and the economic dependency of many nations in the global South on global financial institutions such as the World Bank and the International Monetary Fund.

These global economic concerns might seem a far cry from Marx's account of industrial production in nineteenth-century western Europe. Yet this is not to suggest that the division of labour described by Marx has simply vanished. Indeed, what is crucial for Spivak is that the conditions of industrial production and labour in nineteenth-century western Europe, with which Marx was preoccupied, have been gradually replaced by a flexible, non-unionized, and casual form of work that often targets women and children in the global South. In saying this, however, Spivak is not claiming to represent the female proletariat. As discussed in the previous chapter, Spivak is cautious and sceptical of any move to represent such subaltern constituencies as objects for political transformation; indeed to speak for such subaltern constituencies is to run the risk of preserving the condition of their exploitation and oppression. Instead, by rethinking Marx's labour theory of value and his description of the AMP from the imagined standpoint of the gendered subaltern in the contemporary global economy, Spivak develops a theoretical idiom that is appropriate to engage with the singularity of the gendered subaltern's position in the global economy. Indeed in *A Critique of Postcolonial Reason*, Spivak praises Marx's prescience in *The Communist Manifesto* (1848) for anticipating the increasing importance of women's labour power in modern industry (*CPR*, 167). In this respect, Spivak engagement with Marx's thought demonstrates the continuing importance of Marx's labour theory of value to the contemporary global economy. Before examining the significance of this claim in more detail, however, I assess Spivak's critique of the AMP and her deconstructive re-thinking of Marx's labour theory of value.

Marx and the Asiatic mode of production

One of the major limitations with Karl Marx's thought for many postcolonial theorists and Subaltern Studies historians lies in the Eurocentrism of Marx's materialist conception of history. For Marx history is a sequence of different stages, or modes of production, which develop chronologically from primitive forms of accumulation such as the 'Asiatic mode of production' to the advanced industrial capitalist economies of nineteenth-century western Europe. Such a developmental model of history clearly reproduces a Eurocentric vision of world history because it defines western capitalist societies as more developed than non-western societies. Indeed, the postcolonial theorist Edward Said in *Orientalism* (1978) criticized Marx's 'Romantic Orientalism' on the grounds that it reproduced an image of Asia as 'fundamentally lifeless' and subordinated to despotism, even as Marx condemned the 'vilest interests' of British rule in India.[9]

Like Said, Spivak notes how the AMP marks the limit of Marx's analysis for postcolonial thought. However, Spivak is careful to emphasize that the 'Asiatic mode of production' is not a fully elaborated theory or concept in Marx's work, but a 'notorious phrase that Marx probably used only once' (*CPR*, 71). This single usage occurs in the preface to *A Contribution to the Critique of Political Economy* (1859), in which Marx argued that 'In broad outlines Asiatic, ancient, feudal and modern bourgeois modes of production can be designated as progressive epochs in the economic formation of society'.[10] While Marx may not have elaborated on the phrase in much detail, its syntactic location in a progressive historical paradigm suggests that the AMP stands as a metonym for Asia's social and economic 'backwardness' within Marx's materialist conception of history.

Such a position is further borne out in Marx's writings on British colonialism in India, where Marx laments the dissolution of family communities and domestic industry in rural Indian villages, which had formerly sustained 'hand-weaving, hand-spinning and hand-tilling agriculture',[11] but also emphasizes that 'these idyllic village communities, inoffensive though they may appear, had always been the solid foundation of Oriental despotism'.[12] In this respect, Marx could be seen to repeat the orientalist rhetoric of European colonial modernity exemplified in the work of Kant and Hegel, for example, as well as British liberal economists such as Adam Smith and John Stuart Mill (among others).

Instead of merely rehearsing the postcolonial critique of the Eurocentric narrative of colonial modernity put forward by Said and others, Spivak asks whether we should 'resurrect' the AMP in order to understand 'globality' (*CPR*, 72). By doing so, Spivak reads Marx's 'largely unsatisfactory formulation' of the Asiatic mode of production against the grain of the European narrative of colonial modernity. This latter reading strategy approaches the AMP as a sign of difference at the origin of colonial modernity, which cannot be simply foreclosed on the grounds that it is precapitalist or primitive. Instead, the AMP provides Spivak with a productive critical problem for tracing the foreclosure of the subaltern woman from contemporary critical thought.

Significantly, Spivak's deconstructive reading also departs from earlier twentieth-century Marxist-Leninist scholarship on the Asiatic mode of production. As Spivak suggests, much of this scholarship has tended to argue that Marx's account of the AMP is 'empirically or theoretically insufficient' (*CPR*, 79). Indeed readers of Marx from Plekhanov and Lenin through to Karl Wittfogel, Stephen Dunn, Barry Hindess and Paul Hirst have variously struggled to articulate precisely what Marx meant by 'Asiatic' and furthermore how the phrase 'Asiatic mode of production' can be used to designate widely divergent modes of production in terms of economy, exploitation and land-ownership, across differences in space, time and culture.[13]

Spivak judiciously questions whether such attempts to 'prove that the AMP is or is not empirically and/or theoretically valid' by 'filling up the gaps in the knowledge available to Marx' (*CPR*, 85) are worthwhile. Instead, by reading the AMP as a deconstructive sign of difference at the origin of Marx's mode of production narrative, she suggests that Marx's philosophical system is marked by 'the desire to theorize the other' (*CPR*, 79). In saying this, Spivak is not suggesting that Marx was successful in his 'desire' to 'theorize' or know 'the other', but merely noting that his work is marked by this 'desire'.

Starting with a discussion of Marx's distinction between Species-Life and Species-Being in *The Economic and Philosophical Manuscripts* (1844), Spivak contends that Marx's definition of Species-Being is indebted to classical German philosophy. This debt is significant because it reveals how Marx, like Kant and Hegel before him, attempted to universalize the historical experiences of the masculine, European subject ('Man'). In Marx's argument 'Man is a species-being, not only because he makes the species – both his own and those of other things – his object, but also – and this is simply another way of saying the same thing – because he looks upon himself as the present, living species, because he looks upon himself as a *universal* and therefore free being.'[14] Indeed Marx defined Species-Being as the human subject's unique capacity for self-reflection as an individual member of a species.

Furthermore, Spivak argues that Marx attempted to 'insert the historical narrative within philosophy' (*CPR*, 78). Although Spivak does not specify which 'historical narrative' she is referring to here, given the context of the discussion about the AMP in which this sentence occurs, it seems reasonable to assume that she is alluding to Marx's mode of production narrative. So by inserting that narrative within the logic of Hegelian dialectics, Marx attempted to 'verify' the truthfulness of Species-Being. Yet, Spivak suggests, in so doing Marx 'perceives that, given social inequity, it is not possible for each human being to take himself (we would add 'or herself') as the *correct* general case of being-human as such' (*CPR*, 78). Such a revelation challenges the universalism of the ethical subject of German enlightenment philosophy, and 'introduces difference within the self-sameness or self-identity of the normative (ethical?) subject' (*CPR*, 78).

Despite Marx's attempt to annul this general and as-yet-unspecified category of difference and to establish a universal humanist subject through recourse to German Enlightenment philosophy, Spivak argues that Marx's thought is irreducibly marked by this abstract category of difference. Indeed, her parenthetical suggestion that Marx's normative subject is also 'ethical' suggests that Species-Being would be ethically responsible to different histories of labour and production. Furthermore, Spivak proceeds to label this abstract category of difference: 'The Asiatic Mode of Production, however brief its appearance, is the name and imaginary fleshing out of a difference in terms that are consonant with the development of capitalism and the resistance *appropriate* to it as "the same"' (*CPR*, 79). In so doing, Spivak situates Marx's conceptual account of difference in relation to the history of colonial modernity and contemporary geopolitical power relations.

This relationship between the conceptual structure of Marx's thought and the history of colonial modernity is further clarified in a subsequent analysis of a passage from Marx's posthumously published collected notebooks, the *Grundrisse* (1941), which is often cited by Marxist scholars to exemplify the Asiatic mode of production. In a section from 'Notebook IV', entitled 'Forms which Precede

Capitalist Production', Marx describes different forms of production and land-ownership in precapitalist societies. One of the examples Marx cites is 'most of the *Asiatic* land forms' in which the 'comprehensive unity' of a community 'appears as the sole proprietor or higher proprietor', and this property is 'mediated *for* him through a cession *by* the total unity [. . .] realized in the form of the despot'.[15] As a consequence, the individual members of this communal property are 'in fact propertyless'. To be more precise: 'property' for these individuals is 'the relation of the individual to the *natural* conditions of labour and of reproduction as belonging to him, as the nature given inorganic body of his subjectivity'.[16]

For Spivak, Marx's description of an Asiatic mode of production in this extract recalls the distinction between Species-Life and Species-Being in *The Economic and Philosophical Manuscripts*: 'It is almost as if Species-Life has not yet differentiated itself into Species-Being' (*CPR*, 80). By comparing the forms of production and land-ownership in 'Asiatic societies' to Species-Life, or the basic need to preserve life through a 'continuing dialogue' with nature,[17] Spivak suggests that Marx excludes the AMP from the developmental logic of his mode of production paradigm. Like some of Marx's other commentators, Spivak notes how the passage in the *Grundrisse* is 'not an explanation' of the Asiatic mode of production (*CPR*, 81).

Yet Spivak's reading of this passage is significantly different from that of earlier commentators. In her argument, the problem with Marx's account of the AMP was that it attempted to 'fit historical presuppositions into a logical mode' (*CPR*, 81). It is for this reason that the difference between Species-Life and Species-Being is 're-cast as a sequential (historical) story as well as a spacing (geography)' (*CPR*, 81).

This recasting of the difference between Species-Life and Species-Being in Marx's later work does not simply signal the negation of the AMP. Rather the AMP is a name that 'inhabit[s] the pre-historical or para-geographical space/time that mark[s] the outside of the feudalism-capitalism circuit' (*CPR*, 83). It is this exclusion of the AMP as a precapitalist mode of production from the Eurocentric mode of production narrative that constitutes the coherence and closure of Marx's evolutionary model of history. For Spivak, however, the problem with Marx's account of the AMP was less 'due to his being a nineteenth-century European' than a result of his attempt to explain his theory of political economy and history in the philosophical language of Hegelian dialectics (*CPR*, 90).

For Marx, this attempt to explain history in terms of philosophy draws on Hegel's dialectical account of the human subject's development of absolute knowledge in *The Phenomenology of Spirit* (1807). In plain terms, the dialectic refers to a philosophical method in which concepts are defined through the negation of two antithetical positions. For example, in *The Phenomenology of Spirit* Hegel described how the human subject's achievement of absolute knowledge was predicated on a series of dialectical struggles: between the master and the slave; lordship and bondage; the family and civil society. Each of these struggles had to be overcome or 'sublated' in order to attain absolute knowledge. Marx borrows this dialectical method from Hegel in order to account for the historical division of labour between the dominant, property-owning classes and the oppressed and dispossessed working classes. In Marx's materialist conception of historical progress, each stage or mode of production from the 'Asiatic' mode and feudalism through to capitalism and socialism is overcome or 'sublated' by the proceeding mode of production.

For Spivak, however, Marx's attempt to explain the historical mode of production narrative in Hegelian terms is inadequate after the collapse of the former Soviet bloc and the global expansion of capitalism since the last two decades of the twentieth century. For this reason, Spivak substitutes the deconstructive term *différance* for sublation 'as the name of the relationship between capitalism and socialism' (*CPR*, 70). As discussed in the previous chapter, the term *différance* was coined by Derrida, and denotes the persistent reversal and displacement of a binary opposition. In the case of that between socialism and capitalism, the term designates the persistent and open-ended political task of reversing and displacing the capital relationship in the pursuit of social justice. Furthermore, by substituting the term *différance* for sublation, Spivak also challenges Marx's argument that 'more primitive' modes of production are completely overcome or negated by 'more advanced' modes of production. Contra Marx, Spivak thus suggests that the AMP does not simply disappear in the face of global capitalism.

Indeed, what is at stake in Spivak's deconstructive reading of the AMP is an attempt to 'work at the deconstructive "new politics of reading," which involves an effort to enter the protocols of Marx's text in order to re-inscribe it for use' (*CPR*, 91). This deconstructive strategy of reading is subsequently clarified in a reference to Derrida's *Positions* (1972), in particular to the new use of 'a name X as a *lever of intervention*, in order to maintain a grasp on the previous organization, which is to be transformed effectively'.[18] In the case of Marx's theory of the AMP, this deconstructive reading strategy allows Spivak to suspend moral judgement of Marx's Eurocentrism in order to re-inscribe Marx's thought for use in the contemporary era of 'planetary financialization' (*CPR*, 70).

As Spivak points out in *A Critique of Postcolonial Reason*, her previous engagements with Marx's work focused on his account of Value. In essays such as 'Scattered Speculations on the Question of Value', 'Limits and Openings of Marx in Derrida' and 'Ghostwriting', Spivak traces the ambivalence of use value in Marx's theory of value. In *A Critique of Postcolonial Reason*, Spivak supplements this reading of value with a reading of the Asiatic mode of production. Before examining the significance of this supplementary reading in more detail, I now examine Spivak's deconstructive readings of Marx's theory of value.

Deconstructing value

Like the deconstructive reading of the Asiatic mode of production in *A Critique of Postcolonial Reason*, Spivak's readings of Marx's labour theory of value are primarily concerned to demonstrate the critical and political relevance of Marx's thought in the contemporary era of global capitalism. Indeed, Spivak often emphasizes that subaltern women in the global South are the agents of production for contemporary global capitalism. Yet this is not to suggest that her readings of Marx's labour theory of value simply represent the productive body of the subaltern woman as the source of value under contemporary capitalism. For to do so would be to repeat the act of ethical violence against the subaltern that Spivak attributes to western intellectuals such as Michel Foucault and Gilles Deleuze in 'Can the Subaltern Speak?'. Instead, Spivak traces the ambivalence of Marx's labour theory of value in order to articulate the singular, embodied knowledge of the subaltern woman, which cannot be accounted for in the economic terms of capitalism (and is explored below).

In chapter 1 of the first volume of *Capital*, Marx lays the foundations for what has since become known as the labour theory of value. Starting with an analysis of the commodity in nineteenth-century European capitalist societies, Marx proceeds to distinguish between use value, or the 'physical property' and 'material content' of a commodity and exchange value, or the universal equivalent that defines the value of a commodity in relation to other commodities of a different type. As he puts it, 'the relation between the values of two commodities supplies us with the simplest expression of the value of a single commodity'.[19] As a relational category, the exchange value of a commodity is thus independent of the physical and material content, or use value of the commodity.

In Marx's argument, exchange value is defined by abstracting the specific form of embodied human labour required to produce the commodity from the commodity form itself. As a consequence, 'there is nothing left of [the concrete forms of labour embodied in the commodity] in each case but the same phantom-like objectivity; they are merely congealed quantities of homogeneous human labour, i.e. of human labour expended without regard to the form of its expenditure'.[20] Yet this is not to say that the signs of embodied human labour are completely erased in the calculation of exchange value. As the adjectives 'congealed' and 'phantom-like' suggest, the commodity is still marked by the 'residue of the products of labour'.[21]

For Spivak, it is the ambivalent status of use value as a spectral presence in Marx's labour theory of value that undermines the total abstraction of labour from the calculation of exchange value. For the use value of labour power embodied in the commodity is also 'the material bearer [*Träger*] of [. . .] exchange value'.[22] As such, the use value of labour power has no positive presence in the circulation of commodities. It is perhaps for this reason that Spivak argues in 'Limits and Openings of Marx in Derrida' that Marx left 'the slippery concept of use value untheorized' (*OTM*, 97). Yet Marx's apparent refusal to theorize use value is also crucial to Spivak's deconstructive reading of Marx.

For Spivak it is the 'slippery idea' of the use value of labour power in Marx's work that both enables and threatens the smooth running of capitalism (*OTM*, 106). On the one hand 'labor-power as commodity is sublated into (exchange[able]) value by being negated as use value' (*OTM*, 106). Yet on the other hand the use value of labour power continues to haunt the exchange value of the commodity. For this reason, use value cannot be accounted for in the rational terms of political economy. As the Marxist thinker G. A. Cohen noted in 1978, 'Political economy examines not the content or substance or body, but exchange-value and capital [. . .] it is beyond political economy's brief to consider use-value "as such" '.[23] For Marx, by contrast to the established views of political economy, 'use-value plays a far more important part than it has in economics hitherto'.[24]

For some readers of Marx the use value of labour power is interpreted as a mythic origin of political economy that both precedes and is outside exchange and commodity circulation. In this reading, the use value of labour power is equated with the romantic anti-capitalism that can be detected in some of Marx's earlier writings. In his *Economic and Philosophical Manuscripts*, for example, such a vision is exemplified in a passage describing a socialist utopia in which the worker lives in a state of unalienated labour and subsists on the use value of his own labour power. As suggested above, Marx went on to revise this position in his later economic writings. Yet because the use value of labour power continues to have this connotation of romantic anti-capitalism, some commentators have excluded use value in favour of a more scientific account of capital circulation. As Spivak notes, ' "Scientific socialism" contrasts itself to a "utopian socialism" committed to such a restoration by presupposing labor outside of capital logic or wage labor' (*IOW*, 161).

Certainly, Marx suggested in the *Grundrisse* that 'use-values circulated without market exchange in earliest history' and that the 'first instance of market exchange is trade between independent tribes'.[25] Yet to claim that Marx's critique of political economy is simply 'a question of restoring a society of use value' (*IOW*, 161) overlooks Marx's argument that 'Capital consumes the *use*-value of labour power' (*IOW*, 161). Indeed for Spivak, Marx's argument constitutes an 'aporetic moment' (*IOW*, 161) in the utopian socialist caricature of Marx's labour theory of value because it ignores how the use value of labour power is consumed by the exchange value of a commodity.

Spivak's claim that Marx's account of use value is an 'aporetic moment' (*IOW*, 161) in Marx's labour theory of value challenges the scientific readings of that theory which test its truth claims by attempting to calculate the relative prices of commodities and the rate of profit in terms of use value.[26] Such scientific readings often conclude that the labour theory of value is flawed because the use value of labour power is not necessary to calculate the prices and surplus value of commodities. In Spivak's argument, by contrast, the use value of labour power is precisely incalculable because it is abstracted from the exchange value of the commodity. The critical task instead is to attend to Marx's argument that 'the twofold nature of labour contained in commodities' is 'crucial to an understanding of political economy'.[27]

It is this double meaning of labour in Marx's analytic of the commodity that prompts Spivak to treat use value as a deconstructive lever rather than a stable philosophical concept: 'For use value in the classic way of deconstructive levers, is both outside and inside the system of value determinations' (*IOW*, 162). Use value is outside that system 'because it cannot be measured according to the labor theory of value' (*IOW*, 162). Yet at the same time, use value is not '*altogether* outside the circuit of exchange' (*IOW*, 162). The use value of labour power thus serves to disrupt what Spivak calls the 'continuist version' of capital circulation (*IOW*, 155–6).

The continuist paradigm of capital circulation is based on a partial reading of Marx, which excludes the ambivalent category of use value from the calculation of exchange value, its representation as money, and the subsequent transformation of money into capital. Against this partial interpretation, Spivak traces the ruptures in Marx's reasoning in order to re-articulate the spectral presence of the use value of labour power contained in the commodity.

At stake in this re-articulation of the ghostly presence of the use value of labour power is an attempt to account for new forms of exploitation and precarious labour under contemporary global capitalism, such as subcontracting, casual contracts and non-unionization. For Spivak, however, such a critical and political task is hampered by Marx's argument that there is no philosophical injustice in the capital relation between workers and capitalists (*OTM*, 107). In the terms of Enlightenment rationality upon which Marx based his analysis of capital, the wage labour contract seems just and ethical because it is grounded in a humanist discourse of universal rights. As Dipesh Chakrabarty has argued in *Rethinking Working-Class History* (1989), 'the concept of "abstract labor" is an extension of the bourgeois notion of the "equal rights" of "abstract individuals", whose political life is reflected in the ideals and practice of "citizenship"'.[28]

What is more, Spivak argues that it is the human body's natural capacity to produce more than it requires for its own subsistence that provides a rational and ethical ground for the capital relation. Indeed '[c]apital is only the supplement of the *natural* and *rational* teleology of the body, of its irreducible capacity for superadequation, which it uses as use value' (*OTM*, 107). In plain terms, capitalists do not simply coerce workers to produce more than they are actually paid for; rather capital homogenizes the human body's natural capacity to produce more than it requires to survive. As Marx argued in *Grundrisse*, capital, or surplus value, is no more than the objectification of surplus labour, or the human body's natural ability to produce more than it requires for its own subsistence:

> Within the production process itself, surplus value, the surplus value procured through compulsion by capital, appeared as *surplus labour,*

itself in the form of living labour, which, however, since it cannot create something out of nothing, finds its objective conditions laid out before it. [. . .] This new *value* which confronts living labour as independent, as engaged in exchange with it, as capital, is the *product of living labour*. It is nothing other than the *excess of labour as such above necessary labour* – in objective form and hence of value.[29]

At first glance, Spivak's argument that capital is 'only the supplement of the *natural* and *rational* teleology of the body' might seem to be a deconstructive rephrasing of Marx's claim that capital is 'nothing other than the *excess of labour*', by which he means the surplus labour that workers produce in excess of the labour required for their own subsistence. Yet such a reading ignores how Spivak's employment of the deconstructive term 'supplement' to describe the relationship between capital and surplus labour in Marx's thought challenges the dialectical claims of Marx's argument that capitalism will be sublated or totally replaced by a socialist economy at a determinate point in the future. By emphasizing that capital is only the supplement of the human body's natural and rational capacity to produce more than it needs for its own subsistence, Spivak challenges the assumption that there is an absolute categorical difference between capitalism and socialism.

One might legitimately ask whether Spivak's deconstructive reading of the capital relation in Marx undermines the very theoretical ground for political opposition to capitalism. However, this would be to overlook both the conceptual and the contextual significance of Spivak's argument. Conceptually, Spivak reframes Marx's dialectical approach to social and political change by re-thinking socialism as the *différance* of capitalism (SM, 110–11; GW, 67; *CPR*, 430). Against Marx's argument that socialism is the complete overcoming, or sublation of capitalism, Spivak describes socialism as 'a constant pushing away – a differing and a deferral – of the capital-ist harnessing of the *social* productivity of capital' (*CPR*, 430). What is at stake in Spivak's deconstructive re-thinking of Marx's conception of socialism is an attempt to invent a different spatial and temporal logic for socialism that can push away the *global* capitalist harnessing of the social productivity of capital. Whereas Marx argued that industrial capitalism contains the seeds of its own destruction, and that capitalism would give way to socialism by a process of historical inevitability, Spivak's deconstructive re-thinking of Marx's account of socialism in the era of post-communist globalization is sceptical of the evolutionary narrative

upon which Marx's model of history is based. Moreover, the reason
why Spivak's agonistic pushing away of the global capitalist harnessing of the social productivity of capital is open-ended and indeterminate rather than finite and teleological is precisely because
capitalism is constantly searching around the globe for new labour
markets to harness and exploit. In contrast to Marx, Spivak's vision
of the political future is uncertain about the possibilities of a total
break with capitalism.

Marx and the humanist definition of the social

Another reason for Spivak's conceptual re-thinking of Marx is that
Marx's vision of the social emancipation of the proletariat depended
on a conflation of rational, Enlightenment principles of social rights
with a vague and incoherent humanist definition of the social (*OTM*,
97; SM, 108). For the proletariat to claim 'the social' as a political
goal and to achieve consciousness of itself as a class is an example
of what Spivak calls (in Kantian terms) 'the Enlightenment project
of the public use of reason, but with the proletarian rather than a
bourgeois subject' (SM, 109).

This argument is clearly evinced in Marx's introduction to his
Critique of Hegel's Philosophy of Right (1843), in which Hegel is seen
as positing a false universality in his presentation of the 'particular'
class interests of the bourgeoisie as if they were the 'universal rights
of [nineteenth-century German] society'.[30] Against this false universalism, Marx called for the 'dissolution of society as a particular
class' in favour of the proletariat, or 'a class of civil society which
is not a class of civil society, a class which is the dissolution of all
classes'.[31]

Spivak does not object to Marx's re-thinking of the rational,
enlightenment definition of 'the social' from the standpoint of the
proletariat *per se*. Rather she argues that it is Marx's unexamined
humanism that impedes the call for the dissolution of the class
structure of bourgeois civil society (*OTM*, 97; SM, 109). In the introduction to his *Critique of Hegel's Philosophy of Right*, for instance,
Marx equated the dissolution of bourgeois society by the proletariat
with the 'total redemption of humanity'.[32] Such examples of Marx's
untheorized humanism are dangerous in Spivak's account because
the meaning of the word 'humanity' is vague and therefore open
to abuse by particular hegemonic groups.

Moreover, it is against the conflation of a rational, Enlightenment definition of 'the social' and an unexamined humanism in Marx's work that Spivak proposes a re-thinking of socialism as the *différance* of capitalism. Whereas Marxist-humanist critiques of capitalism, such as Georg Lukács's critique of reification, tend to assume 'a binary opposition between labour and commodity', Spivak emphasizes that 'Marx's notion of the use of reason as class consciousness in a socialized society [. . .] was the recognition that labor as a particularization of labor power was a commodity' (SM, 110). In other words, by emphasizing that the value of commodities is produced by labour, Marx encouraged the workers to recognize themselves as agents of capitalist production instead of as victims of exploitation.

As mentioned above, the spectral presence of the use value of labour power contained in the commodity continues to haunt the capital relation. What is crucial in Spivak's re-thinking of use value as a deconstructive lever is that this spectre of the use value of labour power can be used to push against the transformation of surplus labour into capitalism. In 'Ghostwriting', for instance, Spivak proposes that the 'future socialist must use capital carrying the subjectivity of "the social", as rationally spectralized, rather than that of capital' (GW, 74). In other words, if 'capital' is haunted by the spectre of the worker's labour power, then this spectre can be transformed into a rational political programme for the social redistribution of capital rather than being commodified as abstract labour.

Against the humanist reading of Marx, which assumes a binary opposition between socialism and capitalism, Spivak emphasizes that 'capital accumulation is indispensable to socialism' (GW, 74). Citing a passage from Marx's *Capital*, Spivak suggests that the critical task of Marxist thought is to strip ' "both wages and surplus-value, necessary labour and surplus labour [. . .] of their specifically capitalist character" ' (Marx, vol. III, chap. 51; cited in GW, 74). By reducing the capital relation to 'the degree needed to [. . .] form an insurance and reserve fund' and 'for the constant expansion of reproduction to the degree determined by social need',[33] Marx called on the proletariat to manage the capital relation for social equality and redistribution rather than for profit.

After the collapse of Soviet communism, the global restructuring of industrial and agricultural production by multinational corporations and financial organizations such as the World Bank and the International Monetary Fund, and the superexploitation of non-unionized, subcontracted female labour in the global South, Marx's labour theory of value may appear to be obsolete and his programme for the social redistribution of wealth a distant pipe-dream. Yet it is precisely the contemporary superexploitation of subaltern women in the international division of labour that makes Spivak's deconstructive re-thinking of Marx's labour theory of value imperative. In 'Scattered Speculations on the Question of Value' Spivak insists that 'any critique of the labor theory of value, pointing at the unfeasibility of the theory under post-industrialism, or as a calculus of economic indicators, ignores the dark presence of the Third World' (*IOW*, 167). Just as Marx emphasized that the masculine, industrial working-class subject of nineteenth-century Europe is 'the source of value' for industrial capitalism, so Spivak argues that the 'so-called "Third World" [. . .] produces the wealth and possibility of the "First World"' (*PCC*, 96). In saying this, Spivak also challenges the view of the Third world as a primitive, pre-modern or underdeveloped space outside the circuits of capitalism, which is epitomized in Marx's idea of the Asiatic mode of production.

The gendered international division of labour

Spivak's invocation of the gendered international division of labour certainly demonstrates the continuing relevance of Marx's labour theory of value to the gendered and geographical dynamics of contemporary global capitalism. However, the casual and non-unionized conditions of labour for many women (and children) employed in sweatshops and free-trade zones and other forms of subcontracted labour in the global South would seem to make it difficult for such workers to organize and protest against their exploitation, let alone to promote the social redistribution of capital.[34]

The plight of subaltern workers in the global South has also been the focus of concern for writers such as Saskia Sassen and Naomi Klein. In Sassen's *Globalization and its Discontents* (1998), there is a systemic relation between the growth of export production in Third-world countries and the massive increase in Third-world immigration to the United States on the one hand, and the incorporation of Third-world women into global structures of wage labour on the other.[35] For Sassen, the 'expanded incorporation of women into wage labour is a global process that assumes specific forms in different locations'.[36] There are, nevertheless, structural similarities between the exploitation of immigrant women's labour power in the

United States and the use of women's labour in the service economy and free-trade zones in the global South. In both instances, Sassen contends that women fulfil the global economy's demand for a non-unionized, casual and low-paid labour force.

Whereas Sassen's book examines the connections between migrant labour and women's wage labour, Klein's *No Logo* (2000) explores how global corporations, which market brands such as Nike sportswear and Gap clothing, have tried to efface the manufacturing of their commodities by subcontracting production to free-trade zones in Indonesia and Vietnam.[37] In common with US-based organizations such as the United Needle and Textile Workers' Union and Students against Sweatshops, Klein has advocated a political strategy that seeks to expose how particular multinational corporations produce their commodities by subcontracting manufacturing to companies in the global South that force subaltern women to work under conditions of non-unionized, sub-minimum wage labour. Such a strategy of 'outing' the exploitative labour practices of particular corporations seeks to encourage a practice of ethical consumerism among citizens in North America and Europe. And, in doing so, both Klein and the anti-sweatshop movements claim to speak and act on behalf of the subaltern worker in the global South.

It is precisely such transparent claims to 'speak for' subaltern workers in the global South that Spivak's deconstructive rethinking of Marx seeks to challenge. In *A Critique of Postcolonial Reason*, for example, Spivak criticizes the 'moral imperialism' of 'boycott politics' (*CPR*, 415). Focusing on the emergence of a public discourse in the US media during the 1990s around the exploitation of child labour in the Bangladeshi garment-manufacturing industry, Spivak criticizes the racism of benevolent liberal reformers, who supported 'sanctions against Southern garment factories that use child labor' (*CPR*, 416). Spivak equally condemns the exploitation of child labour. However, she also questions the efficacy of sanctions against Bangladeshi garment factories that use child labour on the grounds that such sanctions do nothing to redress the broader absence of unionized labour laws or infrastructure reforms in countries such as Bangladesh.

Spivak's critique of the 'moral imperialism' associated with 'First-world' anti-sweatshop campaigns for consumer boycotts of certain commodities that are produced by 'Third-world' workers under conditions of sweated labour has been taken up in critiques of the contemporary anti-capitalist movement. The British cultural critic

Jeremy Gilbert has questioned the political efficacy of the anti-sweatshop crusade on the grounds that its appeal to the ethical subjectivity of the First-world consumer is incommensurate with 'the desire of third-world workers to improve their pay and conditions'.[38] In a more generous reading of the moralizing rhetoric of the anti-sweatshop movement ('The Sweatshop Sublime', 2002), the American cultural critic Bruce Robbins characterizes the First-world consumer's contemplation of the magnitude of the world economic system and the international division of labour as a contemporary example of Kant's theory of the sublime.[39] Robbins acknowledges that there is no guarantee that a First-world consumer's contemplation of what he aptly calls the 'sweatshop sublime' will necessarily lead to their political mobilization; indeed, in many cases, a consumer's experience of the 'sweatshop sublime' may lead to political paralysis and inaction. Yet, for Robbins, it is precisely the experience of hesitancy, self-questioning and doubt associated with the sublime that complicates the 'tempting simplicity of action'.[40]

Significantly, Robbins cites Spivak's *A Critique of Postcolonial Reason* to support his argument. In particular, he juxtaposes Spivak's critique of Kant's foreclosure of the native informant in his analytic of the sublime with her critique of the 'boycott politics' associated with the North American anti-sweatshop movement and western human rights discourse. In doing so, Robbins concludes that in Spivak's *Critique*, 'Kant's analytic of the sublime does the same thing that western human rights discourse does when addressed to Bangladeshi sweatshops: it flattens out the complexity and difference of Third World society to suit a First World standard of ethical rationality'.[41]

What Robbins calls the sweatshop sublime may provide an ethical structure through which the First-world consumer can respond to the exploitation of Third-world labour. Yet this structure simultaneously forecloses the agency and voice of the Third-world worker. What is more, the ethical structure of the sweatshop sublime offers no viable political alternative for infrastructural reform or the social redistribution of capital in postcolonial nation-states such as Bangladesh or Vietnam.

The limitations of this 'First World standard of ethical rationality' are further elaborated by Ian Baucom in a discussion (published in *Nepantla*, 2000) of the Nike Corporation's public-relations campaign to clean up its reputation as a company that operates ' "without any regard for people in developing countries" '.[42] In Baucom's account, the rhetoric of Nike's public-relations campaign draws on an ethical language of responsibility and global citizenship, which seems to be based loosely on the work of Spivak and Levinas. In doing so, the campaign responds to the charges made by anti-sweatshop activists using the same language of ethical responsibility in its public address that the activists themselves used against the Nike Corporation in the early 1990s. Unsurprisingly, Nike's rhetorical strategy is not matched by a reform in its use of superexploited Third-world women workers in free-trade-zone garment-industry sweatshops. Instead, the campaign advocates indebtedness through a corporate-sponsored programme of microlending as a solution to women's exploitation and poverty. As Baucom puts it, 'subalternity is refitted for capital, educated, made responsible, presentable, [and] recoded for membership within a global community of finance-capital-citizenship whose identity document is a sound credit record'.[43]

It is in response to such examples of what Baucom calls the refitting of subalternity in the contemporary global capitalist circuits of production, exploitation and debt that Spivak's deconstructive reading of Marx should be understood. At times Spivak's reading of Marx might appear to suggest that the regulation of labour laws and the social redistribution of capital through infrastructure and state welfare in the global South remains a viable alternative to the expansion of a global financial market driven by debt and consumerism. In *A Critique of Postcolonial Reason*, for instance, Spivak argues that the 'possibility of persistently redirecting accumulation into social redistribution can be within [the] reach [of new immigrants in the global North] if they join the globe-girdling Social Movements in the South through the entry point of their own countries of origin' (*CPR*, 402). Yet Spivak is also sceptical of whether a programmatic socialist alternative to capitalism such as social redistribution is possible in the era of post-Soviet global capitalism. Instead Spivak's later work has tended to focus on the slow, painstaking work needed to establish ethical singularity with the subaltern (*IM*, xxiv).

So far this chapter has considered how Spivak's deconstructive reading of Marx's account of the Asiatic mode of production has challenged the Eurocentric notion that the Third world exists in a primitive, pre-modern space outside the sphere of capitalism. I have also suggested that Spivak's deconstructive reading of Marx's labour theory of value is precisely concerned with how the labour power of the female proletariat of the global South has been incorporated into the global economy. Such a rethinking of Marx's labour theory of value in terms of the gendered and geographical dynamics of the international division of labour also reveals how the Asiatic mode of production is crucial to the contemporary global economy.

Spivak has expanded this focus on economic theories of value and labour to include an analysis of how the lives and bodies of different subaltern constituencies are subjected to the value coding of western development agencies and Non-Governmental Organizations. Spivak's concern with reproductive rights, population control and post-Fordist homeworking cannot really be accounted for in the narrow economic terms of Marx's labour theory of value. It is perhaps for this reason that Spivak turns to *Anti-Oedipus* (1972) by Gilles Deleuze and Felix Guattari, which includes a re-thinking of Marx's labour theory of value and his materialist conception of history.

Deleuze and Guattari and the re-thinking of value

Deleuze and Guattari re-write Marx's labour theory of value by 'applying it to the production and appropriation of the value-form in affective and social rather than merely economic coding' (*OTM*, 62). This extension of Marx's argument beyond the 'merely economic' would seem to account for what Spivak calls 'the new socialization of the reproductive body' (*CPR*, 68). This 'socialization' denotes the regulation of women's reproductive bodies in the global South, which Spivak registers through a taxonomy that includes reproductive rights, surrogacy, transplant, population control and post-Fordist homeworking (*CPR*, 68). As discussed in chapter 5 below, Spivak's concern with population control and women's reproductive rights complicates the moral agenda of western feminism towards women in the global South. For the purposes of this chapter, however, suffice to say that Spivak's concern with the reproductive bodies of subaltern women in the global South clearly works to complicate the narrow definition of productive labour that underpinned Marx's labour theory of value, and parallels a broader concern with the biopolitical control of populations outlined in the work of Michel Foucault, Michael Hardt and Antonio Negri, as well as that of Gilles Deleuze and Felix Guattari.[44]

For Spivak, Deleuze and Guattari re-conceptualize Marx's modes of production narrative as a discontinuous process of desiring production that is inscribed and regulated by a surface of decoding, which they call the 'deterritorialized socius'.[45] This re-thinking of value coding and the rejection of the evolutionist model that underpins Marx's modes of production narrative alters the minor place of the Asiatic mode of production in Marx's ethnocentric conception of history. As a consequence 'Deleuze and Guattari [. . .] can see the Asiatic Mode as a place of constant connections rather than an unbridged and unbridgeable gulf' (*CPR*, 108).

Spivak finds Deleuze and Guattari's reassessment of the Asiatic mode of production valuable because they are 'able to hint at an approach to a "third world" full of agents of coding' (*CPR*, 108). One of the reasons why Deleuze and Guattari can only 'hint' at such an approach is that they are 'not specialists of Asia' and thus cannot translate the desiring production of the Third-world subject into a common language that is intelligible to other agents of coding, reproduction or production (*CPR*, 108). This translation problem points towards a broader linguistic and epistemological limit in counter-globalist activism and the representative claims of certain Non-Governmental Organizations, which Spivak has elsewhere called transnational illiteracy.

If, as Marx suggested in *Capital* (vol. I), the exchange value of a commodity is defined by abstracting the use value of labour power contained in the commodity, this process of abstraction might be understood as a process of translation into a common language: the common language of exchange value. Yet this common language of commodities clearly effaces the multiple histories of labour that went into the manufacturing of commodities. As discussed below, Spivak's discussion of transnational illiteracy and her plea for western Marxists and global justice activists to learn the languages of the global South is consistent with her commitment to achieving ethical singularity with the subaltern. Indeed, it is this commitment that links Spivak's engagement with Marx's labour theory of value and the Asiatic mode of production to her critique of transnational illiteracy. For in the process of finding a new idiom appropriate to address the singularity of the subaltern, Spivak also produces a theoretical vocabulary that can account for different histories of subaltern labour.

Transnational illiteracy and the translation of subaltern labour

What Spivak means by transnational illiteracy is partly explained in *A Critique of Postcolonial Reason*: she criticizes benevolent liberal activists and reformers in the global North, who claim to speak for disempowered subaltern groups in the South, yet have no knowledge of the economic and social circumstances of such groups or willingness to learn the language and culture of the subaltern constituencies for whom they claim to speak. For Spivak such transnational illiteracy is epitomized by liberals who supported the US Senate's sanctions in 1993 against garment factories in the global South, those using child labour without considering the economic or material impact on the children who become unemployed as a result of these sanctions. In Spivak's argument, it is 'complicity with racism' that 'allows the benevolent transnationally illiterate liberal to stop at supporting sanctions against garment factories that use child labor' (*CPR*, 416).

Against the damaging effects of the benevolent liberal's transnational illiteracy, Spivak suggests that the transnational literacy of the educated new immigrant dwelling in the global North could serve the social and economic interests of the poorest women and children in the global South. As Mark Sanders observes in an essay on *A Critique of Postcolonial Reason*, published in *Interventions* (2002), the transnationally literate New Immigrant is a privileged figure in Spivak's re-writing of Marxism as a setting to work of deconstruction.[46] Neither Sanders nor Spivak fully explains why the transnationally literate New Immigrant is a possible source of agency for the subaltern in the global South. Yet it can be inferred from the logic of their arguments that if the New Immigrant in the global North is literate in the subaltern language of the Southern nation from which they immigrated and has an understanding of the economic reality of the subaltern, then the New Immigrant has the capacity to act in a way that is ethically responsible to the singularity of the subaltern.

Transnational literacy may not sound like the most obvious or effective strategy for achieving economic justice, or the social redistribution of capital, for the subaltern. However, Spivak's imperative to political collectives or networks, which claim solidarity with the subaltern, to learn the languages of the global South is crucial if those collectives or networks are to act in a way that is ethically responsible to the social and political world of the subaltern.[47]

Another way in which transnational literacy could work to produce a form of collective political action that is responsible to the singularity of the subaltern lies in the potential of transnational literacy to translate the singular histories and situated knowledges of subaltern labour, which are often relegated to the status of precapitalist in Marx's mode of production narrative. As

Dipesh Chakrabarty has argued in *Provincializing Europe* (2000), a critique of Marx from the standpoint of the subaltern worker in postcolonial India: 'the transition from "real" to "abstract" [labour] is [. . .] also a question of transition/translation from many and possibly incommensurate temporalities to the homogenous time of abstract labor, the transition from nonhistory to history'.[48]

In Chakrabarty's argument, the Marxist model of the commodity as abstract labour cannot adequately translate the singular and heterogeneous histories of subaltern labour. As a consequence, the secular historical narrative of commodity production is haunted by these singular, heterogeneous and (in some cases) non-secular histories of subaltern labour. Chakrabarty cites *The Devil and Commodity Fetishism* (1980), a book by the anthropologist Michael Taussig, whose work on the tin mines of highland Bolivia revealed that some Bolivian tin miners performed rites to Tio, an Incan devil spirit, to protect them from physical danger in the mines. In these rites the Tio 'stands as a custodian of the meaning of Indian submission and loss of control over the life they constantly call for'.[49] By constructing the Tio in this way, the tin miners refashioned the image of the Incan spirit of evil and the Christian myth of redemption to 'give poetic expression to the needs of the oppressed'.[50] What is more, such a poetic expression defined the tin miners' political organization and struggle against the destructive power of commodities and capitalism in terms of 'myths of creation and in rituals of work that oppose the form that modern production has taken to an earlier organic form'.[51] In Taussig's account, this framing of the Bolivian tin miners' alienated labour is 'an indictment of an economic system which forces men to barter their souls for the destructive powers of commodities'.[52] Yet such myths and rituals do not provide an escape from capitalist social relations; rather they 'oppose the exploitative and fragmented form that [the Bolivian peasants' social life] has taken' under global capitalism.[53]

For Chakrabarty, Taussig's research on the myths and rituals of the Bolivian tin miners exemplifies how European colonialism, and the expansion of global capitalism that it inaugurates, has failed to completely eradicate the subaltern forms of political consciousness, organization and resistance that are heterogeneous to the temporality of capitalism. In Chakrabarty's argument, it makes no sense to think of such forms of subaltern labour as primitive or precapitalist in the sense of a period of time that is 'simply chronologically prior on an ordinal, homogeneous scale of time'[54] (as Marx does). Rather Chakrabarty contends that precapitalist 'can only be imagined as something that exists within the temporal horizon of capital and that at the same time disrupts the continuity of this time by suggesting another time that is not on the same, secular, homogenous calendar'.[55] This heterogeneous and non-secular form of time 'could be entirely immeasurable in terms of the units of the godless, spiritless time of what we call "history", an idea already assumed in the secular concepts of "capital" and "abstract labour".[56] It is for this reason, Chakrabarty suggests, that subaltern labour can be understood only in relation to the historical narrative of commodity production as 'a Derridean trace of that which cannot be enclosed, an element that constantly challenges from within capital's and commodity's – and by implication, history's – claims to unity and universality'.[57] In other words, by re-conceptualizing the term precapitalist as a Derridean trace of heterogeneous forms of subaltern labour rather than a primitive stage in the linear history of global capitalist accumulation, Chakrabarty provides a critical vocabulary for articulating different histories of subaltern labour.

It is precisely such histories of subaltern labour that Spivak's transnationally literate New Immigrant intellectual could work to translate. Such a practice of translation would take place against the grain of what Chakrabarty calls the 'transition/translation from [the] many and possibly incommensurate temporalities' of subaltern labour 'to the homogenous time of abstract labor'.[58] Indeed, through the labour of translation, Spivak suggests that the transnationally literate New Immigrant could begin to challenge the stereotypes of the postcolonial world as a place without socioeconomic organization before the colonial expansion of European capitalism, or as a place without theoretical sophistication. Such a translational reading strategy might also articulate and value the singular and heterogeneous forms of subaltern labour that are abstracted in the contemporary global circulation of commodities. By developing a translational reading of Marx's labour theory of value, which can account for the coexistence of 'precapitalist' modes of production such as the AMP alongside contemporary global capitalist regimes of production, Spivak invents a theoretical language that is appropriate to address the singular forms and conditions of subaltern labour.

4

Subaltern Studies and
the Critique of Representation

Spivak's ongoing critical engagements with Marxism, feminism, deconstruction and psychoanalysis are crucially informed by a political and intellectual commitment to disenfranchised groups in the global South. Yet her writing has also always demonstrated an acute awareness of the ethical dangers associated with representing the disenfranchised from the standpoint of a relatively empowered, diasporic intellectual in the western academy. As a consequence, Spivak's work is marked by a tension between a commitment to social and political change for disenfranchised constituencies and an ethical responsibility to produce a critical vocabulary that is appropriate to engage with the particular social, historical and economic circumstances of subaltern subjects. Such a vocabulary has questioned whether the representation of the subaltern by intellectuals is a desirable political goal. This tension in Spivak's writing has produced several complex and challenging theoretical interventions, which have expanded and developed the historiographic methodology of the Subaltern Studies collective, a group of historians who were originally concerned to recover the histories of peasant insurgency in colonial South Asia.

Before examining Spivak's contribution in more detail, I now trace the genealogy of the term 'subaltern' in the work of Karl Marx, Antonio Gramsci and the Subaltern Studies collective.

The subaltern: Genealogy of a concept

According to the *Oxford English Dictionary* the term 'subaltern' has three distinct meanings: it is conventionally understood as a synonym of subordinate, but it can also denote a lower-ranking officer in the army, or a particular example that supports a universal proposition in philosophical logic. Spivak's use of the term is primarily informed by the work of the Italian Marxist thinker Antonio Gramsci on the rural-based Italian peasantry and the research of the international Subaltern Studies collective on the histories of subaltern insurgency in colonial and postcolonial South Asia. In his *Prison Notebooks* (1929–35) Antonio Gramsci uses 'subaltern' interchangeably with 'subordinate' and 'instrumental' to describe 'non-hegemonic groups or classes'.[1] While the English translators of Gramsci's *Prison Notebooks* found it difficult to 'discern any systematic difference in Gramsci's usage between [. . .] subaltern and subordinate',[2] some commentators have argued that Gramsci used the term as a code-word for the more familiar Marxist 'proletariat' in order to smuggle his manuscript past the prison censor during his incarceration under Mussolini's fascist government. Yet for other social theorists such as Ernesto Laclau and Chantal Mouffe, Gramsci's account of the historical failure of a class alliance between the industrial proletariat based in Northern Italy and the rural peasantry in Southern Italy works to complicate the founding assumption of Marxist-Leninist thought that working-class subjects are *a priori* revolutionary in character as a necessary consequence of their economic conditions.[3] For this reason, it is hard to read Gramsci's use of the term subaltern only as a simple code-word for the more familiar Marxist category of proletarian; rather it seems to precisely denote subordinate groups such as the rural peasantry in Southern Italy, whose achievement of social and political consciousness was limited and their political unity weak. In so far as the subaltern had not achieved consciousness of their collective economic and social oppression as a class, the subaltern is quite different from the industrial proletariat. As David Arnold has observed in his contribution to *Mapping Subaltern Studies* (2000):

> In dealing with peasants and other groups in a society, like that of nineteenth-century Italy or India, that had not become wholly capitalistic, the language of subalternity might generally be more appropriate than that of class [. . .]. Gramsci's use of the term 'subaltern' further invites us to appreciate the common properties of

subordinate groups as a whole – the shared fact of their subordination, their intrinsic weakness, their limited strengths. The special,
revolutionary character of the industrial proletariat is correspond-
ingly played down.[4]

It is this sense of the subaltern – as a general category of subordination – that informs the work of the Subaltern Studies collective.
Drawing on Gramsci's account of the rural peasantry in Southern
Italy in his 'Notes on Italian History' and 'Some Aspects of the
Southern Question', as well as the work of the British Marxist historians Eric Hobsbawm and E. P. Thompson, the Subaltern Studies
collective use the term as a 'name for the general attribute of subordination in South Asian society whether this is expressed in
terms of class, caste, age, gender and office or in any other way'.[5]
Crucially, the Subaltern Studies historians sought to emphasize how
the concept of the subaltern signified the social and demographic
difference between the elite and the rest of the population in South
Asia. As Ranajit Guha has argued, what elite historiography ignores
is 'the politics of the people', or 'the domain of Indian politics in
which the principal actors were [. . .] the subaltern masses and
groups constituting the mass of the labouring population and the
intermediate strata in town and country – that is, the people'.[6] This
is not to suggest that the category of the subaltern is synonymous
with the people, however. As Spivak argues in 'Scattered Speculations on the Subaltern and the Popular', 'Subaltern in the early Guha
was the name of a space of difference [. . .]. Although Guha seems
to be saying that the words "people" and "subaltern" are inter-
changeable, I think this is not a substantive point for him' (SSSP,
476). Crucially for Spivak, 'Subalternity is a position without
identity' (SSSP, 476).

'A new constellation of the political': The Subaltern Studies collective

The Subaltern Studies historians have been primarily concerned to
research the social and political practices of those groups who are
unable to represent themselves as a class or social group in elite
historiography. An illuminating example of this approach is provided in an essay by Sumit Sarkar, published in 1984: it discusses
subaltern militancy during the period between the Swadeshi
movement and the non-cooperation movement in colonial Bengal

(1905–22). In Sarkar's argument, the political organization and radical activities of the masses tended to be discontinuous with the nationalist agitation of the elite: 'During the anti-Partition agitation the masses appeared irritatingly inert to the more radical activists, for despite the formulation of a theory of "extended boycott" or "passive resistance" which demanded popular participation and often anticipated the methods of Gandhism, the movement seldom went beyond the confines of the *bhadralok* [elite Hindu] groups'.[7] This is not to suggest that the masses' lack of enthusiasm for anti-Partition agitation was simply a sign of their political apathy during this period. As Sarkar proceeds to argue, the political militancy of the subaltern classes often tended to focus on economic issues such as the price of agricultural rent and taxes, as well as labour disputes over wages. In one public demonstration, the class character of this militancy was evident from the way that a Swadeshi crowd turned on the elite *bhadralok* members during the demonstration: 'In Calcutta during 2–4 October 1907, following a clash between the police and a Swadeshi crowd at Beadon Square, the Bengali bhadralok found themselves being beaten up and their property looted by what a non-official enquiry committee described as "large numbers of low class people, such as mehtars, dhangars, sweepers, etc." '[8] While nationalist politicians represented these examples of subaltern insurgency as expressions of communal violence against Hindus, Sarkar contends that such representations 'ignored pre-existing structures of exploitation'.[9]

Sarkar's analysis, which describes the early phase of the nationalist movement in India, is exemplary of the Subaltern Studies collective's approach in that it emphasizes that subaltern insurgency is contingent, non-systematic and heterogeneous to elite nationalist forms of resistance. Indeed Sarkar adds the important qualification that narrow economic accounts of subaltern insurgency such as Marxism cannot account for 'the multiplicity of types of subaltern activity and their interpenetration'.[10]

By focusing on South Asian history from the standpoint of the subaltern, the Subaltern Studies historians have persistently sought to challenge the elitism of bourgeois nationalist historiography, which has its roots in a British colonial ideology. What is more, many Subaltern Studies historians have rejected the characterization of peasant consciousness as pre-political or semi-feudal in the work of elite historians, and argued instead that the 'nature of collective action against exploitation in colonial India was such that it effectively led to a new constellation of the *political*'.[11]

Just as Gramsci argued that the subaltern historian should attend to '[e]very trace of independent initiative on the part of subaltern groups',[12] so Guha emphasized the imperative to focus on the 'vast areas in the life and consciousness of the people'[13] that could not be accounted for by the state. Yet the historical methodology used by the Subaltern Studies collective to recuperate the consciousness and agency of the elite differed significantly from that of Gramsci. As Chakrabarty observes in a collection subtitled *Essays in the Wake of Subaltern Studies* (2002), Guha's methodology for attending to the histories of subaltern resistance and insurgency in colonial India was from the standpoint of the subaltern rather than that of the elite. It drew partly on a structuralist model of reading the colonial archives, which was incompatible with the positivist approach to history predominant in the work of Marxist English historians such as Thompson and Hobsbawn, whom Guha also cites as important influences on his historical methodology. By adopting this model of reading '*Subaltern Studies* historiography [was left] open to the influences of literary and narrative theory'.[14]

Since Guha's book *Elementary Aspects of Peasant Insurgency in Colonial India* (1999) contains only a few scattered references to the work of Ferdinand de Saussure, Claude Lévi-Strauss and Roland Barthes, it may seem inaccurate to describe his approach to subaltern insurgency as structuralist. Yet it was Guha's attempt to identify the 'general form' of peasant insurgency rather than 'a series of specific encounters' that distinguished his approach as structuralist.[15] As Sarkar observes in *Writing Social History* (2000), Guha 'used some of the language and methods of Lévi-Straussian structuralism to unravel what *Elementary Aspects* claimed was an underlying structure of peasant insurgent consciousness, extending across more than a century of colonial rule and over considerable variations of physical and social space'.[16] Certainly, Guha's positivist approach to recovering the social and political consciousness of the subaltern was somewhat incommensurate with his structuralist approach to peasant insurgency. And, as I now go on to suggest, it was partly this incommensurability in the work of Guha and others that prompted Spivak's critical engagement with the Subaltern Studies collective.

'Deconstructing historiography'

In an interview originally published in the journal *Polygraph* in 1989 (reprinted in *The Postcolonial Critic*), Spivak explains that she likes the term 'subaltern' because it is more flexible than 'proletarian', which conventionally denotes the masculine working-class subject of nineteenth-century Europe (*PCC*, 141). Like Guha, Sarkar, Chakrabarty and Arnold, Spivak traces how 'subaltern' has become transformed by the Subaltern Studies collective into a category that is clearly distinct from 'proletariat'. Yet Spivak's approach is not entirely in agreement with the work of the Subaltern Studies historians. Indeed, Spivak's essay 'Subaltern Studies: Deconstructing Historiography' offers a productive critique of the theoretical methodology and gender politics of the early Subaltern Studies historical research between 1982 and 1986.

Spivak's critique of the Subaltern Studies historians in 'Deconstructing Historiography' focuses on a discrepancy that she identifies between practice and methodology. More specifically, Spivak notes a tension between the claims of some of the early Subaltern Studies historians to offer a structuralist account of insurgency, which examines how subaltern insurgency was coded in the dominant colonial archives, and a positivist desire to recover the will and consciousness of the subaltern insurgent. Furthermore, Spivak examines what is at stake in Guha's criticism of Marx's mode of production narrative and his preference for a model of colonial power and domination, which Guha attributes to the work of Foucault.

Spivak praises the work of Ranajit Guha, Dipesh Chakrabarty, Partha Chatterjee and others for challenging the elitism of bourgeois nationalist historiography on the grounds that it ignores the political agency of subaltern groups. What is more, she identifies how historians such as Guha question whether the Marxist theory of historical change can account for subaltern insurgency. Spivak claims that 'the insertion of India into colonialism is generally defined as a change from semi-feudalism to capitalist subjection' (*IOW*, 197), a change that she attributes to Marx's materialist view of history as a series of modes of production from feudalism to capitalism. Yet, she argues that the Subaltern Studies historians revise this definition in two crucial ways. Firstly, they reframe social and political change 'in relation to histories of domination and exploitation rather than within the great modes-of-production narrative'; and secondly, they argue that 'such changes are signalled or marked by a functional change in a sign system' (*IOW*, 197). This rejection of a generalized Marxist 'mode-of-production narrative' in favour of a model of power and domination that is akin to the work of Foucault, alongside an approach to historical change that focuses on 'a functional change in sign system', might suggest that the Subaltern Studies historians view instances of subaltern insurgency in a broadly structuralist way. Yet, as Spivak proceeds to point out, their claims to recover the consciousness of the subaltern often fall back on a positivist approach to the subjectivity and consciousness of the subaltern. Such an approach is closer to the traditional Marxist one, which assumes that positive, objective evidence of subaltern insurgents can be recovered from studying colonial archives.

The attempt by the Subaltern Studies historians to recover the political consciousness and will of the subaltern as a positive object of knowledge is borne out by empirical evidence such as the analysis of rumours in the work of Shahid Amin and Ranajit Guha, or David Hardiman's collection of village-level data about peasant nationalism in Gujarat. In Spivak's argument, such a methodological approach is problematic insofar as it risks objectifying the subaltern and thereby perpetuating the very subordination that the historians criticized in both colonial discourse and bourgeois nationalist historiography. For in 'refusing to acknowledge the implications of their own line of work' Spivak contends that the historians would ' "insidiously objectify" the subaltern, control him through knowledge even as they restore versions of causality and self-determination to him, [and] become complicit, in their desire for totality (and therefore totalization), with a "law [that] assign[s] a[n] undifferentiated [proper] name" to "the subaltern as such" ' (*IOW*, 201).

Rather than simply repeating the errors that the Subaltern Studies historians identify in bourgeois nationalist historiography, however, Spivak argues that it is more productive to read their use of a positivist methodology supported by empirical evidence as strategic. This reading emphasizes how the historians acknowledge the impossibility of recovering the political consciousness of the subaltern from the archives of colonial discourse at the forefront of their research, instead of simply claiming to recover the consciousness of the subaltern as a positive object of knowledge.

As mentioned above, Ranajit Guha's emphasis on the negativity of the subaltern's consciousness gestures towards the limitations of a model of historical change, which privileges the subaltern subject as an agent rather than an effect of a dominant historical discourse. While the early work of Guha and others emphasizes that it is still possible to recover the political will and presence of a rebel consciousness from the colonial archives, Spivak argues that concepts such as 'will' and 'presence' are a 'theoretical fiction' and that 'the actual practice' of the historians is closer to deconstruction' (*IOW*, 198). As Spivak admits, this reading clearly goes 'against the grain' of the early Subaltern Studies historians' methodology. Indeed the crucial difference between Spivak's understanding of their 'actual practice' and their theoretical methodology is that she reads the political will and consciousness of the subaltern insurgent as 'an effect of the subaltern subject-effect' (*IOW*, 204), which is produced by the discourse of colonialism.

Instead of simply trying to recover the political consciousness of the subaltern and thereby remaining complicit with the power structures that they seek to criticize, Spivak argues that the historians 'undo a massive historiographic metalepsis and "situate" the effect of the subject as subaltern' (*IOW*, 205). 'Historiographic metalepsis' here means the substitution of an effect for a cause in the writing of a historical event, as happened in the reports, letters, minutes, despatches, laws and other documents representing subaltern insurgency from the perspective of dominant institutions such as the police, military and state bureaucracy, which the subaltern historians used as primary sources. In the process the subaltern insurgent is constructed as a sovereign subject, who is retrospectively framed as the single cause of a political uprising, strike or demonstration.

Spivak thus aligns the methodology of the Subaltern Studies historians with the deconstructive critique of originary truth and presence. Such an equation of the subaltern with Derrida's deconstructive thought might seem to be opposed to the historians' political aims to re-write history from the viewpoint of the subaltern rather than that of the political elite. That is to say, by rejecting the idea that the subaltern's will, voice and consciousness can ever be fully recovered as a positive presence, Spivak could be seen to undermine the very foundation upon which the Subaltern Studies project is based.

Yet as Spivak has argued in 'Scattered Speculations on the Subaltern and the Popular' the desire among some Subaltern Studies scholars to represent the subaltern as a coherent political agent is 'only constative' and does not address 'the political strategy that appropriates the disenfranchised' (*SSSP*, 477). Against the positivist desire to recover the fixed presence of the subaltern's consciousness from the official records of subaltern insurgency, Spivak argues that ' "the subaltern" cannot appear without the thought of the "élite" ' (*IOW*, 203). As a consequence 'subaltern consciousness [. . .] is never fully recoverable [. . .] it is effaced even as it is disclosed [. . .] it is irreducibly discursive' (*IOW*, 203).

It is partly for this reason that Spivak compares the Subaltern Studies historians' methodology to Derrida's deconstruction of metaphysics in *Of Grammatology* and *Margins of Philosophy*. Just as Derrida argues that philosophical truth is an effect of writing and representation, so the historians argue that the subaltern subject is an effect of hegemonic history. Yet by positing this analogy with deconstruction, Spivak could be seen to deny the subaltern any ontological existence outside the dominant discourses that represent her.

What is crucial for Spivak, however, is that the subaltern is radically heterogeneous to dominant systems of western knowledge and meaning, including ontology. This position does not only refuse the authority of hegemonic historical writing, but also disrupts the philosophical logic that underwrites it. In philosophical logic, the conventional definition of the subaltern refers to a particular example that supports a universal proposition.

Against that definition, Spivak contends that the subaltern refuses any relationship of exemplarity. Rather than a specific empirical social subject or group, the subaltern is perhaps better understood as a singular category, which is unverifiable (SSSP, 475). For Spivak, the term singular is taken from Gilles Deleuze's *The Logic of Sense* (1969), in which Deleuze argues that the singularity is 'essentially pre-individual, non-personal and a-conceptual'.[17] For Deleuze, the singular is 'quite indifferent to the individual and the collective, the personal and the impersonal, the particular and the general – and to their oppositions'.[18] Following Deleuze, Spivak argues that the singular is 'not the particular because it is an unrepeatable difference that is, on the other hand, repeated – not as an example of a universal but as an instance of a collection of repetitions' (SSSP, 475). Indeed, it is this sense of singularity – 'as an instance of a collection of repetitions' – that corresponds to Spivak's account of subalternity: 'If the thinking of subalternity is taken in the general sense, its lack of access to mobility may be a version of singularity' (SSSP, 475). Furthermore, it is this 'lack of access to mobility' that defines subalternity in general for Spivak and prevents it from being 'generalised according to hegemonic logic' (SSSP, 475). In this respect, the subaltern's 'lack of access to mobility' and 'hegemonic logic' suggests a formal correspondence between subalternity and singularity. Yet Spivak also qualifies this apparent correspondence by suggesting that the contamination of the general sense of subalternity by the narrow sense contravenes the 'philosophical purity of Deleuze's thought' (SSSP, 476).

Significantly, Spivak's account of the term 'subaltern' also corresponds with Derrida's use of it to describe the deconstructive concept of the supplement: 'compensatory and vicarious, the supplement is an adjunct, a subaltern instance which takes-(the)-place'.[19] For Derrida the supplement is a pre-ontological entity or infrastructure, which cannot be grasped as a positive thing in the terms of philosophical discourse. As a 'subaltern instance', the supplement stands as a limit, or a condition of possibility, which defines the coherence of western philosophical truth, but cannot be grasped as a concept in itself.

By drawing this analogy between the supplement and the subaltern, I do not mean to suggest that Spivak simply conflates the philosophical and political connotations of subalternity. Rather, Spivak suggests that the logic of exclusion that both defines and threatens the coherence of western philosophical discourse is equivalent to the political logic of exclusion that defines the hegemonic discourse of elite bourgeois nationalist historiography. Put in a different way, the singularity of the subaltern does not exemplify the universal rule of hegemony, but rather threatens its coherence by remaining heterogeneous to hegemonic structures of representation.

For some critics, for example Benita Parry, Arif Dirlik and Peter Hallward, Spivak's theoretical account of the subaltern's heterogeneous position fails to offer an effective model for the social and political empowerment of subaltern groups. Parry, using the phrase 'The subaltern cannot speak', has stated that Spivak effectively writes out 'the evidence of native agency recorded in India's 200 year struggle against British conquest and the Raj';[20] and Hallward has argued that in Spivak's account of ethical singularity 'organised political mobilisation would seem to be doomed from without'.[21] In response to such charges, Spivak has emphasized that deconstruction is a sophisticated interpretative approach to philosophical and literary texts, and as such it cannot ground a political programme. Moreover, a deconstructive approach to subaltern insurgency is not meant to preclude the possibility of insurgency or organized political resistance to an oppressive regime; rather, deconstruction offers a way of theorizing the conditions of possibility for subaltern insurgency. In a subsection of her article 'Deconstructing Historiography', for instance, Spivak identifies a parallel between Guha's account of the important political role played by rumour in the communication and organization of peasant insurgency in colonial

India and Derrida's deconstruction of the speech/writing dichotomy in *Of Grammatology* and 'Signature Event Context' (1977). In Spivak's reading of Guha, rumour lacks a clear, identifiable origin or source; it does not belong to 'any *one* voice-consciousness' (*IOW*, 213). In this respect, the structure of rumour in the mobilization of peasant insurgency movements in colonial India resembles Derrida's argument that writing is a structureless structure that contains no determinate origin or end. For the speaker of rumour is always part of a broad network of utterances that cannot be traced back to an original source. Such an account of rumour may not fit with the positivist tradition in conventional Marxist historicism, which seeks to recover a single historical actor behind different historical events. Yet, this deconstructive approach also reveals how the history of subaltern insurgency in colonial India cannot be grasped within that same positivist tradition in Marxist historicism, and requires a more situated approach to subaltern insurgency.

Spivak's deconstructive reading of the early Subaltern Studies historians' methodology is more than a difference in theoretical approach. As I go on to argue, Spivak's critical engagement with the work of the Subaltern Studies collective has been increasingly concerned with the marginalization of women and the structural inability of the subaltern to represent herself.

'Can the Subaltern Speak?'

Towards the end of 'Deconstructing Historiography', Spivak notes how the Subaltern Studies group 'is scrupulous in its consideration towards women' (*IOW*, 215). Yet she adds that 'they overlook how important the concept-metaphor woman is to the functioning of their discourse' (*IOW*, 215). To support her argument, Spivak invokes several examples from *Subaltern Studies* I–III (a continuing series begun in 1982, with Ranajit Guha as editor of the first six volumes), including Partha Chatterjee's analysis of communal violence, Gyanendra Pandey's essay on cow protection, David Arnold's account of the rebellious hill men of Gudem, and David Hardiman's reading of the Patidar organization. Spivak contends that all of these writers display 'indifference to the subjectivity, not to mention the indispensable presence, of the woman as crucial instrument' in the histories of peasant insurgency (*IOW*, 216).

This critique is significant because it helps to clarify what underpins Spivak's deconstructive reading of the methodology. As mentioned above, Spivak is broadly in agreement with the group's political aims to recover the histories and historians' practices of subaltern insurgency. However she specifically questions whether the historians' positivist model of subjectivity and consciousness is adequate to account for the histories and practices of subaltern women. This concern is expanded and developed in Spivak's famous essay 'Can the Subaltern Speak?', to which I now turn.

The essay begins with an argument that some French poststructuralist critiques of the western humanist subject and theories of representation are complicit in the global economic interests of the west and the legacy of European colonialism. This appears to complicate Spivak's position in 'Deconstructing Historiography', where she draws on the poststructuralist thought of Foucault and Derrida to criticize the implicit assumption of the Subaltern Studies historians that a coherent subaltern subject with a rational political programme can be recovered from the dominant historical reports of subaltern insurgency in colonial India.

'Can the Subaltern Speak?', however, centres on the role of the radical western intellectual rather than the subaltern historian as a spokesperson or proxy for oppressed or disempowered groups. Invoking a conversation between Deleuze and Foucault about the relationship between theory and political movements, Spivak argues that while these thinkers offer a radical critique of the western humanist subject in theory, their account of political practice effectively re-centres the 'subject of the West, or the West as Subject' (CSS, 271). As Spivak puts it:

> The theory of pluralized "subject-effects" gives an illusion of undermining subjective sovereignty while often providing a cover for this subject of knowledge. Although the history of Europe as Subject is narrativized by the law, political economy, and ideology of the West, this concealed Subject pretends it has "no geo-political determinations." The much-publicized critique of the sovereign subject thus actually inaugurates a Subject. (CSS, 271–2)

In Spivak's reading, Deleuze and Foucault reject the idea of a sovereign subject on the grounds that it cannot account for the heterogeneity of networks of power, desire and interest. What Foucault and Deleuze mean by 'network' in this context is a web of social and political relations that both produce and are produced by human subjects. The network differs from more deterministic paradigms of society and politics because it emphasizes the constitutive role of the subject in the production of power relationships. In this respect, both Foucault and Deleuze depart from the vertical model of power exemplified by the Marxist argument that social relationships are defined and determined by an economic base.

As a model of power relationships, the network may be a more sophisticated and therefore more appropriate concept metaphor to account for different examples of subject constitution in advanced capitalist societies than the spatial metaphor of the base/superstructure in Marxist thought. Yet, as Spivak contends, both Deleuze and Foucault 'ignore the question of ideology and their own implication in intellectual and economic history' (CSS, 272). As a consequence, Spivak argues that both Foucault and Deleuze are incapable of addressing contemporary forms of economic exploitation. In her reading of Deleuze's contribution to the conversation, for instance, Spivak argues that his 'reference to the worker's struggle [. . .] is obviously a genuflection' that ignores the globalization of capital and the international division of labour (CSS, 272). Such a criticism of Deleuze's pious but Eurocentric invocation of the worker's struggle might suggest that Spivak has rejected the broadly poststructuralist position adopted in 'Deconstructing Historiography' in favour of a more materialist position that is concerned with the plight of superexploited workers in the sweatshop floors and free-trade zones of the global South. Indeed, at one point in the essay, Spivak frames the conversation between these thinkers in terms of a 'race for the "last instance" [. . .] between economics and power' (CSS, 274).

The reference to the "last instance" of the economic invokes the work of the French Marxist thinker Louis Althusser as a counterpoint to the privileging of power relationships in the work of Foucault and Deleuze. In his essay 'Ideology and the Ideological State Apparatuses' Althusser carefully scrutinized the topographical metaphor of the base/superstructure in Marxist thought. In Althusser's account that metaphor figures the social as an 'edifice containing a base (infrastructure) on which are erected the two "floors" of the superstructure'.[22] The spatial dimension works to emphasize the dependency of the superstructure (which includes culture, education, politics and religion) on the economic base, or what Althusser calls 'determination in the last instance'.[23]

Spivak is certainly critical of Foucault and Deleuze's blindness to the international division of labour in their claim that the oppressed can know and speak their own conditions. Spivak acknowledges the risk of seeming to adopt an economic reductionist argument by invoking this discussion. Yet Spivak justifies this by saying that

Deleuze and Foucault 'forget at their peril that this entire over-determined enterprise [the international division of labour] was in the interest of a dynamic economic situation requiring that interests, motives (desires) and power (of knowledge) be ruthlessly dislocated' (CSS, 280). In other words, by invoking Althusser's discussion of economic determinism 'in the last instance' Spivak argues that Foucault and Deleuze overlook the global economic division of labour in their account of the political subject as a space of power, desire and interest.

Spivak's critique of Deleuze and Foucault centres on their suggestion that 'theory is a relay of practice' (CSS, 275), and that the oppressed can know and speak for themselves. In doing so, Spivak suggests that these two French intellectuals conflate the desire of the oppressed with the interests of the radical intellectual to construct an undivided political subject: 'the oppressed [who] can know and speak for themselves' (CSS, 279). The crucial problem for Spivak in this account of political action is that it re-introduces 'the individual subject through totalizing concepts of power and desire' (CSS, 279). What is more, the effacement of the intellectuals as absent representatives 'marks the place of "interest"' (CSS, 279). Such a model of political agency is unsatisfactory both because it assumes that the political desire of the oppressed and the political interests of the intellectual are identical, and because it falls back on a fixed and stable notion of the self that is prior to representation.

To counter this problem, Spivak offers a deconstructive reading of the term 'representation' in the original German edition of Marx's *Eighteenth Brumaire of Louis Bonaparte* (1852). Against the 'running together' of the difference between 'representation as "speaking for" as in politics, and "re-presentation," as in art or philosophy' (CSS, 275), which she identifies in the Foucault–Deleuze conversation, Spivak emphasizes the significance of the double meaning of 'representation' in German: *Vertreten*, or political representation, where an elected political representative steps into the shoes of her constituency; and *Darstellen*, or representation in the aesthetic and philosophical sense.

Spivak further elaborates on this distinction by attributing the words to different types of public rhetoric. *Vertreten* carries strong suggestions of substitution, and belongs to a constellation of rhetoric as persuasion; *Darstellen* belongs to a constellation of rhetoric as tropology (CSS, 276). Spivak suggests that the 'post-Marxist description of the scene of power' in the Deleuze-Foucault exchange masks a 'much older debate' about the political role of the intellectual and the artist that extends back to ancient Greek rhetoric (CSS, 276). Citing the figures of the 'poet and the sophist, the actor and the orator', Spivak indirectly evokes Plato's exclusion of poets from the Greek *polis* in *The Republic* to demonstrate how political representation and aesthetic representation are related, but are not the same. Indeed by conflating these two senses of representation (which are clearly differentiated in Marx's *Eighteenth Brumaire*) 'in order to say that beyond both is where oppressed subjects speak, act and know for themselves' (CSS, 276), Spivak argues that in the unguarded context of a conversation about the relationship between intellectuals and political struggle Deleuze and Foucault fall prey to 'an essentialist, utopian politics' (CSS, 276).

Spivak's reading of Marx as a proto-deconstructive theorist of representation against the 'essentialist, utopian politics' of Deleuze and Foucault (*CSS*, 276) reverses the popular understanding of Marx as a somewhat utopian political thinker and political economist, and that of Deleuze and Foucault as anti-essentialist, postmodern thinkers. Yet as I go on to argue, this reading of Marx is better understood as a proto-deconstructive reading, which allows her to articulate the singular position of the gendered subaltern subject on the other side of the international division of labour.

The extract from *The Eighteenth Brumaire* on which Spivak focuses in 'Can the Subaltern Speak?' concerns Marx's description of the small peasant proprietor of mid-nineteenth-century France. In Marx's account, this rural group may form a class insofar as its members 'live under economic conditions of existence' that place them in 'inimical confrontation' with 'other classes'.[24] Yet this descriptive notion of class in terms of 'economic conditions of existence' provides no guarantee that the peasants will achieve class consciousness. As Marx goes on to say, 'In so far as [. . .] the identity of [the] interests [of the small peasant proprietors] fails to produce a feeling of community [. . .] they do not form a class'.[25]

By contrast, Spivak reads Marx as a proto-deconstructive theorist of representation, who is mindful of the ethical dangers of speaking for others. While such a reading serves Spivak's ethical agenda in 'Can the Subaltern Speak?', it is important to note that this reading signals a departure from Marx's original argument. As the Marxist literary critic Neil Larsen has pointed out in *Determinations* (2001), Spivak isolates the passage in *The Eighteenth* where Marx says 'they cannot represent themselves; they must be represented',[26] in order to highlight what she calls the two constellations of representation.

Yet in doing so, Larsen contends that Spivak overlooks Marx's argument that it is 'the still primitive, under-socialized labor of the *Parzellenbauern* that ultimately determines its failure to become a class "for itself" and hence its reduction to a mere object of politics, of the class will of others'.[27]

In *The Eighteenth Brumaire of Louis Bonaparte* Marx is certainly concerned with the revolutionary potential of the proletariat to become a universal class, and to effectively dissolve the division of labour that structured nineteenth-century French society. And Spivak's purpose in 'Can the Subaltern Speak?' is to trace the historical, economic and geopolitical conditions that prevent the agency and voice of the gendered subaltern subject on the other side of the international division of labour from being represented. For this reason Spivak's reading of the double meaning of representation in Marx's account of French agrarian peasants is perhaps best understood as a proto-deconstructive reading. This would be consistent with Gramsci's account of subaltern groups such as the rural peasantry in Southern Italy, whose achievement of class consciousness was limited. Indeed, as Spivak put it, Gramsci's 'work on the "subaltern classes" extends the class-position/class-consciousness argument isolated in *The Eighteenth Brumaire*' (CSS, 283). Furthermore, Spivak's reading of *The Eighteenth Brumaire* does not simply elide the significance of labour in Marx (as Larsen suggests in his reading of 'Can the Subaltern Speak?'), but rather points towards a more nuanced articulation of Marxist and postcolonial theory that is able to account for the singular position of the gendered subaltern subject.

Spivak further clarifies this point in 'Scattered Speculations on the Subaltern and the Popular', in which she argues that Marx's account of the way in which the French agrarian smallholders understand themselves as a class is constative, but not performative (SSSP, 476). In other words, the peasants were able to describe themselves as a class, but this self-description was not recognized as a meaningful speech act: the statement of class consciousness (constative) is not transformed into a speech act (performative), and as a consequence, the agency of the French agrarian peasants is not recognized. It is precisely the failure of Subaltern Studies historians and French intellectuals to attend to this difference between the constative description of the subaltern as a class and the institutionally validated recognition of that constative description as a performative speech act that Spivak criticizes in 'Can the Subaltern Speak?'.

Just as 'Deconstructing Historiography' identifies the limitations of a positivist methodology in the work of the Subaltern Studies historians, so Spivak's critique of Foucault and Deleuze and their transparent model of political action focuses on the ' "pure form of consciousness" ' (CSS, 286) that underpins their argument that the oppressed can speak and know their own conditions. What is more, Spivak repeatedly criticizes Foucault and Deleuze for ignoring the international division of labour in their account of political action. As a result of this omission the oppressed subjects whom they discuss are restricted 'to the exploiters' side of the international division of labor' (CSS, 280).

Such an invocation of the international division of labour could be taken as a sign of Spivak's affiliation with a Marxist model of economic determinism. However, Spivak is careful to emphasize that the economic is placed ' "under erasure" ' in her critique of Foucault and Deleuze (CSS, 280). By framing the category of the economic in the deconstructive terms of placing-under-erasure, Spivak distances herself from the economic determinism of Marxism, even though she stresses that the economic factor is 'irreducible' (CSS, 280).

Yet what is at stake in Spivak's discussion of the economic is more than a difference in theoretical position. Indeed, Spivak's upbraiding of Foucault and Deleuze for ignoring the international division of labour in 'Can the Subaltern Speak?' works to challenge the universal claims that they make on behalf of oppressed social groups, for example prisoners, the mentally ill and homosexuals in western Europe, to represent and know their own conditions. That is to say, by ignoring the global restructuring of the economy in the aftermath of colonialism and the international subcontracting of production to a cheap and non-unionized labour force in the 'postcolonial world', Spivak finds Deleuze and Foucault unable to account for the superexploitation of the subaltern woman in the global South (CSS, 288).

Yet 'Can the Subaltern Speak?' is not merely concerned to expose Eurocentric blind spots in western critical theory. Instead, Spivak cites the conversation between Foucault and Deleuze to exemplify a broader ethical and methodological problem facing contemporary left-wing intellectuals who are concerned to address the oppressed, a problem she also identifies in the work of western feminist intellectuals.

In a discussion of the Subaltern Studies collective, for instance, Spivak criticizes the 'essentialist and taxonomic' (CSS, 284–5) methodology outlined in Ranajit Guha's introduction to *Subaltern Studies I* (1982). As discussed above, Spivak argues that the positivist methodology informing the group's early work is not only inadequate to describe the consciousness of the subaltern, but also 'keeps the male dominant'; as a result, 'the subaltern as female is even more deeply in shadow' (CSS, 287).

Spivak is clearly committed to articulating the agency and experience of disempowered subaltern women. However, she is also wary of repeating the same methodological and ethical pitfalls that she identifies in the work of the Subaltern Studies collective and in the Foucault-Deleuze conversation. Such caution is expressed in Spivak's questioning of a 'global alliance politics among women of dominant social groups interested in "international feminism" in the comprador countries' (CSS, 288). The danger with such a model of international feminism is that it can tend to privilege gendered oppression as a ground of political alliance, and thereby efface the complicity of western feminists in imperialist regimes of knowledge and power.

To counter the problem of speaking for the subaltern woman, and thus constituting her as a passive object of imperialist knowledge and power, Spivak develops an ethical strategy for reading the clandestine presence of the subaltern woman in the archives of imperialism and anti-colonial insurgency. Focusing specifically on the debate around *sati*-suicide (or the self-immolation of widows) that took place between East India Company officials, Brahmin pundits, the masculine Indian bourgeoisie, and British missionaries, Spivak traces the silencing of the subaltern woman.

Characteristically, Spivak draws on an eclectic range of theoretical sources to elaborate this reading strategy. Among them is a formulation by the French Marxist literary critic Pierre Macherey: ' "what is important in a work is what it does not say" ' (CSS, 286). Such an approach serves to elucidate a crucial task facing historians and critics: of how to read and measure the silencing of subaltern women in dominant historical archives. Yet, Spivak's reading strategy is most clearly and fully elaborated in her application of Derrida's concept of the *tout autre* ('absolute other') and his discussion of the hieroglyphist prejudice in *Of Grammatology*, Jean-François Lyotard's concept of the *différend* (1983), Sigmund Freud's essay 'A Child is being Beaten' (1919) and Sarah Kofman's *The Enigma of Woman* (French original 1980).

Spivak's reading of Freud offers an important point of entry into her subsequent reading of *sati* and the subaltern woman freedom fighter, Bhubhaneswari Bhaduri. Citing Kofman's reading of Freud's representation of femininity in *The Enigma of Woman*, Spivak argues that 'the deep ambiguity of Freud's use of women as scapegoat is a reaction-formation to an initial and continuing desire to give the hysteric a voice' (CSS, 296). In so doing, Spivak posits an analogy between Freud's desire as a psychoanalyst to 'give the hysteric a voice' and Spivak's desire to give the subaltern woman a voice in history (*CSS*, 296). Concurrently, Spivak recognizes that her desire to 'give the subaltern a voice in history' is shaped by the same 'masculine-imperialist ideological formation' that shaped Freud's account of hysteria (*CSS*, 296). By declaring her complicity in that formation, Spivak marks the limitations of her analysis. As part of this strategy, Spivak invents a sentence summarizing the repression of Hindu widow sacrifice by British colonialism that is inspired by Freud's 'A Child is being Beaten' to predicate the history of repression described by many of his patients. That sentence is: ' "White men are saving brown women from brown men" ' (CSS, 297).

Before examining the significance of the sentence in detail, however, I now briefly assess the relevance of Freud's work to Spivak's reading strategy. In 'A Child is being Beaten', Freud investigates the history of repression that lies behind patients 'who seek analytic treatment for hysteria or an obsessional neurosis and confess to having indulged in the phantasy: "A child is being beaten" '.[28] While Freud does not explicitly state that he constructed the sentence to describe the phantasy, it is intimated in his indirect reporting of the various phantasies described by the patients. In this respect, Spivak is correct to emphasize that Freud constructed the sentence 'out of the many similar substantive accounts his patients gave him' (CSS, 297). What is crucial, however, is that Freud revealed how 'beating-phantasies have a historical development which is by no means simple, and in the course of which they are changed in most respects more than once – as regards their relation to the author of the phantasy, and as regards their object, their content and their significance'.[29] The short sentence 'a child is being beaten', thus conceals many complex layers of repression, sublimation and desire.

It is Freud's attempt to track the historical development of beating-phantasies and their subsequent repression that prompts Spivak to produce something appropriate to 'explain the ideological dissimulation of imperialist political economy' and to outline the history of repression that lies behind the sentence ' "White men are saving brown women from brown men" ' (CSS, 296–7). Just as Freud's analysis of beating-phantasies reveals a complex history of repression and sublimation embedded in the statement 'a child is being beaten', so Spivak's analysis of 'the ideological dissimulation of imperialist political economy' reveals an analogous history of mistranslation and legislation, which Spivak describes as a history with a double origin (CSS, 297). It is to this 'history with a double origin' that I now turn.

The sentence 'white men are saving brown women from brown men' has its origins in early nineteenth-century British colonial discourse about widow sacrifice in India, as well as the classical and Vedic past of Hindu India. The British abolished *sati* in 1829. In this respect Spivak might at first appear to repeat the civilizing rhetoric of British imperialism, and to rehearse the stereotype of Hindu patriarchal customs and laws as retrograde and barbaric. Yet the British colonial mistranslation and prohibition of *sati* is part of a broader historical narrative of epistemic violence in which the East India Company translated, systematized and classified Indian society and culture in an attempt to rule Bengal according to indigenous laws and customs. What is more, the sentence conceals a history of collaboration between colonial officials and Brahmin pundits (religious experts from an elite Hindu caste) about the scriptural and legal basis of *sati*.

Indeed, after the East India Company acquired the right to collect revenues in 1765, Warren Hastings, then governor-general of Bengal, adopted a policy of non-interference in native customs, and 'argued that the imposition of an alien legal system would be regarded as tyrannical by indigenous peoples'.[30] For this reason, the East India Company formed a judicial system based on Muslim and Hindu law. The formation of such a judicial system in late eighteenth-century Bengal was thus partly motivated by the political expedience of the colonial state.

By privileging ancient Sanskrit scriptures as authoritative legal texts, the East India Company sought to codify and normalize Hindu law in a written form. Yet this British translation and codification of Hindu scriptures into writing did not conform to the performative structure of the source texts. As Spivak points out, at 'the end of the eighteenth century, Hindu law [. . .] operated in terms of four texts that "staged" a four-part episteme defined by the subject's use of memory: *sruti* (the heard), *smriti* (the remembered), *sastra* (the learned-from-another), and *vyavahara* (the performed-in-exchange)' (CSS, 281). In the process of transcription, Spivak argues, the performative structure of this 'four-part episteme' was increasingly subordinated to the rigid structures of western writing.

For Spivak, the British colonial administration thus exemplifies what Derrida describes in *Of Grammatology* as 'the ethnocentrism of the European science of writing in the late seventeenth and early eighteenth centuries' (CSS, 294). More specifically, Derrida identifies three kinds of 'prejudice' operating in European histories of writing – theological, Chinese and hieroglyphist. Whereas European theology and Chinese language could be codified in writing, '"Egyptian"' script is too sublime to be deciphered' (CSS, 293). Rather than being the object of ethnocentric scorn, however, the 'hieroglyphist prejudice' manifested towards Egyptian script 'takes the form of a hyperbolic admiration'.[31]

By drawing a parallel between the 'hieroglyphist prejudice' of western grammatology towards Egyptian writing and the British textual translations of Sanskrit scriptures, Spivak implies that the British codification of (and tacit admiration for) ancient Sanskrit scriptures is bound up with the ethnocentric history of writing that Derrida criticizes. Such a view is further borne out by Sandyha Shetty and Elizabeth Bellamy in their article for *Diacritics* (2000), a detailed reading of the fourth section of 'Can the Subaltern Speak?': 'Along with Greek, Hebrew, Egyptian and Chinese texts – ancient scripts that Western philology ethnocentrically incorporated into its "domestic outline" – Spivak would appear to be adding the badly mistranslated and misinterpreted texts of Sanskrit to Derrida's list of key "prejudices" in the history of writing'.[32] By extending Derrida's critique of the western science of writing to include the 'British law's ethnocentric violence to the archive of Hindu antiquity', Shetty and Bellamy argue that Spivak effectively adds the category of 'imperialist prejudice' to Derrida's list of analytic categories in *Of Grammatology*.[33]

As the feminist historian Lata Mani argues in *Contentious Traditions* (1998), the legislation on *sati* in early nineteenth-century colonial India was framed in terms of its adherence to the scriptures rather than as a moral argument by a 'western, Christian sensibility horrified by a practice so cruel to women'.[34] As a result, the East India Company established a 'distinction between legal and illegal burnings', which accommodated some burnings as 'ritual' and penalized others as 'crime'.[35] This legal distinction complicates the mythology surrounding the prohibition of widow self-immolation as part of the civilizing mission of British colonialism, which is epitomized in Spivak's sentence 'white men are saving brown women from brown men' (CSS, 297).

The fourth section of 'Can the Subaltern Speak?' traces the historical repression and disappearance of the subaltern woman's agency and voice in the dominant representation of widow self-immolation. Like Mani, Spivak notes how 'the British in India collaborated and consulted with learned Brahmans to judge whether *suttee* [a variant transliteration of *sati*] was legal by their homogenized version of Hindu law' (CSS, 301). One consequence of this collaboration was that the British in India appeared to condone the practice. Yet when the law was eventually passed to prohibit the practice of *sati* in response to mounting pressure from the British government, evangelical missionaries and Indian anti-*sati* campaigners such as Rammohun Roy, this 'long period of collaboration was effaced' (CSS, 301). By marking the effacement of this period of collaboration Spivak discloses one of the double origins of the history underpinning her invented sentence.

The other origin is embedded in a palimpsest of ancient Hindu scriptures and subsequent misreadings of these texts. Spivak examines two of the many ancient texts of Hindu antiquity that were often cited by both colonial officials and their Brahmin informants as authoritative scriptural sources to determine the legality of Hindu widow sacrifice: the *Dharmasastra* and *Rg-Veda*. In the discourse on sanctioned suicides in the *Dharmasastra*, 'the self-immolation of widows seems an exception to the rule' (CSS, 299). While the 'general scriptural doctrine' of this text holds that 'suicide is reprehensible', Spivak argues that there are two particular instances in the ancient Hindu scripture where suicide is permitted: 'the discourse on sanctioned suicide and the nature of rites for the dead' (CSS, 299). In the 'discourse on sanctioned suicide', Spivak notes how the taking of one's life is justified through a paradoxical process of enlightenment wherein the knowing subject 'comprehends the insubstantiality or mere phenomenality (which may be the same thing as nonphenomenality) of its identity' (CSS, 299).

Yet this philosophical justification of suicide 'does not accommodate the self-immolating woman' (CSS, 299). As Spivak suggests, the scriptures are less clear about the exceptional circumstances under which women can kill themselves; indeed the sanctioning of widow self-immolation 'belongs in the area of *sruti* (what was heard) rather than *smirti* (what was remembered)' (CSS, 299). By referring back to the different performative genres of the scriptures, Spivak foregrounds the heterogeneity of the scriptures and implicitly questions their legitimacy as a reliable textual source for nineteenth-century Hindu civil law. In this respect, Spivak's reading strategy seems to resemble the approach of Rammohun Roy, who in 1820 wrote a pamphlet against widow burning to expose the ambivalent presentation of widow burning in the scriptures.[36]

Nevertheless, Spivak argues that according to the *Dharmasastra* the exceptional condition under which women's suicide is sanctioned is at the sacred place of her dead husband's funeral pyre (CSS, 300). In this situation, the widow's legal subjectivity is displaced from her self onto the husband's act of truth-knowledge and the sacred place of the funeral pyre. In this sense, the law on sanctioned suicide requires that the widow abdicates legal responsibility for her life and thus denies her agency in the killing of her self.[37] That is to say, the woman stands as a representative figure that 'can only act out the dead husband's "piety of place" within the context of the husband's death'.[38] Before I examining the significance of women's paradoxical freedom in the legal discourse on widow sacrifice, I now assess Spivak's commentary on another important scriptural source: the *Rg-Veda*.

The *Rg-Veda* is a collection of ancient hymns, which is also one of the oldest of the *Vedas*.[39] Spivak contends that a particular verse that outlines the rites for the dead, translated by a legal scholar of the late-fifteenth to early-sixteenth century, includes a crucial passage, which has been mistranslated. Spivak suggests that this translator reads the passage as if it were addressed to a widow: the figure of a living husband has been mistaken for a dead husband. What is more, by misreading the Sanskrit word *agré* (meaning 'first') as *agné*, which means 'O fire', some commentaries have transformed the verse into an injunction for widow self-immolation on their husband's funeral pyre (CSS, 304). In the same passage, Spivak further draws attention to the connotations of the Sanskrit word *yoni*, which signifies house or dwelling place, but can also mean 'genital' (CSS, 42). The double meaning of this word here can serve to reinforce the domestic sphere as a site of social reproduction. However Spivak also suggests that the word's 'syntactic proximity to the word *agré* (often misread as *agné* or "fire")' serves to legitimize the legal sanction of *sati* as widow self-immolation.[40]

What Spivak's readings of the *Dharmasastra* and the *Rg-Veda* reveal is the absence of a stable legal foundation sanctioning widow self-immolation in the scriptures of Hindu antiquity. Instead widow self-immolation is sanctioned either by a series of misreadings of ancient scriptures or as an 'exceptional signifier of [the widow's] desire', which exceeds 'the general rule for a widow's conduct' (CSS, 300). Consequently, the agency and voice of women is subordinated to a hermeneutic debate about the status of *sati* in the scriptures.

Spivak acknowledges that there were cases in Bengal where male relatives of the widows coerced them into performing *sati* in order to gain their inheritance. Certainly, some upper-caste Hindu or *bhadralok* advocates of widow immolation privileged the ritual practice of *sati* over its ambivalent scriptural foundation, and one pro-*sati* advocate even defended 'as customary the tying of widows to the pyre'.[41] These advocates also rejected the scriptural argument that the act of *sati* should be based on the widow's free choice. Yet such arguments did not reflect the general position of the Brahmin pundits; indeed, as Spivak reminds us, it is important to note that 'the self immolation of widows was not *invariable* ritual prescription' (CSS, 301).

Spivak identifies 'two contending versions of freedom' as the source of antagonism between the East India Company and the Indian *bhadralok* who advocated *sati* (CSS, 301). From the standpoint of those who advocated *sati*, the woman's paradoxical freedom to choose to die was codified as a 'dutiful act of religious volition'.[42] From the point of view of East India Company officials before the prohibition of *sati* in 1829, the question of whether an act of widow self-immolation conforms to Hindu scriptures is dependent on whether the widow freely chooses to relinquish her legal subjectivity and life. For this reason, the East India Company appointed magistrates to supervise the immolation and to ensure that the widows chose to die of their own volition. If the magistrate dissuaded the widow from proceeding with the ritual after choosing to perform it, this decision was perceived as 'a mark of real choice, a choice of freedom' (CSS, 301).

It is between these 'two contending versions of freedom' that Spivak defines the place of female subjectivity. Invoking Lyotard, Spivak argues that 'the constitution of the female subject *in life* is the place of the *différend*' (CSS, 301). For Lyotard the *différend* denotes the 'inaccessibility of, or untranslatability from, one mode of discourse in a dispute to another' (CSS, 300). By applying this concept to the incommensurability of the two 'contending versions of freedom' that struggled to define and constitute the subjectivity of the widow in life, Spivak emphasizes that the voice and agency of the subaltern woman is marginalized. In both arguments, the 'testimony of the woman's voice consciousness' is not available: '[a]s one goes down the grotesquely mistranscribed names of these women, in the police reports included in the records of the East India Company, the sacrificed widows, one cannot put together a "voice"' (CSS, 297). This silencing of the subaltern woman's body and voice by the competing discourses of the East India Company and the pro-*sati* campaigners clearly accords with Lyotard's account of the *différend* as that which cannot be communicated through existing idioms.[43]

To counter the founding exclusion of women's voice and agency from the debate about *sati*, Spivak marks 'the place' of the subaltern woman's ' "disappearance" with something other than silence and nonexistence'; that 'something' is 'a violent aporia between subject and object status' (CSS, 306). Spivak's allusion to the deconstructive concept of aporia serves to emphasize that the 'figure' of the subaltern woman continues to act and live on even if she disappears from the dominant archives of patriarchy and imperialism. In this context, the term aporia denotes a logical contradiction, which constitutes the legislative discourse about *sati*, but cannot be comprehended as a positive presence according to the rules of that discourse. Such an argument works to complicate Mani's claim that 'the women who burned were neither the subjects nor even the primary objects of concern in the debate on [the prohibition of *sati*]. They were, rather, the ground for a complex and competing set of struggles over Indian society and definitions of Hindu tradition'.[44] For Spivak, the subaltern woman-as-aporia is not merely the ground (as Mani suggests), but the founding conditions of possibility for the debate on *sati*. From the standpoint of the subaltern woman, this aporetic experience of *sati* may be circumscribed by the competing discourses of imperialism and indigenous patriarchy; it is not, however, entirely determined by these discourses. In the deconstructive terms of Spivak's argument, the concept of aporia thus marks the paradoxical (non)place that the subaltern woman occupies at the non-originary origin of the discourse on *sati*.

By marking the founding aporia that underpins discourses on *sati*, Spivak exposes the interventionist possibilities for re-writing the dominant patriarchal and imperialist scripts of *sati*-suicide from a postcolonial feminist standpoint. Such interventionist possibilities are developed further in the final section of 'Can the Subaltern Speak?', where Spivak turns to the case of Bhubaneswari Bhaduri, a young woman who hanged herself in her father's apartment in North Calcutta in 1926 (CSS, 307). This tragic act was a 'puzzle' for her family because it defied the sanctioned motives for female suicide in Hindu culture such as 'illicit pregnancy'; as she 'was menstruating at the time' this explanation was not viable (CSS, 307).

It was discovered over ten years later that Bhubaneswari was a member of the *samitis*, the organizations involved in the armed struggle for Indian independence.[45] She had 'finally been entrusted with a political assassination' which she was unable to execute (CSS, 307). This failure clearly precluded Bhubaneswari's representation as a heroic, fighting mother figure in Hindu nationalist mythology. Nevertheless, Spivak suggests that Bhubaneswari killed herself as a sign of commitment to the nationalist cause.[46]

In response to the 'inexplicable' circumstances of Bhubaneswari's death, Spivak further conjectures that Bhubaneswari had consciously waited for the onset of menstruation in order to re-write the prescribed codes of *sati*-suicide. Spivak describes Bhubaneswari's embodied act of waiting as a 'displacing gesture' because it reverses the 'interdict against a menstruating widow's right to immolate herself' and the prescription that 'the unclean widow must wait, publicly, until the cleansing bath of the fourth day, when she is no longer menstruating, in order to claim her dubious privilege' (CSS, 308). In other words, by committing suicide during menstruation, Bhubaneswari effectively offered an already articulated response to the interpretation of her death, and thereby discredited the argument that her suicide was a pre-emptive response to the familial shame associated with an illicit pregnancy (CSS, 308). As a consequence, the singular circumstances of Bhubaneswari's death are not intelligible within the social codes of family honour and patriarchal devotion. Instead, her suicide was *both* a sign of her commitment to the nationalist cause *and* a refusal to carry out an act of revolutionary terrorism. Yet it is precisely because this embodied act of re-writing cannot be understood as a speech act within the available public codes of female insurgency that Spivak argues that the gendered subaltern cannot speak: 'the singular woman [. . .] attempted to send the reader a message, as if her body were a "literary" text. The message of the woman who hanged herself was one of unrecognisable resistance' (SSSP, 478).

Despite Bhubaneswari's attempt to re-write the 'social text of sati-suicide in an interventionist way' and to inscribe a message on her body, Spivak concludes that 'the subaltern as female cannot be heard or read' because this message cannot be recognized as a speech act or a sign of Bhuvaneswari's agency (CSS, 308). Spivak's concluding statement that the 'subaltern cannot speak' (CSS, 308) has often been taken to mean that the subaltern is incapable of speaking or acting. Indeed Benita Parry has argued that 'Spivak in her own writings severely restricts [. . .] the space in which the colonised can be written back into history, even when "interventionist possibilities" are exploited through the deconstructive strategies devised by the post-colonial intellectual'.[47] In a similar vein, Bart Moore-Gilbert's *Postcolonial Theory* (1997) argues that dominant historiography has acknowledged the resistance of subaltern women, ranging from 'Nanny, the guerrilla leader of the Maroon uprisings of 1773, through the bazaar prostitutes' role in the 1857 "Mutiny" and the Nigerian market woman protesters of 1929 to the "bandit queen" Phoolan Devi'.[48] Such comments emphasize the importance of examining the histories of anti-colonial insurgency from the standpoint of the subaltern rather than the elite (a view broadly shared by both Spivak and the Subaltern Studies historians). However, these criticisms can also elide the situated theoretical framework that Spivak carefully establishes in 'Can the Subaltern Speak?' and 'Deconstructing Historiography'.

Bart Moore-Gilbert also identifies a contradiction in Spivak's deconstructive critique of the Subaltern Studies collective's positivist methodology and the transparent model of representation that informs the Foucault-Deleuze conversation on the one hand and her speculative reading of Bhubaneswari Bhaduri's embodied act of writing in 'Can the Subaltern Speak?' on the other. According to Moore-Gilbert, Spivak's reading of Bhubaneswari Bhaduri's suicide 'restores to her all the qualities of self-consciousness and free will which she has dismissed in Western humanist (and anti-humanist) models of the oppressed subject'.[49] As a consequence '[Spivak] claims to reveal the "true" motivation behind Bhubaneswari's suicide'. Furthermore, 'this politically comforting reconstruction of motive [. . .] makes Bhaduri "signify" (if not literally speak), in apparently blatant contradiction of the assertion that the subaltern "as female cannot be heard or read"'.[50]

What this reading crucially ignores, however, is Spivak's insistence that Bhaduri's embodied act of re-writing the social text of *sati*-suicide is not recognized or 'heard' as a sovereign speech act within the Indian public sphere at the time of Bhubaneswari's death. In an interview with Donna Landry and Gerald McLean, Spivak subsequently clarifies this position, arguing that ' "the subaltern cannot speak" [. . .] means that even when the subaltern makes an effort to the death to speak, she is not able to be heard, and speaking and hearing complete the speech act' (*SR*, 287).

By distinguishing between Bhuvaneswari's embodied act of writing and the failure to register this embodied articulation as a public act of representation or a sovereign speech act, Spivak offers an important riposte to critics such as Parry and Moore-Gilbert (among others). In making this distinction, Spivak clearly accepts that subaltern women can and do act and speak in ways that frequently resist the patriarchal authority of the state; however, she also emphasizes that the sovereign and embodied acts of subaltern women are often not audible or intelligible in the systematic terms of dominant representation.

What is more, Spivak's reading of Bhubaneswari Bhaduri's cryptic inscription of her commitment to the anti-colonial nationalist cause is not simply a positivist truth claim (as Moore-Gilbert suggests), but an inventive reading strategy informed by deconstruction. As mentioned above, Spivak explicitly refers to Lyotard's concept of the *différend* and Derrida's deconstruction of the ethnocentric history of writing in 'Can the Subaltern Speak?' as key theoretical concepts for elaborating this reading strategy. Just as Lyotard emphasizes the imperative to invent idioms in order to articulate experiences that are not communicable through existing idioms, so Spivak emphasizes the importance of inventing a 'new idiom' for articulating the singular position of the subaltern.[51]

The ethical-political dimension of Derrida's thought provides Spivak with a theoretical frame of reference to formulate this new idiom. As she argues in 'Can the Subaltern Speak?': 'Derrida marks radical critique with the danger of appropriating the other by assimilation' (*IOW*, 308). This ethical caution against speaking for the oppressed has continued to inflect Spivak's textual and political engagement with subalternity, and has allowed her to acknowledge complicity as a postcolonial intellectual with dominant systems of representation and power at the forefront of her critical interventions.

In *A Critique of Postcolonial Reason*, however, Spivak has also acknowledged a debt to the later work of Paul de Man on ethics and allegory. In so doing, Spivak has expanded the emphasis of her ethical engagement from the realm of Derrida's deconstruction of western metaphysics to de Man's deconstructive reading strategies.[52] While there is of course an area of overlap between the work of these two thinkers, there are also significant differences between them. While Derrida's work provides Spivak with an ethical frame of reference for guarding against the dangers of representing the oppressed, it is de Man's work on allegory as 'speaking otherwise' that has provided her with a new idiom for articulating the singularity of the subaltern.

Many critics have suggested that the density of Spivak's prose works to impede the articulation of the subaltern's agency and voice. Yet such criticisms tend to ignore the careful and situated negotiation of theoretical concepts and histories of subaltern insurgency that characterize Spivak's interventions. As argued throughout this chapter, Spivak's deconstruction of the positivist and essentialist paradigms of representation that underwrite the claims of many benevolent left-wing intellectuals to speak for the oppressed is primarily motivated by an ethical and political commitment to the empowerment of the subaltern. Indeed for Spivak, the urgent critical and political task facing postcolonial critics and intellectuals is to invent a new idiom that is appropriate to articulate the singular histories, practices and agencies of the subaltern.

5

Transnational Feminism

Throughout her intellectual career, Gayatri Spivak has been at the forefront of feminist debates about the empowerment and agency of women in her essays and interventions. Alongside feminist theorists such as Chandra Talpade Mohanty, Nawal El Saadawi and Rajeswari Sunder Rajan, Spivak has also been persistently critical of western feminism's historical complicity with imperialism and the tendency of some western feminist thinkers to ignore the specific social, cultural and historical circumstances of non-western women's lives. Such a view is exemplified in Spivak's criticism of bourgeois female individualism in Charlotte Brontë's novel *Jane Eyre* and in her critique of Julia Kristeva's book *About Chinese Women*. As discussed in chapter 1, Spivak's reading of *Jane Eyre* identifies how the social mobility of Brontë's protagonist is made possible by the spoils of colonialism. Similarly, Spivak's reading of Julia Kristeva in 'French Feminism in an International Frame' analyses the imperialist determinants of western feminism. More specifically, Spivak identifies how Kristeva's ahistorical representation of Chinese women falls back on orientalist stereotypes of Chinese culture and history that are clearly at odds with the anti-colonialist agenda of Kristeva's thought.[1] Such a criticism of western feminist thought has contributed to the emergence of a transnational approach in feminist thought, and foregrounded the importance of social, cultural and political differences between women.

This chapter focuses on the development of such an approach in Spivak's engagement with feminist thought. Starting with a discussion of Spivak's concept of strategic essentialism and her critique of feminism's complicity in imperialism, I go on to consider how Spivak's thought has negotiated the tensions between feminism and decolonization, and defined the position of women in the contemporary global economy. What underpins each of these critical engagements is a commitment to achieving a relation of ethical singularity with the gendered subaltern.

Strategic essentialism

Spivak's discussion of strategic essentialism has had a significant impact on feminist debates about the formation of the gendered subject, and with the use of woman as a category to implement social and political change. In plain terms, essentialism refers to those fixed and seemingly natural foundations or essences that define human identity. As Freud argued in his essay 'On the Universal Tendency to Debasement in the Sphere of Love' (1912), 'anatomy is destiny'.[2] What Freud meant is that human behaviour and identity are determined by the anatomical essences with which all humans are born. One of the most obvious examples is that of sexual difference, because it might provide a biological explanation for social and cultural differences between men and women.

Since Freud, feminist theorists have questioned whether anatomical or biological differences determine human identity, and have emphasized that social and cultural influences play an important role in its formation. In what could be read as a riposte to Freud's 'anatomy is destiny', Simone de Beauvoir asserted in *The Second Sex* (1949) that 'one is not born, one becomes a woman'.[3] Such an argument has led feminist theorists to distinguish between the biological category of sex and the social and cultural category of gender. In so doing, feminists have argued that differences between men and women are based on the social and cultural construction of gender by patriarchal institutions such as the family, the school, the church and the media rather than an essential biological category that is prior to social and cultural influence.

By emphasizing that gender is a social and cultural construction rather than a biological essence, some feminist theorists have suggested that gender differences are part of a dominant patriarchal construction of social reality, rather than a natural fact. The problem with this approach is that it assumes that by simply declaring that patriarchal institutions construct gender differences between men and women, both patriarchal institutions and the traditional gender roles that they support will disappear. This view clearly underestimates the power and authority of patriarchal institutions such as the family, the church and the education system to construct and maintain patriarchal gender roles. It is for this reason that feminist theorists such as Judith Butler have emphasized that dominant discourses shape and determine the formation of gendered subjectivity through the repetition of speech acts. Such speech acts include the statements 'it's a girl' or 'it's a boy', which are conventionally uttered by midwives or parents on the birth of children in western culture to categorize human subjects according to gender. In Butler's account, such speech acts do not merely describe the gendered identity of the bodies to which they refer, but also constitute those subjects as gendered.

If Butler's theory of gendered subject constitution in *Gender Trouble* (1990) and *Bodies that Matter* (1993) offers a nuanced account of how gendered subjects are constituted in and through the discourse of social institutions, Spivak's theory of strategic essentialism explores the ways in which that gendered subjectivity can be mobilized as part of a political strategy. Indeed, Spivak's account of strategic essentialism is precisely an attempt to develop a more situated account of the agency of relatively disempowered social groups such as women, the colonized or the proletariat. As Spivak asserts in an interview with Ellen Rooney: 'If one is considering strategy, one has to look at where the group – the person, the persons, or the movement – is situated when one makes claims for or against essentialism. A strategy suits a situation; a strategy is not a theory' (*OTM*, 4).

Spivak's discussion of strategic essentialism was first developed in her critique of the Subaltern Studies collective. In 'Deconstructing Historiography', for instance, Spivak identifies a tension between the proto-deconstructive methodology of the Subaltern Studies historians and the related theoretical language. Against the grain of that methodology, Spivak proposes what she calls the '*strategic* use of positivist essentialism in a scrupulously visible political interest' (*IOW*, 205). Spivak uses the term 'essentialism' to guard against the regulative use of essentialist categories as master concepts in social movements such as Marxism, feminism or nationalism: 'The strategic use of an essence as a mobilizing slogan or masterword like *woman* or *worker* or the name of the nation is, ideally, self-conscious for all mobilized. This is the impossible risk of a lasting strategy' (*OTM*, 3).

For Spivak the concomitant risk is that the essentialist use of masterwords such as woman, worker or nationalist to mobilize the disempowered groups may ossify into a fixed identity, which can ultimately perpetuate the subordination of the groups they claimed to emancipate. This problem is self-evident in the mobilization of women as a group in nationalist movements such as the Algerian decolonization movement during the 1950s, a context that has partly informed Spivak's re-thinking of western feminism. As the feminist theorist Marnia Lazreg has argued in *The Eloquence of Silence* (1994), 'women's entry in the [Algerian] decolonization movement was revolutionary in the sense that it upset patterns of gender relations as we have known them since at least the second half of the nineteenth century'.[4] In this respect, the essentialist strategy of mobilizing women in the Algerian war of independence as bomb carriers, messengers and assassins may seem to have been successful. The mobilization of women in the resistance movement was certainly important in the Algerian national liberation struggle between 1956 and 1962. Yet the passing of the family code in 1984 effectively undermined women's social and legal rights in Algerian society. As Lazreg explains, the code 'institutionalized the unequal status of women in matters of personal autonomy, divorce, polygamy and work outside the home'.[5] While the mobilization of women during the Algerian liberation struggle can be understood as essentialist – because it exploited the western perception of women's physical appearance and social status in Algeria in order to smuggle arms and medicine and to pass behind military checkprints – that strategy offers no guarantee that women will be empowered as a result of their mobilization. As Spivak puts it, 'A strategy suits a situation; a strategy is not a theory' (*OTM*, 4).

Women and decolonization

The mobilization of women in the armed resistance struggle against French colonial rule may have been an effective strategy for the nationalist political agenda. The passing of the family code in Algerian law, however, suggests that women's active participation in the nationalist struggle did not simply lead to women's social empowerment after independence. This is not to say that women were simply passive victims of a patriarchal system in postcolonial Algeria. Indeed, as Marie-Aimée Hélie-Lucas has observed, during 1982 veteran women who fought in the Algerian liberation struggle organized a protest against the proposal to introduce the family code.[6] As I will now argue, the work of Hélie-Lucas has had a significant influence on Spivak's thought in the late 1980s because it enabled her to re-think the possibility of an alliance politics between different feminist constituencies.

In 'Bound and Gagged by the Family Code' (1987), Hélie-Lucas emphasizes the importance of internationalism among women's groups in the struggle to change the family code in Algeria. In contrast to what she described as the blind nationalism of her earlier thinking, Hélie-Lucas affirmed the value of an internationalist feminist politics that acknowledged differences in wealth and class between women. For Spivak, such arguments are significant because they open a space for 'exchange between metropolitan and decolonized feminisms' (*OTM*, 144). This possibility of an 'exchange' also signals a shift in Spivak's position *vis-à-vis* the possibilities of transnational alliances between western feminisms and decolonized feminisms.

In 'French Feminism in an International Frame', Spivak suggests that the complicity of French feminist theorists such as Julia Kristeva in the rhetorical structure of colonialism undermines the possibility of a dialogue between Kristeva and the Chinese women whom she seeks to address in *About Chinese Women*. In contrast 'French Feminism Revisited' seems to signal a shift in Spivak's position because it considers the possibility of a dialogue between the French feminist Hélène Cixous and the Algerian feminist Marie-Aimée Hélie-Lucas. To support her argument, Spivak cites the following passage from Cixous' essay 'The Laugh of the Medusa' (1975), in which Cixous offers an account of women's position as a subject of history:

> As subject for history, woman always occurs simultaneously in several places. Woman un-thinks or squanders the unifying, ordering history that homogenizes and channels forces, herding contradictions into the practice of a single battlefield. In woman, the history of all women blends together with her personal history, national and international history. *As a fighter*, woman enlists in all liberations. She must be far sighted. Not blow for blow. She foresees that her liberation will do more than modify relations of force or toss the ball over to the other camp; she will bring about a mutation in human relations, in thought, in all practices: it is not only the question of a class struggle, which she sweeps along in fact into a much vaster movement. Not that in order to be a woman-in-struggle(s) one must leave the class struggle or deny it; but one must open it up, split it, push it, fill it with the fundamental struggle so as to prevent the class struggle, or any other struggle for the liberation of a class or people,

from operating as an agent of repression, pretext for postponing the inevitable, the staggering alteration in relations of force and in the production of individualities. (Cixous, cited in *OTM*, 158)

What is striking about this passage is not only its polemical tone, but also the injunction to the feminist subject to re-organize the concepts and categories of left-wing political thought in general and the class struggle in particular. Cixous' call to split the class struggle is not simply a call to divide that struggle, but a plea to prevent it from ossifying into a repressive political system, which defers social transformation or 'the staggering alteration in relations of force and in the production of individualities'.

For Spivak, Cixous is not simply offering a feminist political programme with a predetermined goal; rather, what Cixous does in this passage is to offer a 'narrativization or figuration of woman that would be appropriate for this new story' (*OTM*, 158). The reason why this process of 'narrativization and figuration' is significant is because it offers a 'persistent critique of history' (*OTM*, 159). In other words, Cixous' feminist subject alters the structure of history, which universalizes the struggle of a particular masculine subject: 'The general point is that the appropriate subject *for* such a new story is the one that makes visible all the plural arenas that are suppressed when history is written with the representative man as its subject' (*OTM*, 158). By making visible these plural arenas, Spivak argues that Cixous is able to construct a plural subject, or an 'agent of pluralization [and] alteration' (*OTM*, 159). For Spivak this task of conceiving such a plural agent 'may be a requirement in decolonized feminism' (*OTM*, 159).

Spivak's wager is that Cixous' deconstructive re-thinking of woman as a plural subject *for* history might work in the interests of decolonized feminism. This wager is posed in the following question: 'Is Cixous able to become part of the body of the struggle for national liberation, or against imperialism?' (*OTM*, 159). Spivak acknowledges that Cixous' writing about postcolonial nations in her Indian and Indonesian plays 'is shaky' and that 'one does not hear her name in activist circles in Algeria' (*OTM*, 159). Yet in the next section of her essay, she spells out the implications of Cixous' re-thinking of feminist subjectivity for postcolonial feminism via a reading of Hélie-Lucas. One particular aspect of Cixous' argument, which Spivak identifies as important for Hélie-Lucas as well as Cixous, is the production of individualities. What Cixous means by individualities is the singularity of a non-subjected body. This concept is clearly distinct from the abstract liberal humanist concept of the individual, which is tethered to the axis of the nation-state. Yet the production of individualities is necessarily shaped by the social, political and cultural context in which it is situated.

There may seem to be certain structural similarities between the logic of repression and exclusion that Cixous attributes to the historical narrative of the European class struggle and Hélie-Lucas' analysis of women's position in postcolonial Algerian society. However, Spivak is careful to emphasize that the argument 'from plurality becomes something different in the hands of Marie-Aimée Hélie-Lucas' (*OTM*, 160). The difference to which Spivak refers here is the 'repressive logic' of the Algerian liberation struggle, which used women instrumentally. In the context of postcolonial Algeria, Hélie-Lucas emphasizes that women's rights are always suspended: the defence of women's rights is always regarded as ' "a betrayal – of the people, of the nation, of the revolution, of Islam, of national identity" ' (Hélie-Lucas, cited in *OTM*, 161). Against this postponement of women's rights, Hélie-Lucas calls for an internationalist outlook in feminist politics, which is grounded in a principle of ethics: ' "We should link our struggles from one country to the other for reasons of *ethics*. . . . We have everything to gain in being truly internationalist" ' (Hélie-Lucas, cited in *OTM*, 161).

Feminist internationalism

By 'truly internationalist' Hélie-Lucas means more than a 'Marxist ideal of internationalism-after-national-liberation'; for her, internationalism seeks to question the emancipatory value of nationalism 'when it interferes with the production of female individualities' (Hélie-Lucas, cited in *OTM*, 162). Such a model may share affinities with Cixous' production of subjectivities. Yet, Spivak argues that Hélie-Lucas' 'model of true inter-nationalism' also signals 'the (gendered) internationality of Islam' (*OTM*, 163). In doing so, Spivak suggests that Hélie-Lucas' internationalism involves reclaiming Islam from 'Islamic patriarchy' or 'the (masculinist) demonized image that is projected in the West' (*OTM*, 163). This international Islamic feminist approach resonates with the work of Maghrebi writers such as Assia Djebar and Fatima Mernissi, and with that of the Egyptians Leila Ahmed and Nawal El Saadawi.

Such a situated feminist approach to Islam is clearly very different from the cultural context in which Cixous calls for a new subject to alter the structure of history in 'The Laugh of the Medusa'. Yet, there are certain structural similarities between the work of Cixous and Islamic feminist intellectuals. As Miriam Cooke has argued in *Women Claim Islam* (2001), many Islamic feminist writers including Assia Djebar, Nawal El Saadawi and Leila Ahmed 'describe the Prophet Mohammad as the leader of a feminist revolution that was almost immediately betrayed'; in so doing, '[t]hey tell stories that expose current corruption and create possibilities for imagining alternative futures'.[7] Significantly, Cooke's description of how Islamic feminist writers re-define Islam can be seen to parallel Cixous' vision of history. What is more, Cooke's argument that Islamic feminism is 'a contingent, contextually determined strategic self-positioning'[8] resonates with Cixous' plural vision of a feminist political future which enables the production of individualities.

Spivak does not really expand on Hélie-Lucas' contribution to the formation of an international network of Islamic feminism in 'French Feminism Revisited'. The final section of the essay turns instead to the ethical dimension of French feminist thought. Although Spivak does not explicitly state why she turns to ethics in that essay, one possible explanation can be inferred from her reference to Hélie-Lucas' claim that '[w]e should link our struggles from one country to the other for reasons of *ethics*' (*OTM*, 161). For if ethics – as defined by French poststructuralist thinkers such as Levinas and Derrida – is understood as a respect for the singular alterity of the other, then Spivak's turn to ethics at this point in the essay can be read as an attempt to investigate the relationship between singular feminist individualities in greater depth. Indeed, it is precisely this ethical model of subjectivity that Spivak attributes to Hélie-Lucas' model of international feminism.

To address the ethical dimension of international feminism in greater depth, Spivak turns to the work of Luce Irigaray, in particular *An Ethics of Sexual Difference* (1984). Starting with Irigaray's observation that ' "sexual difference is the limit to ethics" ' (*OTM*, 165), Spivak proceeds to examine how Irigaray 'undoes' the heterosexist, male-identified subject of ethics in the work of Levinas. Irigaray takes issue with Levinas's exclusion of the maternal-feminine body in his account of the formation of ethical subjectivity. In response to this exclusion, Irigaray re-inscribes the space of the maternal body as 'the impossible threshold of ethics' (*OTM*, 168). Irigaray does so because the maternal body provides tactile and biological support for the subject, yet the maternal body ceases to have exactly the same intimate, physical relation with the subject once it is born. To be more precise, Irigaray invokes the fecund caress of an unborn child by the maternal body to exemplify the latter's importance in giving life to the ethical subject. In Irigaray's argument, the sexual embrace of that caress might seem to connote the intimacy of an ethical encounter between the self and the other as outlined by Levinas. Yet the ' "memory of the flesh as the place of approach" ' is forgotten in Levinasian ethics (Irigaray, cited in *OTM*, 168). This forgetting of the maternal body and the fecund caress ' "risks suppressing alterity, both God's and the Other's" ' (Irigaray, cited in *OTM*, 168). By re-asserting the materiality of the maternal body in the formation of the ethical subject, however, Irigaray demystifies the mystical structure of Levinasian ethics, which maintains that the ethical call of the other is prior to that of the self. If Levinas's account of the formation of the ethical subject is mystical this is precisely because it lacks any reference to a specific embodied subject. To counter this problem, Irigaray embodies this ethical formation of the subject by re-inscribing the maternal body.

But how exactly does this intimate and embodied account of an ethics of sexual difference relate to Hélie-Lucas' model of feminist internationalism? Spivak does not answer this question directly in 'French Feminism Revisited'. Instead she re-defines the ethical task posed by Irigaray in noting the immensity of inscribing 'the agency of the fecund caress in "woman" collectively' (*OTM*, 169). This task might not seem to correspond directly with Hélie-Lucas' plea for an international feminism. Yet, as Spivak suggests in her conclusion to 'French Feminism Revisited', it is only by learning 'the impossible intimacy of the ethical' (*OTM*, 171) that the coercive structure of political programmes such as nationalism, feminism or socialism can be altered.

An ethics of the gendered subaltern in the fiction of Mahasweta Devi

Spivak's concern with the ethical dimension of feminist thought is developed further in her critical commentary on the fiction of Mahasweta Devi. In 'More on Power/Knowledge' for instance, Spivak applies Foucault's later work on ethics and the practice of freedom to Devi's writing on the condition of subaltern women in postcolonial India. For Foucault, the ethical practice of liberty or freedom necessary to bring about social transformation is not reducible to political programmes of emancipation: ' "Liberty is the ontological condition for ethics. But ethics is the deliberate form taken by liberty"' (Foucault, cited in *OTM*, 42). Foucault supports this theoretical claim with the example of a decolonizing nation, in which the act of national liberation does not necessarily 'define the practices of liberty' for people dwelling in a postcolonial society (Foucault, cited in *OTM*, 46).

Foucault's example is significant for Spivak because it explicitly connects his work on ethics and practices of freedom to the challenges of decolonization. Such an example allows her to draw parallels between Foucault's argument that ethics (rather than politics) is the deliberate form taken by liberty and Devi's articulation of a gendered subaltern space that was untouched by 'the event of political independence' in India (*OTM*, 48). Just as Foucault argued that the event of national liberation did not define the practices of liberty for the people, so Devi encourages readers of her fiction to question the meaning of national liberation from the ethical standpoint of the gendered subaltern. For Spivak, Devi's subaltern characters are 'singular, paralogical figures of women [. . .] who spell out no model for imitation' (*OTM*, 49). The reason why these 'figures of women' are 'singular' and 'paralogical' is precisely because they have no access to the political category of citizenship: they are 'at odds with the project of access to national constitutional agency for the tribal and the outcaste upon which Mahasweta is herself actively bent' (*OTM*, 51). Spivak's reading of the subaltern space occupied by Devi's women characters might appear to offer a theoretical description that contradicts Devi's activist commitment to the political enfranchisement of subaltern groups in rural Bengal. Yet as Spivak argues, this reading of Devi's subaltern characters is better understood as 'a critical *rapport sans rapport*' (*OTM*, 51).

Spivak does not really define the significance of *rapport sans rapport* in 'More on Power/Knowledge'. However, the meaning of the phrase can be elucidated by a brief consideration of Spivak's discussion of ethical singularity as the experience of the impossible in her preface to Devi's *Imaginary Maps*. For Spivak, the social, linguistic and historical knowledge necessary for ethical dialogue between groups on both sides of the subalternity/hegemony divide makes the possibility of such a dialogue seem rather remote. Spivak is careful to distinguish what she calls the experience of the impossible in the deconstructive sense – of the painstaking labour required to establish an ethical dialogue with the subaltern – and impossibility as it is conventionally understood.

The phrase *rapport sans rapport* was first developed by Maurice Blanchot in *The Space of Literature* (1955) to describe the absence of relation between the living self and the dying self or the other at the moment of death. As Blanchot explains, 'It is the fact of dying that includes a radical reversal, through which the death that was the extreme form of my power not only becomes what loosens my hold upon myself by casting me out of my power to begin and even to finish, but also becomes that which is without any relation to me – that which is stripped of all possibility – the unreality of the indefinite'.[9] Subsequently, following an engagement with the work of Levinas, Blanchot went on to re-think the complex ethical relationship between the subject and the other.[10] In *The Infinite Conversation* (1969), for example, Blanchot argued that the relation without relation describes the irreducible separation of the subject and the other, which paradoxically defines the relation between the self and the other. As Blanchot puts it: '[F]or me the other is at one and the same time the relation of inaccessibility to the other, the other that this inaccessible relation sets up, and, nonetheless, the inaccessible presence of the other – man without horizon – who becomes relation and access in the very inaccessibility of his approach.'[11]

Although Spivak does not actually cite Blanchot, what she means by relation without relation is the impossible experience of an encounter between the self and the inaccessible presence of the other. Such an aporetic model of an ethical dialogue may seem to be opposed to the urgent political demand for the social and economic empowerment of subaltern groups, as discussed in chapter 2. Yet the problem with existing models of social and economic empowerment is that they tend to construct the subaltern as a tragic victim who needs to be saved by a relatively empowered intellectual or activist. Spivak's model of ethical dialogue as an experience of the impossible is thus intended to address the singular position of the gendered subaltern rather than colonizing the experience of the gendered subaltern as an object of knowledge.

The importance of Spivak's ethical criticism of western feminism is more clearly exemplified in her recent discussions of women and globalization. In 'Claiming Transformation', Spivak contends that women are the target of contemporary international civil society, by which she means the 'United Nations and the powerfully collaborative Non-Governmental Organizations (NGOs)' (CT, 123). While international civil society might appear to work in the interests of subaltern constituencies in the global South, many of the organizations that constitute international civil society are ultimately limited by the fact that they offer no 'realistic plans for infrastructural change' (CT, 123). As a consequence, the development policies of international civil society seem to aid and abet the economic dependency of many countries in the global South on organizations such as the World Bank and the International Monetary Fund, which serve the financial interests of donor countries in the North.

Significantly, it is women in particular who are targeted in many of the recent development policies of the United Nations and Non-Governmental Organizations. One of the more controversial programmes to target rural women in the global South is microcredit: a programme in which 'the grass-roots rural woman [. . .] receives weekly credit from a local or global NGO, to be repaid weekly, at a rate lower than the money lender's, but higher than the rate of commercial credit' (CT, 124). Microlending programmes such as the Grameen Bank could be seen to empower rural 'subaltern' women in Bangladesh and India because they encourage the establishment of micro-enterprises that are organized and managed by rural women. However, these microcredit programmes tend to focus on microlending as an inherent form of empowerment for rural women rather than perpetuating a relation of debt. What the example of microcredit programmes illustrates is the way in which the feminist rhetoric of women's empowerment has been appropriated by the development policies of international civil society. For Spivak, such policies are worrying because they do nothing to promote the economic sovereignty or social welfare of postcolonial nation-states through investment in infrastructure.

A related and perhaps even more alarming example of the way in which the rhetoric of western feminism has been appropriated by international development policies is the insidious representation of population control and pharmaceutical dumping as a reproductive right for poor women in the global South. Spivak has persistently tried to question the assumption that is prevalent among many western feminists, and especially western feminists involved in implementing international development policies, that reproductive rights are a universal good. Spivak's writing on this subject is partly influenced by the writing of Farida Ahkter, whose speeches and essays on the politics of fertility and population control in Bangladesh have sought to address the damage that western-sponsored aid packages and population control policies from the mid-1960s to the present have done to women in Bangladesh.

As described in Ahkter's *Depopulating Bangladesh* (1992), population control programmes were initially developed in the United
States with the establishment of organizations such as the International Planned Parenthood Federation and the Population Council,
which was funded by the Rockefeller Foundation and the United
States National Academy of Sciences. The primary task of these
organizations was to establish links with political elites in the global
South in order to prepare the ground for the US-sponsored control
of population growth by Third-world governments.[12] In the late
1960s, for instance, when Bangladesh was still East Pakistan, a
Family Planning Board was established with the health minister as
its chairman. This board sent trained female family planning
workers into the rural villages with the intention of educating
women about the use of intra-uterine devices for birth control.
However, this policy was not deemed to be effective in controlling
the population, so financial incentives were used to coerce the
rural poor into accepting contraceptives.[13] After the formation of
Bangladesh in 1971, there was a marked increase in USAID funding
of population control programmes. Akhter cites two reasons for
this: one was that the US wanted to control nationalist movements
and Third-world opposition to the foreign control of resources in
general, and it saw an opportunity to do so by funding population
control activities; the other was that the US government wanted to
help pharmaceutical manufacturers to find new markets for birth
control pills.[14]

Pharmaceutical dumping, or the export of drugs that are known
to be harmful for human consumption, was also practised as part
of the population control programme in Bangladesh. As Akhter
explains, US Federal Drugs Administration stopped clinical trials
on the intravenous contraceptive drug Depo-provera after it was
discovered to be carcinogenic; the drug was nevertheless exported
to Bangladesh and other Third-world countries.[15]

For Akhter, pharmaceutical dumping is only a part of the First
world's programme to control the population of Bangladesh and
to protect its financial interests through development policies.
By flooding Bangladesh with contraceptives, sponsoring the
Bangladeshi government to promote family planning and then
shifting the responsibility for achieving the fertility targets of global
financial institutions to Non-Governmental Organizations, Akhter
argues that First-world development organizations and their donors
have systematically attempted to coerce Bangladeshi women into
accepting birth control. For this reason, Akhter suggests that the

articulation of population control as a reproductive right effaces the global economic and political relationship between the First and Third worlds.

The rhetoric of reproductive rights has its origins in eighteenth-century European bourgeois civil society, in which the topic of the citizen's right to work and vote was hotly debated. When this discourse of rights is applied by development policy makers to women in a militarized, non-democratic and neocolonial society such as Bangladesh, it is generally presupposed that Bangladeshi women are also bourgeois citizens with equal social and economic rights to men, which is clearly not the case. Furthermore, by defining women's rights in the narrow terms of women's reproductive bodily function, Akhter argues that the discourse of reproductive rights reduces women to the status of private property in a patriarchal society rather than empowered subjects with rights.[16]

In common with Akhter, Spivak has also criticized the way in which the discourse of reproductive rights has served the agenda of population control rather than empowering the women that development agencies claim to represent. In a speech delivered at the International Conference on Population and Development, held in Cairo in September 1994, Spivak argued against the reduction of reproductive rights to abortion on the grounds that 'this provides the North with a huge alibi' (PH). For Spivak, the reason why abortion is an alibi is because it fails to address the 'extreme poverty' and 'absence of resources' that 'leads to excessive childbearing as social security' (PH). In other words, by targeting women in the global South as the bearers of responsibility for population growth and poverty, development agencies have tended to ignore the broader macro-economic determinants of underdevelopment in the global South. Indeed, one major contributing factor to the lack of social welfare provision and economic prosperity in many countries of the global South is the World Bank's structural adjustment policies; these require debtor countries, as a precondition of development loans, to invest in export-based manufacturing and to buy imported foreign goods, as well as to control population growth. Rather than addressing the macro-economic determinants of poverty and the absence of social welfare in Bangladesh and elsewhere, Spivak argues that the discourse of reproductive rights, when applied to poor women without any attention to their social and economic circumstances, perpetuates the oppression of the very women that development agencies claim to empower.

For some feminist development scholars, the critique of reproductive rights in development discourse has dangerous practical
consequences for women in the global South. In Santi Rozario's
view, the hard-line opposition of Farida Akhter and FINRRAGE
(the Feminist International Network of Resistance to Reproductive
and Genetic Engineering, with which Akhter is associated) to reproductive rights runs the risk of denying women in the global South
access to contraception. What is more, Rozario contends that such
a hard-line position effectively denies women in the global South
the right to choose whether to use contraception: '[i]n effect
[FINRRAGE] are saying that these poor rural women do not know
what is good for themselves, and [FINRRAGE] are deciding for
them'.[17] In a similar vein, Rayah Feldman has argued that Gayatri
Spivak's claim that 'abortion is immaterial' for women 'in a situation
where extreme poverty makes children mean social security' effectively 'repeats the fallacy that she accuses Northern feminists of
committing, of denying the subjectivity of poor Southern women'.[18]
Against such a fallacy, Rozario has recommended a more nuanced
approach to reproductive rights that offers safe and voluntary
family planning services to women in Southern nations without
social or economic coercion. Such a recommendation may be sound
in itself; however, in continuing to stress the importance of reproductive rights, Rozario forecloses discussion of the broader political
point that Spivak and Akhter have made about how development
organizations aid and abet the economic dependency of Southern
countries on the North by focusing on women's reproductive bodies
as a cause of poverty in the global South.

Spivak's more recent essays and interviews on reproductive rights
and microlending are part of a broader shift in the focus of contemporary feminist thought. Along with postcolonial feminist theorists such
as Chandra Talpade Mohanty, Aihwa Ong, Maria Patricia Fernandez-
Kelly, Trinh T. Minh-ha, Farida Akhter and Swasti Mitter, Spivak is
concerned with how women are placed at the centre of global capitalist relationships. In 'Women Workers and the Politics of Solidarity'
(2003), for instance, Chandra Talpade Mohanty argues that 'Third
world women workers [. . .] occupy a specific social location in the
international division of labour that illuminates and explains crucial
features of the capitalist processes of exploitation and domination'.[19]
By identifying commonalities between Third-world women workers
across geographical and cultural divides, Mohanty constructs 'a way
of reading and understanding the world' which helps to 'envision and
enact transnational feminist solidarity'.[20]

Such an imperative to 'envision and enact transnational feminist solidarity' certainly underpins Spivak's writing on women and globalization. Yet, as suggested in this chapter, her contribution to contemporary feminist thought is primarily concerned with theorizing the ethical conditions of possibility for transnational feminist solidarity and collective political action. In an interview published in the journal *New Formations* in 2002, Spivak was asked to situate her work in relation to a number of socialist-feminist thinkers who are concerned with 'issues as diverse as population control, socialization of reproductive rights and homeworking'.[21] In her response, Spivak defines herself as 'someone who is interested in the speed of changing minds impossibly rather than forming very important collectivities quickly'.[22] As this suggests, it is Spivak's commitment to achieving what she calls a relation of ethical singularity with the gendered subaltern – however impossible this task might seem – that ultimately defines the political significance of her feminist intellectual work. For without the slow and painstaking work necessary to achieve ethical singularity between feminist intellectuals and the subaltern women they seek to address, the political goal of transnational feminist solidarity will continue to perpetuate the objectification and silencing of the gendered subaltern.

6

From a Postcolonial Critique of Reason to A Critique of Postcolonial Reason

The title of Gayatri Spivak's *A Critique of Postcolonial Reason: Towards a History of the Vanishing Present* (1999) signals a clear departure from the orthodoxies of postcolonial theory, with which Spivak had become associated in the 1980s and early 1990s. By defining post-colonial studies as a form of reason, Spivak suggests that this dis-cipline is a coherent, rational system of thought that is analogous to the western philosophical tradition of rational, systematic critique. Furthermore, by defining her own intellectual project as a 'critique' of postcolonial reason, Spivak is alluding to Kant, specifically to his *Critique of Pure Reason* (German originals 1781, 2/1787), implying a parallel between her study and Kant's idea of critique as the sys-tematic attempt to demonstrate the determinate and necessary limits of reason itself from the critical examination of its universal principles.[1]

Yet, while Spivak's critique of postcolonial reason in the twenti-eth century parallels Kant's critique of scepticism and empiricism in eighteenth-century Germany, this is not to suggest that it is a critique in the strict Kantian sense of the term. For Spivak is pre-cisely concerned to scrutinize Kant's universal principles by ques-tioning the ethnocentric assumptions that underpin Kant's subject of Enlightenment humanism. What is more, *A Critique of Postcolonial Reason* examines the way in which the production of postcolonial knowledge in the academies of Europe and North America has become complicit in the narrative of 'the dynamics of the financial-ization of the globe' (*CPR*, 3). In this respect, Spivak's book expands the arguments expounded by Arif Dirlik and Aijaz Ahmad and in

Michael Hardt's and Antonio Negri's *Empire* (2000) that postcolonial studies, by focusing on the history of national liberation struggles, ignores the contemporary economic dependency of many postcolonial nation-states on financial organizations such as the World Bank and the International Monetary Fund.[2]

Why, though, does Spivak describe postcolonial studies as a form of reason? If there is a rationality or reason underpinning postcolonial studies it cannot be neatly separated from the legacy of western colonial knowledge and power. It is precisely for this reason that Spivak turns to the critical resources of western rationality – which she aptly names the 'axiomatics of imperialism' – to trace the postcolonial theorist's complicity in the economic and social structures of globalization. Spivak repeatedly asserts in her essay collection of 1993, *Outside in the Teaching Machine*, that the political concepts of citizenship, sovereignty and nationhood that define the postcolonial nation-state are products of the eighteenth-century European Enlightenment (*OTM*, 48, 281). *A Critique of Postcolonial Reason* applies a similar strategy to expose how postcolonial discourse is implicated in the critical legacy of European Enlightenment thought, especially the work of Kant, Hegel and Marx. To support this claim, Spivak cites the admonition of the social scientist Carl Pletsch to 'dismantle the Three Worlds paradigm' using the critical tools provided by Kant, Hegel and Marx. Pletsch describes how the Three-worlds paradigm 'came into being and what larger social interests it served'; once one appreciates its strengths and weaknesses one can 'overcome the limitations of such a paradigm by devising another conceptual umbrella for social science that will serve all the useful purposes that the three worlds notion served, without its obvious defects'.[3] In citing Pletsch, Spivak argues that 'these source texts of European ethico-political self-representation [the philosophical work of Kant, Hegel and Marx] are also complicitous with what is today a self-styled postcolonial discourse' (*CPR*, 9).

What is implicit in Spivak's discussion of Pletsch is a suggestion that postcolonial studies is the apotheosis of Pletsch's vision of area studies and development studies because postcolonial studies has sought to 'dismantle the Three Worlds paradigm', and is similarly indebted to Kant, Hegel and Marx. Yet whereas Pletsch invokes their critical tools, Spivak suggests that in the process of dismantling the paradigm, and the limitations that it has imposed on our way of understanding the world, postcolonial studies remains complicit in the western philosophical tradition of critique as developed in the thought of Kant, Hegel and Marx. This relationship of complicity is also a relationship of responsibility to the ideological blind spots and limitations imposed by the explanatory power of post-Kantian thought. As a consequence, Spivak argues that it 'may be interesting to read Kant, Hegel, Marx as remote discursive precursors, rather than as transparent or motivated repositories of "ideas" ' (*CPR*, 3). By treating Kant, Hegel and Marx as 'remote discursive precursors', Spivak encourages readers to 'discover a constructive rather than disabling complicity' between postcolonial studies and post-Kantian philosophy. Spivak goes on to clarify this constructive complicity in her imperative to trace the foreclosure of the native informant in the texts of Kant, Hegel and Marx.

The label 'native informant' is conventionally used in ethnography to describe indigenous people who provide information about non-western societies to western ethnographers. However, as explored below, Spivak also uses the term to denote a marginal figure who is excluded from western philosophical discourse. By arguing that the native informant also plays an important role in the philosophy of Kant, Hegel and Marx, which is nevertheless foreclosed in the rhetoric of these thinkers, Spivak does not simply seek to expose the ideological blind spots of Kant, Hegel and Marx in order to 'reject them as "motivated imperialists" ' (*CPR*, 7). Instead, Spivak acknowledges with Pletsch that 'our sense of critique is too determined by Kant, Hegel and Marx', and thus proposes a deconstructive politics of reading which would 'acknowledge the determination as well as the imperialism and see if the magisterial texts can now be our servants' (*CPR*, 7). In so doing, Spivak recognizes a parallel between the foreclosure of the native informant in the philosophy of Kant, Hegel and Marx on the one hand and the foreclosure of the poorest woman of the South in the rhetoric of development aid on the other.

Spivak's account of the foreclosure of the native informant transforms the postcolonial intellectual's complicity in the financialization of the globe into an intricate reading lesson about how to constructively respond to the singular position of the native informant without blindly falling prey to that foreclosure.[4] The term foreclosure comes from the thought of Lacan via *The Language of Psychoanalysis* (1967), the classic text by Jean Laplanche and J.-B. Pontalis, and denotes a form of psychic defence, which involves the 'rejection of affect' (*CPR*, 4). As Spivak emphasizes, Lacan's use of the term foreclosure in his *Seminar I* expands and develops Freud's discussion of repression in his case study of the wolf-man, 'From the History of an Infantile Neurosis (. . .)'[5] Invoking the Hegelian concept of *Aufhebung*, Lacan emphasizes that repression cannot 'purely and simply disappear, it can only be gone beyond'.[6] In Lacan's reading, foreclosure refers to the 'Something [that] has not yet been got over – which is precisely beyond discourse, and which necessitates a jump in discourse'.[7]

Spivak re-constellates this Lacanian term in order to mark the geopolitical differentiation of the subject of the European Enlightenment. This use of 'foreclosure' has caused confusion for some readers because it raises questions about whether the 'name of Man' (a phrase coined by Spivak to denote the subject of Kantian humanism) is a synonym of the name-of-the-father, and furthermore whether the kinship structures of the native informants she invokes in Kant's *Critique of Judgement* are founded on a patriarchal logic.[8] Such questions as how far the analogy between Kant's 'name of Man' and Lacan's 'name-of-the-father' can be taken, and whether Spivak is using foreclosure in a strictly Lacanian sense to mean the ego's rejection of an incompatible idea together with the affect it produces, are less significant than the way in which Spivak proceeds to marshal the concept of foreclosure to produce a series of readings of Kant, Hegel and Marx.[9]

In a passage that is clearly consistent with Lacan's use of the term in *Seminar I*, Spivak defines foreclosure as that which has been expelled from the Symbolic, yet reappears in the Real (*CPR*, 5). For this reason, it is the Real that 'carries the mark of that expulsion' (*CPR*, 5). Yet the foreclosure that Spivak proceeds to elaborate is not merely psychic (even if it is *analogous to* the psychic process of foreclosure described by Lacan); rather it involves the geopolitical differentiation of the ethical subject of the European Enlightenment tradition. For Spivak 'the "native informant"' is the name for the mark of expulsion from the name of Man' (*CPR*, 6). Yet this name for the mark of expulsion is what crosses out 'the impossibility of an ethical relation' (*CPR*, 6). The native informant would thus seem to operate as a mark of ethical undecidability, which is neither completely excluded from western reason as its grounding condition of possibility, nor is the native informant simply represented as a subject of western rationality.

Before examining the ethico-political implications of the foreclosure of the native informant in more detail, I now assess what is at stake in Spivak's claim that the masculine subject of western reason and the native informant have a different experience of the sublime as defined by Kant.

Kant's *Critique of Judgement* and the axiomatics of imperialism

In *The Critique of Judgement* (1790) Immanuel Kant argued that it was the aesthetic power of judgement that provided a mediating link between the realm of pure reason and practical reason. In so doing, Kant suggested that judgement completed the tripartite system of his critical philosophy: it is the power of judgement that 'provides us with the concept that mediates between the concepts of nature and the concept of freedom'.[10] As some commentators have suggested, however, what Kant revealed in *The Critique of Judgement* was a problem, which he openly admitted in the Preface to the Third Critique: 'given how difficult it is to solve a problem that nature has made so involved, I hope to be excused if my solution contains a certain amount of obscurity, not altogether avoidable, as long as I have established clearly enough that the principle had been stated correctly'.[11]

Judgement is a problem for Kant because it escapes rational explanation in the logical terms of his critical philosophical system. As Howard Caygill contends in his *Art of Judgement* (1989), the power of judgement in itself is 'not open to philosophical understanding'; it 'possesses contradictory properties and is unthinkable'.[12] In a similar vein to Caygill, Spivak also notes the aporetic character of the aesthetic power of judgement, which underpins the system of Kant's critical philosophy, yet cannot be accounted for in the systematic terms of its philosophical logic. In the case of theoretical or pure reason 'art allows the ungrounded play of the concept of nature – by which things can be cognized' (*CPR*, 10). Similarly 'practical reason [. . .] can [. . .] work only by analogy, not through cognition' (*CPR*, 22). In these two examples, it is the non-philosophical realms of art and rhetoric which produce the possibility of cognition.

Significantly, Spivak announces that her reading of Kant's *Critique of Judgement* will be 'mistaken' (*CPR*, 9). In so doing, she acknowledges that her reading of the Third Critique will not adhere to the strictures of philosophical rigour. This admission could be interpreted as a ruse to disavow a deconstructive argument that the structure of Kant's *Critique of Judgement* is founded on an aporia. Yet Spivak's interpretation of Kant goes further than this. Indeed, the wager of Spivak's reading is that 'philosophy has been and continues to be travestied in the service of the narrativization of history'

(*CPR*, 9): here, Kant's critical philosophy provides a rational justification for colonialism as a civilizing mission.

One of the ways in which Kant's Third Critique provides philosophical justification for colonialism is by basing the universal subject of reason on the experience of a white, masculine, bourgeois European subject. Kant uses the experience and knowledge of the human subject in the *Critique of Judgement* as an analogy to explain problems of epistemology. Such an analogy exemplifies what Paul de Man calls Kant's anthropomorphism because Kant treats the discipline of epistemology as if it were a human subject. Rather than ignoring Kant's anthropomorphism in order to trace the metaphors and aporia that underpin Kant's philosophical system, Spivak investigates it in order to account for 'the dissimulated history and geography of the subject in Kant's text' (*CPR*, 16). Spivak is thus able to evaluate who is included and who is excluded from the category of *anthropos* in Kant's philosophical system.

Spivak develops this approach in her reading of Kant's theory of the mathematical sublime, which he defined as 'a feeling of pain arising from the want of accordance between the aesthetical estimation . . . formed by the imagination and the same formed by reason' (Kant, cited in *CPR*, 10). Spivak notes how ' "the feeling of the sublime in nature" is a clandestine metalepsis' (*CPR*, 11). In other words, nature is conventionally believed to be the cause of the human subject's feeling of pain associated with the sublime when this feeling actually 'arises from the imagination's inadequacy, in an aesthetic estimation of magnitude'.[13] Kant acknowledges this metalepsis in section 27 of the *Critique of Judgement*, but refers to it instead as 'a certain subreption', by which respect for the object of nature is substituted for the 'superiority of the rational vocation of our cognitive powers over the greatest power of sensibility'.[14]

It is through the rhetorical operation of this metalepsis or subreption that Kant defines the magnitude of the sublime. The reason why this rhetorical operation is important for Spivak is because it challenges the assumption that Kant's moral subject is universal and *a priori* given. In section 59 of the *Critique of Judgement*, Kant argues that the beautiful is a symbol of the morally good. By highlighting the rhetorical basis of Kant's argument, Spivak questions Kant's claim that aesthetic judgement reveals the supersensible basis of morality: 'Our access to morality is operated by rhetoric and clandestinity' (*CPR*, 12). Whereas for Kant the analogy between aesthetic judgement and morality is merely a procedure of reflection for grasping the supersensible basis of morality, for Spivak it is the analogy between aesthetics and morality in *The Critique of Judgement* that constitutes the basis of moral law.

It is precisely this rhetorical basis of aesthetic judgement that produces the geopolitically divided subject of Kantian humanism. In 'On the Modality of a Judgement about the Sublime in Nature' (*Critique of Judgement*, section 29) Kant says that 'in order for the mind to be attuned to the feeling of the sublime, it must be receptive to ideas'.[15] The capacity for being receptive to ideas and moral feelings may seem to be given by nature, yet, as Spivak notes, this receptivity 'is actualized only by culture' (*CPR*, 12).

It is at this point in Kant's *Critique of Judgement* that the geopolitical differentiation of the Kantian subject is disclosed. Kant suggests that receptivity to ideas and moral feeling are available to all humanity. This claim is undermined, however, by Kant's subsequent assertion that: 'Without *development* of moral ideas, that which we, prepared by culture, call sublime presents itself to man in the raw [*dem rohen Menschen*] merely as terrible' (*CPR*, 13). Spivak picks up on the German adjective *roh* in Kant's original German text, noting that while it is normally translated as 'uneducated', the term 'uneducated' in Kant's work refers specifically to 'the child and the poor'; the 'naturally uneducable' refers to women; and '*der rohen menschen*, man in the raw' connotes 'the savage and the primitive' (*CPR*, 13). That the savage and the primitive experience the sublime 'merely as terrible' reveals how the category of human nature that produces the power of aesthetic judgement is not universal, but culturally specific to Europe. As Spivak puts it, 'It is not possible to *become* cultured in this culture, if you are *naturally* alien to it' (*CPR*, 12).

To further support her argument that Kant's critical philosophy provides a rational justification for colonialism, Spivak turns to the second half of the *Critique of Judgement*, 'The Critique of Teleological Judgement', in which Kant investigates 'the possibility of a purposiveness in nature and of an intelligent author of the world' (*CPR*, 20). In Kant's argument, the final purpose of nature or the existence of God cannot be known or cognized by the human subject *as such*; for the answers to these epistemological questions belong to the transcendent realm of what Kant calls the supersensible. Consequently, 'judgement is forced to assume a supersensible realm underlying all purposive forms in nature, and all purposive activity in the subject'.[16]

In Spivak's deconstructive reading of Kant, however, 'The Critique of Teleological Judgement' does not end with the assumption of a supersensible cause. Citing a passage from section 67 of the

Critique of Judgement, Spivak intimates that Kant's quest for a purposiveness or final cause underlying nature is complicated by the example of the New Hollander (more commonly known as the Australian aboriginal) and the man from Tierra del Fuego. Kant invokes these two figures to support his argument that the ultimate purpose or *telos* of nature is located outside the physical laws of nature. Kant recognizes 'how cattle need grass, and how people need cattle as a means for their existence'.[17] Yet he adds the caveat that 'we cannot arrive at a categorical purpose in this way because we cannot see why people should have to exist (a question it might not be so easy to answer if we have in mind, say, the New Hollanders or the Fuegians)'.[18] Kant's parenthetical invocation of the New Hollander and the man from Tierra del Fuego may indeed support Spivak's observation that these figures are 'a *casual* object of thought' (*CPR*, 26) rather than a paradigmatic example in Kant's argument. Indeed, these figures are invoked to support Kant's broader philosophical view that it makes no sense to think of man as a part of nature if we wish to account for the supersensible origin of nature. For Spivak, however, the relegation of the aboriginal to the category of the natural exemplifies what Kant means by man in the raw in his account of the sublime: 'We find here the axiomatics of imperialism as a natural argument to indicate the limits of the cognition of (cultural) man' (*CPR*, 26).

Kant's theory of aesthetic judgement in the *Critique of Judgement* may seem to provide a set of axioms to justify the civilizing mission of imperialism. However, this interpretation of Kant is a travesty because it wrenches the terms of Kant's theory of aesthetic judgement out of its philosophical frame of reference. What Spivak calls her 'mistaken' reading of Kant does have a precedent, however. As Simon Swift has argued in an article for *Textual Practice* (2005), Kant was involved 'in debates about the growth of philosophical anthropology in the German academy from the 1760s onwards, and in particular during the composition of the *Critique of Judgement* after 1785'.[19] Such an involvement suggests that Kant's critical reason benefited from a dialogue with anthropology rather than simply foreclosing the discourse of anthropology in order to posit a purely philosophical critique of reason (as Spivak suggests). Kant's dialogue with anthropology may indeed reveal a philosopher who is more conscious of cultural difference than Spivak's reading will allow. Yet, as Swift proceeds to explain, Kant's use of these anthropological figures serves the purpose of his own philosophical argument: to demonstrate that 'man himself, if he is regarded as a

part of nature, does not fulfil any extrinsic purpose in the development of culture'.[20] Such a reading may seem to accord with Spivak's
observation that the Australian aborigine and the man from Tierra
del Fuego are 'crucially needed' (CPR, 4) by Kant to demonstrate
how the moral subject of western Enlightenment humanism is
determined by 'his' capacity to make transcendental judgements
about the supersensible cause of nature from the standpoint of
(European) culture. Yet it also shows how these judgements ultimately fail: 'Kant's "native informant" ultimately symbolizes, in
effect, the failure of our species to gain an insight into the cause of
the existence of objects of nature'.[21]

Spivak's reading of Kant's racial politics may seem obvious to
scholars familiar with Kant's theories of cosmopolitanism.[22] Yet the
purpose of Spivak's reading is not simply to expose Kant's racism
and Eurocentrism in his description of the aboriginal as an example
of natural man. If Kant's use of the native informant serves as a
'marker [. . .] for certain founding problems in the attempt to formulate a metaphysics of nature',[23] Spivak's reading of the foreclosure of the native informant in Kant's Third Critique is motivated
by the ethical imperative to transform the postcolonial intellectual's
complicity with the western philosophical tradition into a constructive, but critical relationship.

Since Kant's subject of ethics is also the European subject of
reason 'he' clearly cannot be held up as a model for postcolonial
ethics. Yet, as Spivak reminds us, the ethnocentrism of western
reason continues to inform the benevolent discourses of development and First-world aid. As discussed in chapter 5 the discourse
of reproductive rights is projected as a universal good by some
western feminists without attention to the agenda of population
control; and microlending is articulated as a form of economic
empowerment for Third-world women, when it effectively does
nothing to change the economic dependency of nation-states in the
South on financial organizations such as the World Bank. Spivak
thus defines the critical task facing contemporary postcolonial intellectuals as one of tracing the foreclosure of the native informant
without repeating the conceptual violence committed against her
by western rationality.

It is important to note that the foreclosure of the native informant
that Spivak traces in the work of Kant, Hegel and Marx is not
equivalent to the erasure of the native informant. Rather, the native
informant occupies an (im)possible space of double inscription,
where the native informant is foreclosed, but the marks of that

foreclosure remain legible. It is this legibility that persistently interrupts not only the coherence of western philosophy, but the civilizing mission of imperialism as well as the benevolent rhetoric of contemporary development discourse, reproductive rights, microlending and the US-based anti-sweatshop campaigns.

The task of tracing the legibility of the native informant's foreclosure recalls Spivak's critique, in 'Can the Subaltern Speak?', of left-wing intellectuals and western feminists who attempt to represent the oppressed as positive objects of knowledge without acknowledging their own relatively empowered subject positions. In Spivak's reading of Kant's *Critique of Judgement*, however, the perspective of the native informant is a rhetorical invention rather than a positive object of knowledge. Following Paul de Man's reframing of allegory as permanent parabasis, or the permanent interruption of a main narrative line,[24] Spivak evokes the figure of the native informant through a strategy of reading that attends to the 'source relating "otherwise" [. . .] to the continuous unfolding of the main system of meaning' (*CPR*, 430).[25] While this 'source' cannot be represented or understood in the positive terms of the 'main system of meaning', its non-presence can be evoked through a process of reading the permanent parabasis, or the source, which interrupts the main narrative of meaning.[26]

Freedom and necessity in Jameson and Marx

Spivak's use of de Man's concept of parabasis certainly works to interrupt Kant's reflections on the limitations of human knowledge about the supersensible cause of the natural world with the imagined perspective of the native informant, but it also serves to complicate contemporary discussions of postmodern culture. In chapter 4 of *A Critique of Postcolonial Reason*, Spivak contends that an essay on postmodern culture by the American cultural critic Fredric Jameson, published in *New Left Review* (1984), includes 'the magical invocation of multinational capitalism without attention to its multinational consequences' (*CPR*, 330). Spivak does not explain why this invocation is 'magical'. Yet, she provides a hint by suggesting that Jameson's claim that the decentred network of global capitalism is beyond rational cognition is analogous to Kant's Analytic of the Sublime in the *Critique of Judgement*. As Spivak puts it, 'Jameson's fable [. . .] is not a complete rupture with Kant's Analytic of the Sublime' (*CPR*, 325). This implies that Jameson comprehends the effects of multinational capitalism through an aesthetic framework rather than considering the economic and social impact of global capitalism on the lives of workers in the South. Such a framework might be regarded as 'magical' because it mystifies the social and economic determinants of globalization. To put it in the language of de Manian parabasis, if 'the main system of meaning' (*CPR*, 430) in Jameson's essay is postmodern culture, the 'source relating "otherwise"'' to that system is the proletarian bodies of the global South.

For Spivak, it is not only Jameson's aesthetic and cognitive mapping of multinational capitalism that hampers his attempt to conceptualize the multinational consequences of global capitalism, but also his reading of Marx. At one point in his essay Jameson asserts that 'Marx urges us to think of [the development of capitalism] positively *and* negatively all at once' (Jameson, cited in *CPR*, 326). For Spivak, this reading of Marx arrests the 'dynamics of the dialectic' in Marx's thought (*CPR*, 327), and 'marks the management of a contradiction, the covering-over of a fore-closure' (*CPR*, 330). To counter Jameson's reading, Spivak cites a passage from the third volume of Marx's *Capital*, in which Marx describes the movement 'towards a stage at which compulsion and the monopolization of social development (with its material and intellectual advantages) by one section of society at the expense of another disappears' (Marx, cited in *CPR*, 327). Contra Jameson, Spivak argues that passages such as these illustrate the dynamics of the Marxist dialectic and its imperative to 'sublate the good things *in* capitalism *out* of capitalism' (*CPR*, 327).

This is not to suggest, however, that Spivak is simply defending Marx's dialectics against Jameson's postmodern reading of Marx. Instead Spivak proceeds to find a 'graphematic', or something that makes a mark or inscription, in Marx's argument that the 'true realm of freedom, the development of human powers as an end in itself begins beyond [the realm of necessity]' (Marx, cited in *CPR*, 328). Spivak's reading of Marx may seem tangential not only to the critique of Jameson, but also to her later discussion of the anti-sweatshop campaigns in the United States and the dire consequences of these campaigns for the proletariat in the global South. Yet, as I argue next, Spivak's reading of Marx highlights the limitations of rational political programmes, which fail to examine the 'persistent asymmetry between theory and practice' (*CPR*, 330).

The passage from Marx's *Capital* to which both Spivak and Jameson refer concerns the relationship between necessary labour and freedom. In Marx's argument, necessary labour (or the labour necessary to support a worker's subsistence) is crucial to support the possibility of freedom in a socialist society, and yet that freedom can be achieved only if necessary labour is controlled in a rational way. As Marx puts it, 'The realm of freedom really begins only where labour determined by necessity and external expediency ends; it lies by its very nature beyond the sphere of material production proper'.[27] While Marx recognizes that the 'realm of freedom' is predicated on the realm of necessity (or the realm of labour necessary to support the subsistence of the worker), he also tries to separate these categories by suggesting that the category of freedom starts where the category of necessity ends.

For Spivak, however, freedom and necessity are not separate but rather contaminated by one another at the origin and end of Marx's theoretical formulation. Indeed, this contamination is revealed in Marx's claim that freedom can be achieved only if 'socialized man and his associated producers govern the human metabolism with nature in a rational way, bringing it under their collective control instead of being dominated by it as a blind power'.[28] The metaphor of metabolism is crucial for grasping the mutually dependent categories of nature and the human in Marx's work. As Alfred Schmitt comments in his *Concept of Nature in Marx* (1962), Marx uses the metaphor of metabolism to describe how 'human production itself does not fall outside the sphere of nature'.[29] Spivak expands on Schmitt's reading by arguing that the concept metaphor of human metabolism in Marx's theory of the interaction between nature and the human reveals how 'there is something already dividing the apparently pure formulations of origin and end, the trace of the human in the natural and the trace of nature in the human' (*CPR*, 329).

In Spivak's reading of Marx, this 'larger drama between nature and humanity, with pure nature and pure humanity as limits to rational planning at either side subsumes the narrative of capital itself as one of its moments' (*CPR*, 328). It is against Marx's argument that the true realm of freedom begins beyond the realm of necessary labour and material production that Spivak finds a 'graphematic' in Marx's pure formulations of nature and the human. In the deconstructive terms of Spivak's argument, the graphematic is the mark or inscription of nature in the human and the human in nature.

But how does this deconstructive reading of Marx on nature and the human relate to Spivak's critique of Jameson? Spivak acknowledges that her reading of Marx 'might seem a mere making-esoteric of a political text' (*CPR*, 329). Yet, as Spivak goes on to explain, the place of practice in Marx – by which she means the classic Marxist ideas of 'planned economy or revolution' – ultimately remains bound by the antithesis of nature and the human (*CPR*, 329). In Spivak's reading of Marx 'the subject of this practice, belonging to the bound narratives of modes of production, must be centred in rational management'; and yet this centring of the subject of practice is constantly undermined by the trace of nature in the human and of the human in nature. Such a reading of Marx is intended as a corrective to Jameson's reductive argument that Marx wrestled 'a realm of freedom from the realm of necessity' (*CPR*, 330). Indeed, Spivak contends that the bound logic of Marx's argument will 'not allow' (*CPR*, 330) Marx to separate the realm of freedom from the realm of necessary labour precisely because, as Marx claimed, the realm of freedom can only flourish with the realm of necessary labour as its basis.[30]

By attending to the philosophical nuances of Marx's argument, Spivak certainly complicates Jameson's reading of the same passage. But how does this reading of Marx and Jameson relate to Spivak's broader argument in *A Critique of Postcolonial Reason*, that the perspective of the native informant has been persistently foreclosed? Although Spivak does not address this question directly in that book, her call to examine the 'persistent asymmetry between theory and practice' (*CPR*, 330) as it is figured in Marx's text might also apply to her later discussion of the practice of the US-based anti-sweatshop movement, and its claims to represent the interests of garment manufacturers in the global South by prohibiting child labour in Bangladesh. In Spivak's account, the Harkin Bill passed by the US Senate in 1993 to deter the employment of child labour in garment manufacturing in the global South was primarily a ruse to protect the US labour market: 'The real project is, clearly, that "adult workers in the United States should not have their jobs imperiled by imports produced by child labor in developing countries"' (*CPR*, 417). In response to the 'remote American decision to take their jobs away' (*CPR*, 418) and 'with no infrastructural followup' (*CPR*, 419) to address this, many of these redundant Bangladeshi children were forced into even more precarious and dangerous forms of work.

In theory, the boycotting of child labour may seem like a just and ethical decision; yet in practice, this theory may not actually live up to its ethical promise if there is no attempt to address the macro-economic conditions that make it necessary for children to work in sweatshop conditions, as well as the poverty and absence of infrastructural support for child labourers. To put it in the terms of the Marxist dichotomy of freedom and necessity, in boycotting the products of child labour the US-based anti-sweatshop movement's promises of *freedom* are empty if there is no attempt to address the *necessity* for wage labour or a cognate means of material subsistence in the global South. For just as Marx's realm of freedom – of a planned socialist economy or a revolution – is bound by the realm of necessity (i.e. the realm of necessary labour), so the emancipatory claims of the US-based anti-sweatshop movement are bound by the necessity to make viable economic reforms that would address the macro-economic conditions that force children to work in Bangladesh.

For Spivak, the dichotomy between freedom and necessity that Marx discusses in the third volume of *Capital* is more complex than Jameson suggests. Against Jameson's call to 'think well and ill of capitalism at the same time', Spivak concludes chapter 4 of *A Critique of Postcolonial Reason* with an imperative to the reader. '[A]s the web of text and textile roll out asymptotically', she states, 'Please decide [. . .] if one can stitch together Kant's *Third Critique* and documents like *Chinta* [the Bangladeshi journal]', which addresses debates about child labour in the Bangladeshi garment-manufacturing industry (*CPR*, 421). The embedded subordinate clause in this passage provides an important clue to the rhetorical structure of Spivak's argument in *A Critique of Postcolonial Reason*. By juxtaposing a discussion of the labour politics of textile manufacturing in a Bangladeshi journal with a critique of European philosophy, Spivak asks whether it is possible to logically hold these two discussions together. Furthermore, by using the geometrical figure of the asymptote[31] to describe the relation between labour politics in the global South and the text of European philosophy, Spivak implies that the two discussions are related but separate. The allusion to the asymptote also recalls Spivak's discussion of Paul de Man's rhetorical figure of parabasis, or the 'source relating "otherwise" [. . .] to the continuous unfolding of the main system of meaning' (*CPR*, 430). By bringing these discussions of western theory and global labour politics into close proximity, Spivak ultimately refuses to synthesize them; for to do so would be to 'switch from [a] determinant to [a] reflexive judgement' (*CPR*, 421), and to repeat the foreclosure of the native informant. Furthermore, by encouraging readers to 'decide' whether it is possible to 'stitch' Kant to a Bangladeshi journal, Spivak encourages her readers to question how contemporary theoretical and political discourses persist in the foreclosure of the native informant.

A Critique of Postcolonial Reason and the War on Terror

Spivak's *A Critique of Postcolonial Reason: Towards a History of the Vanishing Present* is primarily a critique of postcolonial studies and its relationship to the systematic inequalities of globalization in the 1990s. As a result of this focus, and because the book was published before the terrorist attacks on America on 11 September 2001, the 'vanishing present' of which *A Critique of Postcolonial Reason* promises to offer a 'history' does not explicitly address the critical relationship between postcolonial studies and the contemporary discourse of global political insecurity, also known as terrorism.

Spivak has addressed the discourse of terrorism in an essay titled 'Terror: A Speech after 9-11' (2004), in which she observes an 'intense resurgence of nationalism' in the United States after those attacks, epitomized by the Patriot Act (T, 84). For Spivak, the Patriot Act exemplifies how nationalism did not disappear with the global financial restructuring of the economy that followed the collapse of the Soviet Union in the 1990s. Rather, as Spivak suggests, the contemporary world economic system was always driven by the economic and geopolitical interests of the United States. Like other intellectual commentators on the terrorist attacks of 11 September 2001 and on the subsequent 'war on terror' – including Noam Chomsky, Slavoj Žižek, Judith Butler, Terry Eagleton and Giorgio Agamben – Spivak addresses the question of whether the terrorist attacks could be understood as a response to globalization and US foreign policy, as well as the ambivalent legal status of the terrorist suspects who were held in a state of indefinite detention in a prison at Guantanamo Bay, Cuba.

Yet Spivak is crucially concerned to articulate an appropriate ethical response to the attacks and to the war on terror. Spivak clarifies what she means by an 'ethical' response by distinguishing it from an 'epistemological construction of the other as an object of knowledge' (T, 83). While '[e]pistemological constructions belong to the domain of the law, which seeks to construct the other as an object of knowledge [. . .] in order to punish or acquit rationally', Spivak argues, the 'ethical interrupts the epistemological in order to listen to the other as if it were a self, neither to punish nor to acquit' (T, 83). Spivak does not actually name the other as a terrorist at this point in her essay; however, this is certainly implicit in what she goes on to say about the ways in which the discourse of terrorism constitutes its object of knowledge. Spivak observes how terrorism is a name for social movements involving physical violence as well as the affect of terror produced by the use of such physical violence (T, 91). In the dominant discourse of terrorism, Spivak contends that these meanings have been conflated so that the word is no more than an antonym for war (T, 92). In this slippage between terror and terrorism, Spivak implies that the other who is constructed as an object of knowledge or a 'terrorist' forecloses an appropriate political and legal response to terrorism. Spivak emphasizes that she is not condoning violence or terrorism: 'I cannot and do not condone violence, practiced by the state or otherwise' (T, 93). Instead, she suggests that an ethical response to terrorism necessitates 'an imaginative exercise in experiencing the impossible [and] stepping into the space of the other' (T, 94).

Spivak attempts to imagine the 'space of the other' by way of an analogy with Kant's theory of the sublime. In her view Kant's theory posits that the human subject's cognitive faculties are unable to understand the magnitude of the sublime object, and the subject is rendered 'stupid' or 'mindless' as a result of this experience (T, 94). In a similar way, Spivak claims that 'single coerced yet willed suicide "terror"' is 'informed by the stupidity of belief taken to extreme' (T, 94). The coercive training of suicide bombers to carry out their deadly missions in the name of a religious belief may seem analogous to the suspension of rational judgement associated with the Kantian sublime. Yet, this analogy cannot account for the way in which that religious belief provides a structure for training human beings to become martyrs. After all, Kant's theory of the sublime was concerned with the faculty of aesthetic judgement, not with suicide bombing.

Spivak does not really develop this analogy in 'Terror: A Speech after 9-11'. Instead, she proceeds to suggest that Kant's reflections on the relationship between reason and the transcendental in his essay 'Religion within the Boundaries of Mere Reason' (1793) complicates the dichotomy between the secular values of the West and the religious values of the Muslim world that is often used as a frame through which to construct terrorism as an object of knowledge.

In 'Religion within the Boundaries of Mere Reason' Kant argued that pure reason is impotent to satisfy its moral needs, and so it supplements this deficiency by borrowing transcendent ideas from theology, which are beyond reason's realm of cognition.[32] Yet this is not to suggest that Kant's theoretical reflections on moral reason have a theological basis. Rather, as Kant explains, reason's use of religion is based on 'a faith which [. . .] we might call *reflective*, since the *dogmatic* faith, which announces itself to be a *knowledge* appears to reason dishonest or impudent'.[33] This reflective faith involves a rhetorical analysis, which Spivak calls a 'de-transcendentalizing' of divine concepts (T, 108). For Spivak, this rhetorical analysis is exemplified in Kant's discussion of effects of grace. In Kant's argument, the '*effects of grace* [. . .] cannot be incorporated into the maxims of reason' precisely because 'our use of the concept of cause and effect cannot be extended beyond the objects of experience'.[34] By defining 'grace' as an effect rather than a divine cause, Spivak argues that Kant reads grace as a rhetorical figure, which is 'something like a metalepsis' or the substitution of an effect for a cause; and, in so doing, Kant comes close to 'de-transcendentalizing Grace' (T, 108).

But what have these reflections on the rhetoric of religion in Kant's essay to do with the suicide bomber? Spivak implies that the sublime stupidity of the suicide bomber is analogous to the dogmatic faith that Kant denigrates when she proceeds to say that 'in the case of suicide bombing we see the recoding of religious narrative as referential in the narrowest sense' (T, 109). Against this dogmatic faith, which treats religious narratives as literal prescriptions of moral action, Spivak suggests that Kant's idea of reflective faith, which she calls 'de-transcendentalizing the radically other' (T, 109), offers a model of humanities teaching: 'a persistent attempt at an uncoercive rearrangement of desires, through teaching reading' (T, 81).

Spivak's discussion of Kant's 'Religion within the Boundaries of Mere Reason' in her 'Terror: A Speech after 9-11' expands and develops her reading of Kant in *A Critique of Postcolonial Reason*. Indeed, Spivak's analysis of the foreclosure of the native informant in Kant's analytic of the sublime is precisely concerned with the way in which the terror of colonial violence, and the foreclosure of that terror, underpins Kant's aesthetic theory. What is more, Spivak's analysis of Bhubaneswari Bhaduri's embodied act of re-writing the ritual of *sati*-suicide in *A Critique of Postcolonial Reason* offers a powerful analysis of women's participation in and resistance to violent nationalist insurgency movements, which are sometimes described as terrorist organizations. I conclude this chapter by examining how

Spivak's revised version of 'Can the Subaltern Speak?' prefigures her recent reflections on terrorism.

'Can the Subaltern Speak?' and the discourse of terrorism

Spivak's account of Bhubaneswari Bhaduri's suicide in the re-worked version of 'Can the Subaltern Speak?', published in chapter 3 of *A Critique of Postcolonial Reason*, exemplifies how some armed anti-colonial nationalist struggles were predicated on the foreclosure of the subaltern woman. In Spivak's account, Bhubaneswari Bhaduri 'hanged herself in her father's modest apartment in North Calcutta in 1926' but attempted to cover up her involvement with an armed resistance movement through an elaborate suicide ritual that *resembled* the ancient practice of Hindu widow sacrifice. 'Nearly a decade later it was discovered that she was a member of one of the many groups involved in the armed struggle for Indian independence' (CSS, 307). Significantly, Spivak has emphasized that the action of Bhubaneswari Bhaduri was inscribed in her body, but 'even that incredible effort to speak did not fulfill itself in a speech act' (*SR*, 289). By retroactively framing Bhubaneswari's suicide as an embodied act, Spivak clarifies her frequently misunderstood argument that the subaltern cannot speak. Moreover, such a statement exemplifies how the sovereign political acts of women are often not intelligible within the patriarchal logic of the state.

Spivak further elaborates on what she means by the foreclosure of the native informant in a related discussion of the clandestine inclusion of women in violent nationalist struggles, which was published in the *Cardozo Law Review* (2001). In this essay, Spivak briefly invokes the figure of the female protagonist in *The Terrorist* (1998), a feature-length film loosely based on the assassination of Rajiv Gandhi by a female suicide bomber in 1991. Since Spivak's reference to the film is supplementary to a detailed reading of Derrida's *Politics of Friendship* (1994), it is worth tracking the connections between the suspenseful moment at the end of *The Terrorist*, where the female protagonist Malli hesitates when she is about to detonate a bomb attached to her body, and the philosophical argument that Spivak addresses in the main body of her essay.

Derrida's *Politics of Friendship* includes a discussion of what is at stake in Carl Schmitt's claim that politics is dependent on the possibility of war; the book makes a decisive distinction between the friend and the enemy and the need to identify the enemy.[35] More importantly, Derrida argues that the figure of woman and the sister are excluded from Schmitt's theories of the political as the absolute enemy or partisan: 'Not even in the theory of the partisan is there the least reference to the role played by women in guerrilla warfare [. . .] and the aftermath of wars of national liberation'.[36] Such a blatant omission of women in Schmitt's theory of the political does not only highlight the active role played by women in violent anti-colonial insurgency (an example of what Schmitt defines as a properly political act), but it also prompts Derrida to raise questions about whether the spectral figure of the absolute enemy in Schmitt's thought, who is 'forced' into a position of 'clandestinity',[37] might actually refer to the position of women in relation to the political. Indeed, Spivak contends that '[o]ne of the greatest merits of *The Politics of Friendship* is its repeated consideration not only of the exclusion of women from the political philosophy of democracy, but also of her appropriation into male lineaments as the price of this inclusion' (SP, 1736).

This clandestine inclusion of woman as a masculine figure in the dominant political philosophy of democracy is developed in a footnote, in which Spivak compares Malli's desistance from the act of suicide bombing in *The Terrorist* to Bhubaneswari Bhaduri's elaborate attempt to disguise her involvement with the violent anti-colonial nationalist independence struggle in India through a suicide ritual that resembled the ancient practice of Hindu widow sacrifice.

What Spivak implies but does not explicitly say is that Malli's last-minute backing away from the suicide-bombing mission in *The Terrorist* can be seen as a resistance to the sacrificial logic that often defines women's participation in violent nationalist conflict according to the masculine rhetoric of heroism. Like Bhubaneswari Bhaduri's 'tragic failure' to re-write the text of *sati*-suicide, however, Malli's refusal to execute the suicide-bombing mission fails to challenge the dominant masculine-centred terms that predetermine her involvement in the struggle. Yet by marking the failure of Bhubaneswari Bhaduri and Malli to transform their embodied acts of resistance into sovereign speech acts, Spivak invents an idiom for re-articulating the agency and lives of such women.

If one of the deconstructive tasks of *A Critique of Postcolonial Reason* is to 'displace the reversal' between colonialism and postcolonial nationalism so that the 'complicity between native hegemony and the axiomatics of imperialism' is revealed (*CPR*, 47), it is figures such as the female freedom fighter as well as the woman of the South that persistently reveal that complicity. Spivak is clearly not defending suicide bombing as a legitimate political strategy any more than she is defending *sati*-suicide in 'Can the Subaltern Speak?'. However, she does raise questions about the way in which the participation of women in nationalist insurgency movements is often foreclosed by these movements. In so doing, Spivak reveals how the singular embodied agency of the female insurgent cannot be accounted for within the systematic terms of rational political programmes such as national liberation. It is this embodied agency of the gendered subaltern that marks the limitations of postcolonial reason.

Conclusion: Transnational Literacy, Subaltern Rights and the Future of Comparative Literature

While the trajectory of Spivak's early critical work was partly concerned with the relationship between literary and cultural studies and European colonialism, her recent work on translation, transnational literacy and subaltern rights signals a shift in emphasis. Spivak's proposal in her lecture series *Death of a Discipline* (2003) – that comparative literary studies should engage with the languages of the global South, which she also names 'subaltern languages' – defines a radical political task for a discipline which is conventionally concerned with reading literary texts written in different languages.

Spivak's defence of comparative literary studies as a training of the imagination in *Death of a Discipline* might at first seem surprising, a move echoing the programme of aesthetic education elaborated by European Enlightenment thinkers such as Friedrich Schiller; Spivak criticizes that programme in *A Critique of Postcolonial Reason*. However, I now argue that what Spivak means by the training of the imagination in *Death of a Discipline* is consistent with the ethical commitment of a singular pedagogical approach underpinning much of Spivak's thought and practice: to learn to learn from the subaltern.

Clearly, Spivak's emphasis on pedagogy does not offer a rational political blueprint to empower or emancipate the subaltern. Yet this emphasis on pedagogy does provide a space for what Spivak calls 'one-on-one epistemic change'.[1] As Spivak explains in an interview with Tani E. Barlow about her pedagogical work in rural schools in India and Bangladesh, this change is 'like training athletes one by one in the hope that when others mobilize them, they will be mobilized more successfully, critically. They will not just be led, or they will not think that they are making choices, when the terms of the choice have been taught them by those who mobilize'.[2] This analogy between 'one-on-one epistemic change' and training athletes certainly helps to elucidate the way in which Spivak's teaching practice in Indian and Bangladeshi schools seeks to educate her students to a point where they are able to identify and question the dominant systems of political representation, which silence and exclude them because of their class position. But to grasp the broader significance of 'one-on-one epistemic change' it is also important to consider how Spivak's discussions of transnational literacy and restricted permeability inform her educational work to combat the class apartheid that is perpetuated by the education system in many rural schools in India and Bangladesh.

Transnational literacy

Spivak first defined what she means by transnational literacy in an essay titled 'Teaching for the Times' (1995), in which she argues that literacy is not simply expertise in another language, but rather 'the skill to differentiate between letters, so that an articulated script can be read, reread, written, rewritten' (TT, 193). More importantly, 'literacy allows us to sense that the other is not just a "voice", but that others produce articulated texts, even as they, like us, are written in and by a text not of our own making' (TT, 193).

To clarify this claim Spivak turns to *Fantasia* (1985), a novel by the Algerian feminist writer Assia Djebar, in which the narrator stages the trauma of being denied access to classical Arabic in French-occupied Algeria. In a passage from a novel called *Embraces*, the French-educated protagonist attempts to translate Eugène Fromentin's story *Un Été au Sahara* (1857) into Arabic for 'Zohra, an eighty-year old rural *mujahida* (female freedom fighter)' (TT, 197). By translating Fromentin's written text into an Arabic story, the narrator also retells the story of two Algerian prostitutes who were murdered by the French army. In doing so, Spivak suggests that Djébar's protagonist privileges the perspective of the two Algerian prostitutes in Fromentin's text, and that in the act of translation the protagonist undoes her amnesia of the Arabic language. Such an example is significant because it stages the delegitimization of a non-European language by a dominant European language. The protagonist thus also works to legitimize the Arabic language, which she has forgotten as a result of French colonial policies. For Spivak, this passage from Djebar's *Fantasia* allows non-Arabic readers to grasp that 'the other is not just a "voice", but that others produce articulated texts' (TT, 193). As I go on to argue, Spivak has proceeded to refine what she means by transnational literacy in her claim that subaltern languages, or the subordinate languages of the global South, have restricted permeability, by which she means that subaltern languages are not widely spoken, read or understood. Before discussing this in more detail, however, I consider Spivak's proposal for the future of comparative literature in *Death of a Discipline*.

Death of a Discipline and the future of comparative literature

Spivak's sensitivity to the traces of Arabic in Djebar's text is significant because it shows how an ethical commitment to the subaltern in Spivak's thought is increasingly linked to questions of translation and transnational literacy. Such a concern is developed further in *Death of a Discipline* (2003), which was originally presented in 2000 as part of the Wellek Library Lectures in Critical Theory at the University of California, Irvine. The title might suggest that this work is a lament or elegy to comparative literature. Yet, as some commentators have pointed out, the word 'death' here refers to what comparative literature 'will do, will be, or rather might do and be, more precisely, might have done or been (in a future anterior sense)'.[3] As Spivak explains, 'For the *discipline* [of comparative literature] the way out seems to be to acknowledge a definitive future anteriority, a "to-come"-ness, a "will have happened" quality' (DD, 6). What the three lectures included in *Death of a Discipline* seek to propose, in other words, is an important yet interminable ethical and political task for the future of comparative literature in an age of post-communist globalization.

Spivak starts by situating her lecture series in relation to the Bernheimer Report on comparative literature of 1995, which focused on the question of whether an emerging interest in multiculturalism and ethnic studies in the US academy might enhance the work of comparison that is central to comparative literary studies.[4] In response to such questions, Spivak reflects on the future of comparative literature in the US academy in the context of funding cuts and the tendency of comparative literature to limit its comparative focus to literatures written in dominant European languages. As a consequence, Spivak is less sanguine about the possibility of a productive dialogue between an Anglophone ethnic studies and comparative literature than some of the contributors to the Bernheimer Report. To counter the financial constraints and Eurocentric limitations in comparative literary studies, Spivak proposes an interdisciplinary link between comparative literature and area studies. Since area studies, as developed in American universities since the Second World War, has traditionally received funding from the US government and the military to investigate non-western societies such as the former Soviet Union, China, South Asia and the Middle East, Spivak suggests that an intellectual encounter with comparative literature may seem to provide a productive opportunity to re-think the intellectual projects and ideological agendas of both disciplines. For if area studies has served the interests of US foreign policy,[5] comparative literary studies can provide that discipline with the critical and linguistic tools necessary to question the 'area' constituted as its object of knowledge and particular expertise. By questioning comparative literature's tendency to focus on literatures written in European languages, area studies can provide comparative literature with a more complex knowledge of the cultures and histories of the global South. As Spivak explains:

> [T]he new step that I am proposing [. . .] would work to make the traditional linguistic sophistication of Comparative Literature supplement Area Studies (and history, anthropology, political theory, and sociology) by approaching the language of the other not only as a "field" language. In the field of [comparative] literature we need to move from Anglophony, Lusophony, Teutophony, Francophony, et cetera. We must take the languages of the Southern Hemisphere as active cultural media rather than as objects of cultural study. (*DD*, 9)

Spivak calls the languages of the Southern Hemisphere subaltern languages presumably because the official languages of national and global political institutions tend to privilege elite national or European languages, and in so doing effectively marginalize the languages of the Southern Hemisphere and restrict the expansion of their literacy.

Spivak's proposal to learn the languages of the global South in order to interrupt and overwrite the global hegemony of European languages may, as Judith Butler has suggested, offer a 'radically ethical framework for the approach to subaltern writing' (*DD*, jacket blurb). Yet for some of Spivak's critics, her faith in the political efficacy of an alliance with area studies (a historically conservative discipline) seems rather idealistic. Haun Saussy, for instance, in an article for *Comparative Literature* (2005), has argued that in the aftermath of the terrorist attacks on the United States of 11 September 2001, the 'call for "patriotism" in scholarship, the demand that national security be the brain directing our organs of research into other countries and cultures, is louder than it has even been in [the United States]'.[6] In this context, he argues that 'Spivak's proposal, advanced in 2000, published in 2003 [. . .] appears extraordinarily utopian'.[7] What this criticism overlooks, however, is the precise deconstructive terms of Spivak's argument and its implications for empowering the subaltern.

Indeed, what is crucial in Spivak's proposal is the idea that 'the traditional linguistic sophistication of Comparative Literature [will] *supplement* Area Studies' (*DD*, 9; italics mine). For Spivak, the word 'supplement', in its strict deconstructive sense, denotes the persistent supplementation of an absent presence at the origin of a metaphysical system of knowledge. Although Spivak does not explicitly say that area studies is a metaphysical system of knowledge in *Death of a Discipline*, one could infer from the deconstructive logic of the statement 'Comparative Literature [will] *supplement* Area Studies' that Area Studies is a metaphysical system of knowledge. And, if the absent presence at the origin of area studies is the subaltern 'languages of the Southern Hemisphere', Spivak's proposal to supplement this absent presence by promoting a close reading of non-European languages is crucial for challenging the monolingualism of area studies and US foreign policy. Furthermore, if we carefully follow the deconstructive logic of Spivak's argument, it becomes clear that Spivak's proposal to supplement area studies with 'the traditional linguistic sophistication of Comparative Literature' is not a utopian programme with a determinate outcome, but rather a slow and interminable attempt to learn to read 'the languages of the Southern Hemisphere as active cultural media' (*DD*, 9).

Such a proposal does not go against the demand for patriotism in scholarship, which Saussy invokes in his critique of *Death of a Discipline*. Rather, in the context of unilateralism and monolingualism in US foreign policy after 11 September 2001, Spivak's proposal would provide the conditions for a more ethical dialogue between area studies and the areas designated as its object of knowledge. Reading between the lines of Spivak's argument, it could also be inferred that since area studies provides the US government and the US military with expert knowledge about a particular region, Spivak's proposal that area studies takes on the task of learning to read 'the languages of the Southern Hemisphere as active cultural media' (*DD*, 9) might also work to promote a more ethical dialogue between the US government and the countries of the global South, some of which it designates as rogue states or terrorist threats.

Teleopoesis and the indeterminate temporality of collective political action

The political implications of Spivak's proposal in *Death of a Discipline* are, however, uncertain, and it is with this uncertainty that Spivak is concerned in her lecture series. She draws on Derrida's discussions of *teleiopoiesis*, community and the indeterminate structure of political responsibility in *The Politics of Friendship* to situate the linguistic and pedagogical task that she proposes in *Death of a Discipline* in relation to questions about the possibility of forming political collectives that are ethically responsible to the subaltern.

In *The Politics of Friendship*, Derrida defines *teleiopoiesis* as 'a messianic structure', which heralds the future and 'engages a bottomless responsibility'.[8] Citing one of the aphorisms in Nietzsche's *Beyond Good and Evil* (1886) – 'Alas! If only you knew how soon, how very soon, things will be – different –'[9] – Derrida argues that the temporal structure of this sentence is unusual because it rhetorically announces the arrival of the future before the sentence describing the future, which is about to arrive, is finished. As Derrida puts it, 'The sentence *speaks of itself*, it gets carried away, precipitates and precedes itself, as if its end arrived before the end'.[10] Derrida names this temporal structure 'teleiopoetic': '*Teleiopoiós* qualifies, in a great number of contexts and semantic orders, that which *renders* absolute, perfect, accomplished, finished, that which *brings* to an end'.[11] Significantly, Derrida does not define the term; instead, he foregrounds the rhetorical process through which *teleiopoesis* enacts its meaning.

Spivak invokes Derrida's *teleiopoesis* to 'buttress' her argument about the future anterior of comparative literature, or to be more precise, what the political effects of her re-thinking of comparative literature will have been for subaltern constituencies at an indeterminate point in the future (*DD*, 29). The reason why Spivak does so, I maintain, is to re-think the temporality of politics and the importance of close reading as a form of ethical responsibility to the subaltern.

Significantly, Spivak's 'buttressing' involves a different transliteration of Derrida's term *teleiopoiesis*, which is itself a mediation of the original Greek term. As Corinne Scheiner explains in a detailed etymological account of the variant forms of *teleiopoiesis*, published in *Comparative Literature* (2005):

> The Greek term τελειοποιησιζ never appears in Derrida's text. Instead, Derrida presents a Latinized French version of it, *téléiopoièsis*, thus beginning with the end, with the translation, not the original. His English translator, George Collins, renders the term as *teleiopoiesis* and Spivak renders it as *teleopoiesis*. In a sense, both of these English versions are incomplete, or modified. The discrepancy between them results from a mechanical practice, a mediation: the Latinization of the Greek term in transliteration. Yet the consequence is not only a change in orthography, but also in meaning. Let us begin at the end, as it were, with the second half of the transliterated Greek compounds: *poiesis* is 'creative production, especially of a work of art' (*OED*), while *poesis* is the 'Greek and Latin word for poesy, formerly sometimes used by English writers' (*OED*). As the preceding discussion has demonstrated, the more flexible *poiesis* is essential to both Derrida's *téléiopoièse* and Spivak's *teleopoiesis*, for *poiesis* – an 'imaginative making' – includes not only poetry – *poesis* – but also reading as a creative, productive act. Returning to the beginning, the difference between the two adjectival or adverbial combining forms that serve as prefixes – *teleio* and *telo* – also results from Latinization. Yet once again the orthographic change affects the meaning. *Téléiopoièse* references the adjectival stem *teleio* deriving from the adjective *teleios* (complete), and therefore translates as the making of all things complete. However, *teleopoesis* is more ambiguous; it may refer either to *teleios*, or to the noun *telos* (end or completion), and thus may translate as the making of ends.[12]

As Scheiner points out, Spivak's rendering of Derrida's term *téléiopoièse* as *teleopoiesis* is subtly different from Derrida's usage, both in spelling and meaning. Certainly, Spivak's re-thinking of comparative literature is interested in 'reading as a creative, productive act' as well as imaginative making.[13] Yet Spivak's use of the stem 'teleo' is not intended to connote 'the making of ends' or the bringing to completion (as Scheiner suggests). Rather, as Spivak explains in an interview with Eric Haynot as a response to Scheiner's article, her usage is more concerned with the distant connotation of the word 'tele'.[14] This connotation is clearly consistent with Derrida's claim in *The Politics of Friendship* that 'the other *tele*' – or the other stem of *téléiopoièse*, which is a prefix meaning 'operating at a distance' – is the 'the one that speaks to distance and the far removed'.[15] Rather than translating Derrida's *téléiopoièse* as a form of teleology, or a programme directed towards a particular point of final completion or a goal, Spivak's *teleopoesis* thus combines the openness and indeterminacy, which 'the other *tele*' connotes, with the sense of 'reading as a creative, productive act' implicit in the word *poiesis*.[16]

Derrida's emphasis on the importance of reading in his discussion of *téléiopoièse* certainly informs Spivak's proposal for comparative literature in *Death of a Discipline*. In her conclusion, Spivak invokes Derrida's claim that '*teleiopoiesis* [. . .] is a messianic structure'[17] to support her injunction 'to keep responsibility alive in the reading and teaching of the textual' (*DD*, 101). This is not to suggest that Spivak's use of Derrida's idea is restricted to the reading and teaching of literary texts, however. We have already seen how Spivak's proposal to learn the languages of the global South could work to expand the literacy of a subaltern language and promote a greater sense of ethical responsibility towards the subaltern through 'the reading and teaching of the textual' in comparative literary studies. In some of her more recent essays, however, Spivak has also suggested that the teaching and reading of subaltern languages might enable a form of collective political action that is more ethically responsible to the subaltern groups with whom political activists campaigning for global economic justice often claim solidarity.

Yet in order to comprehend how the teaching and reading of subaltern languages might enable a more responsible form of collective political action it is important to consider how Derrida's argument in *The Politics of Friendship* informs Spivak's understanding of the temporality of the political and the possibility of forming a more responsible collective. For this reason, the following section considers what Derrida means by the statement that '*teleiopoiesis* [. . .] is a messianic structure' in the context of *The Politics of Friendship* before examining the significance of this discussion for Spivak's imperative 'to keep responsibility alive' in the sphere of extra-state collective political action.

As mentioned above, the statement '*teleiopoiesis* [. . .] is a messianic structure' occurs in *Politics of Friendship*, in an extended commentary on a passage from Nietzsche's *Beyond Good and Evil*, entitled 'On the Prejudices of Philosophers'.[18] Nietzsche was appealing to the new species of philosopher who would, he hoped, continue his philosophical challenge to the Christian tradition of friendship, politics and democracy:

> 'Perhaps! But who is willing to concern himself with such dangerous perhapses! For that we have to await the arrival of a new species of philosopher, one which possesses tastes and inclinations opposite to and different from those of its predecessors – philosophers of the dangerous 'perhaps' in every sense. – And to speak in all seriousness: I see such new philosophers arising.'[19]

In Derrida's reading of this passage, Nietzsche's appeal to the philosopher of the future binds the reader, or addressee, in a structure of responsibility to Nietzsche's idea of what this new species of philosopher should be. What is more, Nietzsche's appeal to this new species of philosopher is also a prophecy, which constitutes the philosopher of the future as a messianic figure.

For Derrida, the act of reading Nietzsche is thus bound up with the 'messianic structure' of Nietzsche's prophetic injunction to the philosophers of the future. Nietzsche's sentence thus declares a responsibility to the new species of philosopher who has not yet arrived, while at the same time inviting readers to become co-signatories in the address to the new species of philosopher, which they may also be. The 'double but infinite responsibility', which Derrida recognizes in the rhetorical structure of Nietzsche's sentence, prompts Derrida to reflect on the conceptual resemblance between Nietzsche's precursory address to the new species of philosopher and what Derrida calls the 'community of those without community'.[20]

For Derrida the paradoxical concept of a 'community of those without community' evokes a discussion about the idea of community among twentieth-century French philosophers such as Georges Bataille, Maurice Blanchot and Jean-Luc Nancy. Derrida refers to a 'language of madness', which cannot be accounted for in the logical terms of an 's is p' proposition.[21] He suggests that there is a correspondence between the *teleiopoetic* structure of Nietzsche's sentence and its precursory address to Nietzsche's absent friends, the new species of philosopher who have not yet arrived, on the one hand; and the paradoxical structure of a 'community of those without community' on the other. For just as the *teleiopoetic* structure of Nietzsche's sentence is predicated on the possibility that a future philosopher might take Nietzsche's text seriously as philosophy, engage with its rhetorical structures and countersign it, so the 'community of those without community' denotes the possibility that a community of thinkers, who are alike only in their singularity, their solitude and their commitment to thinking the conditions of possibility of truth, might also come into being.

Rather than adhering to a particular philosophical opinion or school of thought, this 'community without community' is concerned with the implications of Nietzsche's 'Perhaps' for the future of philosophy and the political. As Derrida explains, 'the friends of the *perhaps* are the friends of truth. But the friends of truth are not, by definition, *in* the truth; they are not installed there as in the padlocked security of a dogma and the stable reliability of an opinion'.[22] Rather, for Derrida, Nietzsche's 'Perhaps' necessitates that the new species of philosopher adopts a language of impossibility and undecidability precisely because those concepts 'might be a condition of decision, interruption, revolution, responsibility and truth'.[23] In the context of this discussion, Derrida's claim that '*teleiopoiesis* [. . .] is a messianic structure' refers to the temporal structure of Nietzsche's 'perhaps', and the implications of Nietzsche's address to the new species of philosopher for the future of democracy and politics.

While Derrida's reflections on Nietzsche and friendship are primarily concerned with the possibility of a future democracy to come at an indeterminate point in the future, Spivak is more concerned with the implications of Derrida's idea that the temporal structure of Nietzsche's 'teleopoesis' is messianic for re-thinking the temporality of the political and imagining a form of extra-state collective political action that is ethically responsible to the subaltern. In a separate but related commentary on Derrida's *The Politics of Friendship*, entitled 'A Note on the New International' (2001), Spivak argues that Derrida's 'critical way of thinking collectivity in the political sphere' is indispensable for imagining alternative forms of collectivity to the '"fake" collectivities [that] are constructed by activist intellectuals at the grass roots, against a globalization about which the rank and file have little intuition' (ANNI, 13). Against what she calls the '"fake" collectivities' that claim to speak in the name of a broader subaltern collective in the global South, Spivak invokes Derrida's 'plea for slow reading, even at a time of political urgency' (ANNI, 15).

Spivak does not explicitly say why Derrida's plea for slow reading in *The Politics of Friendship* might offer a corrective to (what she regards as) the spurious forms of collectivity that many global justice activists based in Europe and North America claim to have with subaltern groups in the global South. Yet her suggestion that 'the patient work of learning to learn from below' is 'a species of reading', which can help to 'mend the torn fabric of subaltern ethics' (ANNI, 15), provides a clue to understanding Spivak's injunction 'to keep responsibility alive in the reading and teaching of the textual' (*DD*, 101). Like Derrida's slow and patient reading of Nietzsche and his teleopoetic address to the new philosophers of the future in *The Politics of Friendship*, Spivak argues that the task of forming collectivities with subaltern groups across the globe can take place only through the process of learning to learn from below, which is itself a 'species' of Derrida's slow and patient reading.

What is more, this work can begin to take place only through an engagement with the subaltern languages of the global South. As a consequence, the 'traditional linguistic sophistication of Comparative Literature' (*DD*, 9) is indispensable for forming a new kind of collectivity with subaltern constituencies precisely because the linguistic skills and competencies of comparative literary studies could perhaps provide activists with a set of critical tools that are responsible to the histories and cultures of the very subaltern constituencies with whom activists often claim collectivity.

The task of close reading in a non-European language that Spivak proposes for scholars and students of comparative literature, as well as global justice activists, is one that she also attempts to put into practice in *Death of a Discipline*. The first lecture in the series, entitled 'Crossing Borders', for instance, offers a close reading of an extract from a novel by the Guadeloupean writer Maryse Condé, *Heremakhonon* (1976): 'an undisclosed West African subaltern speaker' (*DD*, 16) draws attention to the shifting linguistic and ethnic groups in different West African societies, such as the Fulani and the Toucoleur. In Spivak's reading of this passage, the proper names of these languages 'carry the sedimentation of the history of the movement of peoples' in West Africa (*DD*, 18). Furthermore, Spivak argues that the 'movement of peoples and languages' is historically sedimented 'in the translation of this passage from *French* to *English*' (*DD*, 18). This historical sedimentation is significant for Spivak because it exemplifies what she calls the restricted permeability of subaltern languages in an era of globalization.

Restricted permeability

What Spivak means by 'restricted permeability' is clarified in an interview with Meyda Yegenoglu and Mahmut Mutman, which was published in the journal *New Formations* (2002). Against the older definition of subalternity, in which 'the subaltern is precisely outside the circuit of mobility', Spivak argues that the subaltern 'is altogether permeable from above'.[24] In other words, the subaltern has access to the policies of Non-Governmental Organizations and global commodity culture. Yet the influence of subaltern languages and culture on policy making and political reform at the level of the state or the Non-Governmental Organization is restricted. As Spivak puts it, 'the permeability from below up into the dominant *is* not only as restricted as, but more restricted than before'.[25] Although Spivak does not specify a particular time anterior to the present context of the interview, during which the permeability of subaltern languages was less restricted, one could reasonably infer that she means a time before the Bretton Woods agreement and the establishment of the World Bank and the International Monetary Fund, during which India, Algeria, Jamaica and elsewhere were still in the grip of European colonial rule.

What is crucial about the concept of 'restricted permeability', however, is that it conveys the subordinate status of subaltern languages, which are spoken by socially marginalized linguistic communities. By contrast to hegemonic European languages such as English, which have become the international language of power, Spivak argues that subaltern languages do not cross or permeate national and cultural boundaries in the same way, and when they do, they are often ignored. To counter this problem, Spivak contends that the task of the comparative literature specialist is to learn to read these languages as they become historically sedimented in literary texts.

In a reading of Tayeb Salih's novel *Season of Migration to the North* (1969), for example, Spivak openly admits that her knowledge of Arabic 'is minimal' (*DD*, 116). Despite this, she carefully traces the way in which the original Arabic version of the novel foregrounds the subtle codes circumscribing public and private discourses of sexuality in Arab society. She notes how, in the original Arabic version of the novel, the old female character Bint Majzoub uses the archaic language of erotica to silence the male character Wad Rayyes. To quote Salih, 'Wad Rayyes, you're a man who talks rubbish. Your whole brain's in the head of your penis and the head of your penis is as small as your brain' (Salih, cited in *DD*, 60). Spivak proceeds to compare this passage with a phrase attributed to the character Mustafa Sa'eed by a cabinet minister, who symbolizes a corrupt postcolonial elite: 'He used to say "I'll liberate Africa with my . . . ," ' and he laughed so widely you could see the arse of his throat' (Salih, cited in *DD*, 61). She concludes that in 'the book's staging of the two "uses" of the word "penis", "tradition" provides the older woman the possibility of using a word in the private sphere that modernity does not allow the man in the public sphere' (*DD*, 61). In the English translation of Salih's novel, however, this subtle distinction is elided; as a result, 'the gender division of freedom of speech between tradition and modernity is made rhetorically unclear' (*DD*, 61).

These two literary examples show how the restricted permeability of subaltern languages prevents a more sophisticated understanding of the cultures that they represent. Yet it is perhaps not immediately apparent how *Heremakhonon* and *Season of Migration to the North* relate to the broader argument that Spivak makes in *Death of a Discipline* and 'A Note on the New International' about the political necessity to learn to learn from the subaltern. How, in other words, can the practice of close reading that Spivak proposes in *Death of a Discipline* work to empower the disenfranchised?

Righting Wrongs and the task of learning to learn from the subaltern

Spivak elaborates on the political implications of her proposal for comparative literature's ethical vocation in *Death of a Discipline* in 'Righting Wrongs' (2003), an article that was originally presented at the Oxford Amnesty lectures in 2001. She argues that 'the rural poor and [. . .] all species of the sub-proletariat' will remain an 'object of benevolence in human rights discourse' without the recovering and training of the ethical imagination of such subaltern groups (RW, 206–7). To counter this problem, Spivak proposes a re-thinking of the subject of human rights from the standpoint of the rural poor and the sub-proletariat in South Asia. Such a re-thinking demands a new pedagogy that is capable of suturing what Spivak calls the torn fabric of the subaltern episteme. Although Spivak does not specify what it is that has done the tearing, she implies that the divide was caused by centuries of class and caste oppression, as well as the transition from colonial modernity to globalization.

What is crucial, however, is Spivak's attempt to suture this tear through a pedagogy that strives to 'learn well one of the languages of the rural poor of the South' (RW, 208). As Spivak explains: 'for access to the subaltern episteme to devise a suturing pedagogy, you must take into account the multiplicity of subaltern languages' (RW, 208). While this may be a sound ethical principle, Spivak does not really elaborate on how exactly a basic knowledge of subaltern languages would help to alter the class apartheid that perpetuates the disenfranchisement of subaltern groups in rural India. Yet if this call to 'take into account the multiplicity of subaltern languages' is situated in relation to Spivak's discussion of their 'restricted permeability', it becomes clear that promoting the transnational literacy of a subaltern language may provide one strategy for countering the silencing and exclusion of subaltern groups from political representation at a local, national or global level.

As argued in this book, Spivak's theoretical work has always criticized the limits of existing structures of political representation, and carefully elaborated the conditions of possibility for a new idiom in which the subaltern can speak and be heard. Spivak's work on literacy training as a form of pedagogy that can empower the oppressed to recode the representational structures of parliamentary democracy in India expands and develops the ethical commitment to learn to learn from the subaltern that runs throughout her work. The real political outcome of such an ethical commitment may be slow and uncertain, as Spivak herself acknowledges. Yet, as she has cogently argued in her re-thinking of Marxism, feminism, deconstruction and postcolonial studies, this ethical commitment to achieving one-on-one epistemic change is crucial for altering the structures of inequality, which underpin the contemporary global economic system.

Notes

Introduction

1 Pyle, '"By a Certain Subreption"', 186.
2 See, for example, Moore-Gilbert, *Postcolonial Theory*, 74–113; Huddart, 'Making an Example out of Spivak', 35–46; and Hallward, *Absolutely Postcolonial*, 27–35.
3 See, for example, Hallward, *Absolutely Postcolonial*, 27–35; Bhatt, 'Kant's "Raw Man" and the Miming of Primitivism', 37–44; and Chow, *Ethics after Idealism*, 33–54.
4 For a further discussion of the IPTA and India's political theatre, see Bharucha, *Rehearsals of Revolution*, 40–4, 53–4, 57–61.
5 For a further discussion of this, see my *Gayatri Chakravorty Spivak*, 3.
6 Moore-Gilbert, *Postcolonial Theory*, 74–113.
7 See, for example, Ashcroft, *Postcolonial Transformation*, 1–17.
8 Derrida, *Of Spirit*, 40.
9 For more on this troubling and enabling aspect of complicity, see Sanders, *Complicities*, 1–18.
10 For a further discussion of de Man's influence on Spivak's ethics of reading in *A Critique of Postcolonial Reason*, see Sanders, 'Postcolonial Reading'.
11 See Parry, 'Problems in Current Theories of Colonial Discourse', 39; and Chow, *Ethics after Idealism*, 40.
12 See Young, *Postcolonialism*, 339, 350–1.
13 Morton, *Gayatri Chakravorty Spivak*.
14 See Leonard, *Nationality between Poststructuralism and Postcolonial Theory*, 74; Leonard, 'Whose Imprimatur?'.

Chapter 1 Postcolonial Criticism and Beyond

1 Said, *Orientalism*, 12.
2 Dirlik, 'The Postcolonial Aura', 328–56.
3 Macaulay, ed. Young, *Speeches by Lord Macaulay*, 359.
4 Viswanathan, *Masks of Conquest*, 2.
5 Meyer, ' "Indian Ink" ', 66.
6 Meyer, ' "Indian Ink" ', 66.
7 Meyer, ' "Indian Ink" ', 71.
8 Meyer, ' "Indian Ink" ', 75.
9 Meyer, ' "Indian Ink" ', 92.
10 Meyer, ' "Indian Ink" ', 93.
11 Meyer, ' "Indian Ink" ', 92.
12 Meyer, ' "Indian Ink" ', 92.
13 Hulme, 'The Locked Heart', 72.
14 Hulme, 'The Locked Heart', 75.
15 Hulme, 'The Locked Heart', 80.
16 Hulme, 'The Locked Heart', 80.
17 Hulme, 'The Locked Heart', 80.
18 Hulme, 'The Locked Heart', 80–3.
19 Emery, *Jean Rhys at World's End*, 39.
20 Emery, *Jean Rhys at World's End*, 39.
21 Emery, *Jean Rhys at World's End*, 40.
22 Emery, *Jean Rhys at World's End*, 59.
23 Emery, *Jean Rhys at World's End*, 59.
24 Devi, *Imaginary Maps*, 118.
25 Devi, *Imaginary Maps*, 157.
26 Devi, *Imaginary Maps*, 193.
27 Young, *Postcolonialism*, 359.
28 Shetty, '(Dis)figuring the Nation', 67.
29 Lacan, 'A Love Letter', 153.
30 Shetty, '(Dis)figuring the Nation', 70.

Chapter 2 Deconstruction

1 Derrida, 'Letter to a Japanese Friend', in *A Derrida Reader*, ed. P. Kamuf, 275.
2 Derrida, 'As *if* I were Dead', in *Applying: To Derrida*, ed. Brannigan, Robbins and Wolfreys, 217.
3 Derrida, *Of Grammatology*, trans. Spivak, 158. Spivak follows American usage in the phrase 'outside of'; the sentence is quoted elsewhere as 'there is nothing outside the text'.
4 For an overview of such mistaken readings of Derrida, see Bennington, *Legislations*, 11–60.
5 Mowitt, *Text*, 97.

6   Mowitt, *Text*, 44.
7   Mowitt, *Text*, 96.
8   Mowitt, *Text*, 96.
9   Mowitt, *Text*, 103.
10 Davidson, 'Review of *Of Grammatology*', 167.
11 Champagne, '*Of Grammatology*', 741.
12 Donoghue, 'Review of *Of Grammatology*', 32.
13 Donoghue, 'Review of *Of Grammatology*', 34.
14 Donoghue, 'Review of *Of Grammatology*', 34.
15 Saussure, *Course in General Linguistics*, 118.
16 Derrida, *Positions*, 42.
17 Derrida, 'Différance', 13–14.
18 Derrida, 'Différance', 18.
19 Derrida, 'Différance', 17.
20 See Gasché, *The Tain of the Mirror*; Harvey, *Derrida and the Economy of Différance*; Llewelyn, *Derrida on the Threshold of Sense*.
21 Gasché, *The Tain of the Mirror*, 34.
22 Gasché, *The Tain of the Mirror*, 46.
23 Gasché, *The Tain of the Mirror*, 46.
24 Bennington, *Legislations*, 11–49.
25 For more on Spivak's readings of Kant's anthropomorphism in 'Critique of Teleological Judgement', see Swift, *Romanticism, Philosophy, Literature*, pp. 117–21.
26 For more on Spivak's intellectual engagement with de Man's thought, see Spivak, 'Learning from de Man', pp. 21–35.
27 Derrida, cited in de Man, *Blindness and Insight*, 115.
28 de Man, *Blindness and Insight*, 119.
29 de Man, *Blindness and Insight*, 136.
30 de Man, *Blindness and Insight*, 136.
31 Gasché, *The Wild Card of Reading*, 9.
32 de Man, *Aesthetic Ideology*, 147.
33 For a lucid and detailed commentary on de Man's reading of Kant, see Swift, *Romanticism, Philosophy, Literature*, pp. 98–122.
34 Siebers, 'Ethics in the Age of Rousseau', 758–79.
35 Bhabha, *The Location of Culture*, 31.
36 Derrida, *Writing and Difference*, 138.
37 Gasché, 'God, for Example', in *Inventions of Difference*, 156.
38 de Man, *Allegories of Reading*, 300.
39 Keenan, *Fables of Responsibility*, 1.
40 Seth, *Beastly Tales from Here and There*, 130.
41 For more on this topic see Siebers, 'Ethics in the Age of Rousseau', 776–9.
42 Lingis, in Levinas, *Otherwise than Being*, xxxi.
43 Paper presented at the Translating Class, Altering Hospitality Conference at the University of Leeds, June 2002.
44 Derrida, 'Violence and Metaphysics', in *Writing and Difference*, 147–8.

45 Hallward, *Absolutely Postcolonial*, 30.
46 Westphal, *Transcendence and Self-Transcendence*, 100.
47 Pseudo-Dionysius, 'The Divine Names', in *The Complete Works*, 50.
48 For more on Derrida's relation to negative theology, see Coward and Forshay, eds, *Derrida and Negative Theology*; Caputo, *The Prayers and Tears of Jacques Derrida*; and Westphal, *Transcendence and Self-Transcendence*.
49 Derrida, 'Différance', in *Margins of Philosophy*, 6.
50 Hill, *Blanchot*, 171–5.
51 Blanchot, *The Infinite Conversation*, 49–58.
52 Hallward, *Absolutely Postcolonial*, 30. It is worth noting that Hallward's criticism of Spivak – and her engagement with Levinasian ethics – is partly informed by Badiou's critique of Levinas. In a passing comment on Badiou, which could be read as a preliminary response to Hallward's critique, Spivak has argued that Badiou has 'read Levinas too quickly and [has] decided not only that Levinas is only religion [. . .] but that Derrida's interest in Levinas makes Derrida, in the latest phases, only religious and therefore against secularism and against the thinking of ethics and secularism'. See Lyons and Franklin, ' "On the Cusp of the Personal and the Impersonal" ', 214.
53 Hallward, *Absolutely Postcolonial*, 30.
54 See Hallward, *Alain Badiou*, 223–42.
55 Hallward, in Badiou, *Ethics*, xxix–xxx.
56 Hallward, *Alain Badiou*, 115.
57 Hallward, in Badiou, *Ethics*, xxix.
58 Roy, *The God of Small Things*, 263.
59 Roy, *The God of Small Things*, 266.
60 Roy, *The God of Small Things*, 266.
61 Ahmad, 'Reading Arundhati Roy Politically', 103.
62 Ahmad, 'Reading Arundhati Roy Politically', 105.
63 Roy, *The God of Small Things*, 271.
64 Needham, ' "The Small Voice of History" ', 369–91, posits a similar reading of *The God of Small Things* in the use of Guha's idea of a 'small voice of history' to examine the subaltern histories that are articulated in Roy's novel. Although Needham does not specifically address the question of ethics raised in Spivak's work, her claim that *The God of Small Things* points towards the (impossible) possibility of social transformation for subaltern subjects bears a striking resemblance to Spivak's argument.
65 Hallward, *Absolutely Postcolonial*, 34.

Chapter 3   Marxism and Post-Marxism

1 For a further discussion of this problem, see Keenan, *Fables of Responsibility*, 99–133.

2   de Man, *The Resistance to Theory*, 11.
3   Marx, 'Thesen über Feuerbach', *Marx-Engels-Werke*, Band 3, 7.
4   Marx, ed. McLellan, *Selected Writings*, 158.
5   Kemple, *Reading Marx Writing*, 63.
6   Kemple, *Reading Marx Writing*, 63.
7   Indeed this is a view expressed by Keenan, *Fables of Responsibility*, 101–2.
8   Derrida, 'Marx & Sons', 222–3.
9   Said, *Orientalism*, 153–4.
10 Marx, ed. McLellan, *Selected Writings*, 390.
11 Marx, 'The British Rule in India', 122.
12 Marx, 'The British Rule in India', 122.
13 See, for example, Bailey and Llobera, eds, *The Asiatic Mode of Production*; Wittfogel, *Oriental Despotism*; Hindess and Hirst, *Pre-Capitalist Modes of Production*; Dunn, *The Fall and Rise of the Asiatic Mode of Production*.
14 Marx, *Early Writings*, 327.
15 Marx, *Grundrisse*, 472–3.
16 Marx, *Grundrisse*, 472–3.
17 Marx, *Early Writings*, 328.
18 Derrida, *Positions*, 71.
19 Marx, *Capital*, vol. I, 138.
20 Marx, *Capital*, vol. I, 128.
21 Marx, *Capital*, vol. I, 128.
22 Marx, *Capital*, vol. I, 126.
23 Cohen, *Karl Marx's Theory of History*, 103.
24 Cohen, *Karl Marx's Theory of History*, 104.
25 Cohen, *Karl Marx's Theory of History*, 299.
26 See, for example, Elster, *An Introduction to Karl Marx*, 63–70.
27 Marx, *Capital*, vol. I, 131–2.
28 Chakrabarty, *Rethinking Working-Class History*, 226.
29 Marx, *Grundrisse*, 451.
30 Marx, *Early Writings*, 254.
31 Marx, *Early Writings*, 256.
32 Marx, *Early Writings*, 256.
33 Marx, *Capital*, vol. III, 1016.
34 Balakrishnan, ed., *The Hidden Assembly Line*.
35 Sassen, *Globalization and its Discontents*, 111.
36 Sassen, *Globalization and its Discontents*, 130.
37 Klein, *No Logo*, 195–229.
38 Gilbert, 'A Class Performance'.
39 Robbins, 'The Sweatshop Sublime', 84–97.
40 Robbins, 'The Sweatshop Sublime', 96.
41 Robbins, 'The Sweatshop Sublime', 95.
42 Cited in Baucom, 'Cryptic, Withheld, Singular', 414.
43 Baucom, 'Cryptic, Withheld, Singular', 416.

44   See Foucault, *Society Must Be Defended*, 239–64; and Hardt and Negri, *Empire*, 20–41.
45   Deleuze and Guattari, *Anti-Oedipus*, 32–3.
46   Sanders, 'Representation: Reading Otherwise', 202.
47   Such an imperative is also consistent with Nancy's re-thinking of Kant's ethical imperative: as Spivak asserts, 'it is Jean-Luc Nancy's central argument in *L'Impérative Catégorique* that the categorical imperative is the mark of alterity [. . .] in the ethical' (*CPR*, 123).
48   Chakrabarty, *Provincializing Europe*, 92.
49   Taussig, *The Devil and Commodity Fetishism*, 153.
50   Taussig, *The Devil and Commodity Fetishism*, 227.
51   Taussig, *The Devil and Commodity Fetishism*, 153.
52   Taussig, *The Devil and Commodity Fetishism*, xii.
53   Taussig, *The Devil and Commodity Fetishism*, 153.
54   Chakrabarty, *Provincializing Europe*, 93.
55   Chakrabarty, *Provincializing Europe*, 93.
56   Chakrabarty, *Provincializing Europe*, 93.
57   Chakrabarty, *Provincializing Europe*, 93.
58   Chakrabarty, *Provincializing Europe*, 92.

Chapter 4   Subaltern Studies and the Critique of Representation

1   Gramsci, *Selections from Prison Notebooks*, xiv.
2   Hoare and Smith, in Gramsci, *Selections from Prison Notebooks*, xiv.
3   Laclau and Mouffe, *Hegemony and Socialist Strategy*, 12.
4   Arnold, 'Gramsci and Peasant Subalternity in India', 33.
5   Guha, 'Preface', *Subaltern Studies I*, vii.
6   Guha, *Subaltern Studies I*, 4.
7   Sarkar, 'The Conditions and Nature of Subaltern Militancy', 271–2.
8   Sarkar, 'The Conditions and Nature of Subaltern Militancy', 281.
9   Sarkar, 'The Conditions and Nature of Subaltern Militancy', 281.
10   Sarkar, 'The Conditions and Nature of Subaltern Militancy', 286.
11   Chakrabarty, *Habitations of Modernity*, 9.
12   Gramsci, *Selections from Prison Notebooks*, 55.
13   Guha, 'On Some Aspects of the Historiography of Colonial India', 5–6.
14   Chakrabarty, *Habitations of Modernity*, 16.
15   Guha, *Elementary Aspects of Peasant Insurgency*, 11.
16   Sarkar, *Writing Social History*, 87.
17   Deleuze, *The Logic of Sense*, 52.
18   Deleuze, *The Logic of Sense*, 52.
19   Derrida, *Of Grammatology*, 145.
20   Parry, 'Problems in Current Theories of Colonial Discourse', 27–58.
21   Hallward, *Absolutely Postcolonial*, 33.

22 Althusser, *Lenin and Philosophy*, 134–5.
23 Althusser, *Lenin and Philosophy*, 135.
24 Marx, *Surveys from Exile*, 239.
25 Marx, *Surveys from Exile*, 239.
26 Marx, *Surveys from Exile*, 239.
27 Larsen, *Determinations*, 71.
28 Freud 'A Child is being Beaten', 179.
29 Freud, 'A Child is being Beaten', 184.
30 Mani, *Contentious Traditions*, 16.
31 Derrida, *Of Grammatology*, 293.
32 Shetty and Bellamy, 'Postcolonialism's Archive Fever', 35.
33 Shetty and Bellamy 'Postcolonialism's Archive Fever', 35.
34 Mani, *Contentious Traditions*, 15.
35 Mani, *Contentious Traditions*, 25.
36 Mani, *Contentious Traditions*, 55.
37 As Shetty and Bellamy argue, 'the law on sanctioned suicide is con-
    stituted as a denial of women's agency: she can die – but she cannot
    kill her "proper" self': 'Postcolonialism's Archive Fever', 37.
38 Shetty and Bellamy, 'Postcolonialism's Archive Fever', 37.
39 Shetty and Bellamy, 'Postcolonialism's Archive Fever', 40.
40 Shetty and Bellamy, 'Postcolonialism's Archive Fever', 42.
41 Mani, *Contentious Traditions*, 56.
42 Mani, *Contentious Traditions*, 196.
43 Lyotard, *The Différend*, 13.
44 Mani, *Contentious Traditions*, 2.
45 Shetty and Bellamy, 'Postcolonialism's Archive Fever', 46.
46 Indeed Spivak argues that Bhuvaneswari killed herself in an attempt
    to re-write the mythology of the 'blazing, fighting, familial' goddess
    Durga (CSS, 308).
47 Parry, 'Problems in Current Theories of Colonial Discourse', 39.
48 Moore-Gilbert, *Postcolonial Theory*, 107.
49 Moore-Gilbert, *Postcolonial Theory*, 105.
50 Moore-Gilbert, *Postcolonial Theory*, 105.
51 For a further discussion of Spivak's use of Lyotard's concept of the
    différend, see Devedas and Nicholls, 'Postcolonial Interventions',
    73–101.
52 For a more detailed account of the influence of Paul de Man on
    Spivak's work, see Swift, ' "Can the Subaltern Speak?" ', 25–47; and
    Sanders, ' "Postcolonial Reading" '.

Chapter 5   Transnational Feminism

1 For more on the contradiction between Kristeva's left-wing political
   investment in China during the cultural revolution of Mao and
   her orientalist representations of Chinese culture in *About Chinese*

Women, see Lowe, *Critical Terrains*, 136–89. For more on Spivak's critique of *About Chinese Women*, see my *Gayatri Chakravorty Spivak*, 78–84.

2   Freud, 'On the Universal Tendency to Debasement in the Sphere of Love', p. 189.
3   de Beauvoir, *The Second Sex*, 295.
4   Lazreg, *The Eloquence of Silence*, 137.
5   Lazreg, *The Eloquence of Silence*, 151.
6   Hélie-Lucas, 'Bound and Gagged by the Family Code', 3–15.
7   Cooke, *Women Claim Islam*, xxvii.
8   Cooke, *Women Claim Islam*, 59.
9   Blanchot, *The Space of Literature*, 106.
10 For more on the relationship between Blanchot and Levinas, see Hill, *Blanchot*, 170–81.
11 Blanchot, *The Infinite Conversation*, 74.
12 Akhter, *Depopulating Bangladesh*, 4–5.
13 Akhter, *Depopulating Bangladesh*, 6–7.
14 Akhter, *Depopulating Bangladesh*, 8.
15 Akhter, *Depopulating Bangladesh*, 9.
16 Akhter, *Depopulating Bangladesh*, 36.
17 Rozario, 'The Feminist Debate on Reproductive Rights and Contraception in Bangladesh'.
18 Feldman, 'Reply to Gayatri Chakravorty Spivak'.
19 Mohanty, *Feminism without Borders*, 144.
20 Mohanty, *Feminism without Borders*, 144.
21 Yegenoglu and Mutman, 'Mapping the Present', 17.
22 Yegenoglu and Mutman, 'Mapping the Present', 17.

Chapter 6   From a Postcolonial Critique of Reason to *A Critique of Postcolonial Reason*

1   Kant, *A Critique of Pure Reason*, 607, A 761/ B 789.
2   Ahmad, *In Theory*; Dirlik, 'The Postcolonial Aura'; Hardt and Negri, *Empire*.
3   Pletsch, 'The Three Worlds', 588.
4   For a further discussion of this lesson, see Sanders, 'Postcolonial Reading'.
5   Lacan, *Seminar I: Freud's Papers on Technique*, 67.
6   Lacan, *Seminar I: Freud's Papers on Technique*, 67.
7   Lacan, *Seminar I: Freud's Papers on Technique*, 67.
8   See, for example, Rooney, *African Literature, Animism and Politics*, 96–7.
9   Spivak's reading of Kant also recalls Lacan's engagement with Kant in *The Ethics of Psychoanalysis*, even though Spivak does not explicitly refer to *Seminar VII* in her reading. While Spivak's subsequent

discussion of the 'impossibility of ethical relation' between the post-colonial intellectual and the native informant in *Critique of Postcolonial Reason* seems to be primarily influenced by Levinas and Derrida, there are certainly structural homologies between Levinasian ethics and Lacanian ethics. See, for example, Critchley, '*Das Ding*: Lacan and Lévinas', 198–216.

10 Kant, *Critique of Judgement*, 36.
11 Kant, *Critique of Judgement*, 6.
12 Caygill, *Art of Judgement*, 5.
13 Kant, *Critique of Judgement*, 116.
14 Kant, *Critique of Judgement*, 116.
15 Kant, *Critique of Judgement*, 124.
16 Burnham, *An Introduction to Kant's Critique of Judgement*, 121.
17 Kant, *Critique of Judgement*, 258.
18 Kant, *Critique of Judgement*, 258.
19 Swift, 'Kant, Herder, and the Question of Philosophical Anthropology', 219.
20 Swift, 'Kant, Herder, and the Question of Philosophical Anthropology', 226.
21 Swift, 'Kant, Herder, and the Question of Philosophical Anthropology', 228.
22 See, for example, Wood, *Kant's Ethical Thought*, 3; Bernasconi and Lott, eds, *The Idea of Race*.
23 Swift, 'Kant, Herder, and the Question of Philosophical Anthropology', 228.
24 For more on the concept of parabasis, see de Man, *Aesthetic Ideology*, 163–84.
25 For a more detailed discussion of Spivak's engagement with the thought of Paul de Man, see Sanders, 'Postcolonial Reading'; and Sanders, 'Representation', 198–204.
26 For more on Spivak's engagement with de Man's concept of parabasis, see Spivak, 'Learning from de Man', pp. 21–35.
27 Marx, *Capital*, vol. III, 958–9.
28 Marx, *Capital*, vol. III, 959.
29 Schmitt, *The Concept of Nature in Marx*, 77.
30 Marx, *Capital*, vol. 3, 959.
31 'A line that continually approaches a given curve, but does not approach it at any finite distance' (*OED*).
32 Kant, 'Religion within the Boundaries of Mere Reason', 96.
33 Kant, 'Religion within the Boundaries of Mere Reason', 96.
34 Kant, 'Religion within the Boundaries of Mere Reason', 96.
35 Derrida, *The Politics of Friendship*, 106, 130–1.
36 Derrida, *The Politics of Friendship*, 156.
37 Derrida, *The Politics of Friendship*, 157.

Conclusion: Transnational Literacy, Subaltern Rights and the Future of Comparative Literature

1   Barlow, 'Not Really a Proper Intellectual Response', 151.
2   Barlow, 'Not Really a Proper Intellectual Response', 152.
3   Bush, 'Deaths of a Discipline', 208.
4   Bernheimer, ed., *Comparative Literature in the Age of Multiculturalism*, 8–17.
5   Apter, 'Afterlife of a Discipline', 204.
6   Saussy, 'Chiasmus', 236.
7   Saussy, 'Chiasmus', 236.
8   Derrida, *The Politics of Friendship*, 37.
9   Nietzsche, cited in Derrida, *The Politics of Friendship*, 31.
10 Derrida, *The Politics of Friendship*, 31.
11 Derrida, *The Politics of Friendship*, 32.
12 Scheiner, '*Teleiopoesis, Telepoesis,* and the Practice of Comparative Literature', 243.
13 Scheiner, '*Teleiopoesis, Telepoesis,* and the Practice of Comparative Literature', 243.
14 Haynot, ' "The Slightness of my Endeavour" ', 266.
15 Derrida, *The Politics of Friendship*, 32.
16 Scheiner, '*Teleiopoesis, Telepoesis,* and the Practice of Comparative Literature', 243.
17 Derrida, *The Politics of Friendship*, 37.
18 Derrida, *The Politics of Friendship*, 37.
19 Nietzsche, cited in Derrida, *The Politics of Friendship*, 34.
20 Derrida, *The Politics of Friendship*, 37.
21 As Derrida proceeds to explain, both Nietzsche and his philosophical heirs are 'forced [. . .] by the most profound and rigorous necessity' to speak in a 'language of madness', to 'say things as contradictory, insane, absurd, impossible, undecidable as "X without X" ', 'community of those without community', 'inoperative community', 'unavowable community'. See Derrida, *The Politics of Friendship*, 42.
22 Derrida, *The Politics of Friendship*, 43.
23 Derrida, *The Politics of Friendship*, 43.
24 Yegenoglu and Mutman, 'Mapping the Present', 11.
25 Yegenoglu and Mutman, 'Mapping the Present', 11.

References

Writings by Spivak

Myself I Must Remake: The Life and Poetry of W. B. Yeats (New York: Cromwell, 1974) [revised version of PhD dissertation, 'The Great Wheel: Stages in the Personality of Yeats's Lyric Speaker', Cornell University, Ithaca, NY, 1967]

'Translator's Preface' to Jacques Derrida, *Of Grammatology* [1967] (Baltimore: Johns Hopkins University Press, 1976)

'Revolutions that as yet have no Model', *Derrida's Limited Inc.', diacritics*, 10 (4) (winter 1980): 29–49

'Three Women's Texts and a Critique of Imperialism', *Critical Inquiry*, 12 (1) (1985): 243–61

'Imperialism and Sexual Difference', *Oxford Literary Review*, 7 (1–2) (1986): 225–40

In Other Worlds: Essays in Cultural Politics (London: Methuen, 1987) [incl. 'French Feminism in an International Frame', 134–53; 'Scattered Speculations on the Question of Value', 154–75; 'Subaltern Studies; Deconstructing Historiography', 197–221; 'A Literary Representation of the Subaltern: A Woman's Text from the Third World', 241–68]

'Can the Subaltern Speak?', in *Marxism and the Interpretation of Culture*, ed. Cary Nelson and Larry Grossberg (Urbana: University of Illinois Press, 1988), 271–313

The Postcolonial Critic: Interviews, Strategies, Dialogues, ed. Sarah Harasym (London: Routledge, 1990)

'Theory in the Margin: Coetzee's *Foe* Reading Defoe's *Crusoe/Roxana*', in *Consequences of Theory: Selected Papers of the English Institute, 1987–88*, ed. Jonathan Arac and Barbara Johnson (Baltimore: Johns Hopkins University Press, 1991), 154–80

Outside in the Teaching Machine (New York and London: Routledge, 1993) [incl. 'More on Power/Knowledge', 25–51; 'Limits and Openings of Marx in Derrida', 97–119; French Feminism Revisited', 141–71]

'Responsibility', *boundary 2*, 21 (3) (1994): 19–64

'Ghostwriting', *diacritics*, 25 (2) (summer 1995); 65–84

Preface to and commentaries on Mahasweta Devi, *Imaginary Maps: Three Stories*, trans. Gayatri Chakravorty Spivak (New York and London: Routledge, 1995)

'Supplementing Marxism', in *Whither Marxism?*, ed. Steven Cullenberg and Bernd Magnus (New York: Routledge, 1995), 109–19

'Teaching for the Times', in *Decolonizing the Imagination*, ed. Jan Nederveen Pieterse (London: Zed Press, 1995), 177–202

'Public Hearing on Crimes against Women', *Women against Fundamentalisms*, 7 (1995); see http://www.af.gn.apc.org/journal7p3.htm

The Spivak Reader, ed. Donna Landry and Gerald Maclean (London: Routledge, 1996)

A Critique of Postcolonial Reason: Towards a History of the Vanishing Present (Cambridge, Mass.: Harvard University Press, 1999) [incl. revised version of CSS as chapter 3, 'History', 198–311, and appendix, 'The Setting to Work of Deconstruction', 423–32]

'Claiming Transformation', in *Transformation: Thinking Through Feminism*, ed. Sara Ahmed, Jane Kilby, Celia Lury, Maureen McNeil and Beverley Skeggs (London: Routledge, 2000)

'Schmitt and Poststructuralism: A Response', *Cardozo Law Review*, 21 (5–6) (2001): 1723–37

'A Note on the New International', *parallax*, 7 (3) (2001): 12–16

Death of a Discipline (New York: Columbia University Press, 2003) [incl. 'Crossing Borders', 1–23]

'Righting Wrongs', in *Human Rights, Human Wrongs: The Oxford Amnesty Lectures, 2001*, ed. Nicholas Owen (Oxford: Oxford University Press, 2003), 164–227

'Terror: A Speech after 9–11', *boundary 2*, 31 (2) (2004): 81–111

'Learning from de Man: Looking Back', *boundary 2*, 32 (3) (2005): 21–35

'Scattered Speculations on the Subaltern and the Popular', *Postcolonial Studies*, 8 (4) (2005): 475–86

'Touched by Deconstruction', *Grey Room*, 20 (2005): 95–104
'International Public Hearing on Crimes Related to Population Policies', *Re/productions*, 1 [no date]; see http://www.hsph.harvard.edu/grhf-asia/repro/gcspivak.html

Other Works

Aijaz Ahmad, *In Theory: Classes, Nations, Literatures* (London: Verso, 1992)
——, 'Reading Arundhati Roy Politically', *Frontline* (8 Aug 1997): 103–6
Farida Akhter, *Depopulating Bangladesh: Essays on the Politics of Fertility* (Dhaka: Narigrantha Prabartana, 1992)
Louis Althusser, 'Ideology and Ideological State Apparatuses', in *Lenin and Philosophy and Other Essays*, trans. Ben Brewster (New York: Monthly Review Press, 1971), 121–73
Shahid Amin and Dipesh Chakrabarty, eds, *Subaltern Studies IX* (New Delhi, Oxford University Press, 1996)
Emily Apter 'Afterlife of a Discipline', *Comparative Literature*, 57 (3) (summer 2005): 201–6
David Arnold, 'Gramsci and Peasant Subalternity in India', in *Mapping Subaltern Studies and the Postcolonial*, ed. Vinayak Chaturvedi (London: Verso, 2000), 24–49
David Arnold and David Hardiman, eds, *Subaltern Studies VIII: Essays in Honour of Ranajit Guha* (New Delhi: Oxford University Press, 1994)
Bill Ashcroft, *Postcolonial Transformation* (London: Routledge, 2001)
Bill Ashcroft, Alan Lawson and Helen Tiffin, *The Empire Writes Back* (London: Routledge, 1989)
Alain Badiou, *Ethics: An Essay on the Understanding of Evil*, trans. Peter Hallward (London: Verso, 2000)
Anne M. Bailey and Joseph R. Llobera, eds, *The Asiatic Mode of Production: Science and Politics* (London: Routledge and Kegan Paul, 1981)
Radhika Balakrishnan, ed., *The Hidden Assembly Line: Gender Dynamics of Subcontracted Work in a Global Economy* (Bloomfield, CT: Kumarian Press, 2002)
Tani E. Barlow, 'Not Really a Proper Intellectual Response: An Interview with Gayatri Spivak', *positions* 12 (1) (2004): 139–63
Ian Baucom, 'Cryptic, Withheld, Singular', *Nepantla: Views from South*, 1 (2) (2000): 413–29

Simone de Beauvoir, *The Second Sex* [1949], trans. H. M. Parshley (London: Picador, 1988)

Geoffrey Bennington, *Legislations: The Politics of Deconstruction* (London: Verso, 1994)

Robert Bernasconi and Tommy L. Lott, eds, *The Idea of Race* (Indianapolis: Hackett, 2000)

Charles Bernheimer, ed., *Comparative Literature in the Age of Multiculturalism* (Baltimore: Johns Hopkins University Press, 1995)

Homi Bhabha, *The Location of Culture* (London: Routledge, 1994) [incl. 'The Commitment to Theory', 1989]

Gautam Bhadra, Gyan Prakash and Susie Tharu, eds, *Subaltern Studies X* (New Delhi, Oxford University Press, 1999)

Rustom Bharucha, *Rehearsals of Revolution* (Honolulu: Hawaii University Press, 1983)

Chetan Bhatt, 'Kant's "Raw Man" and the Miming of Primitivism: Spivak's *Critique of Postcolonial Reason*', *Radical Philosophy*, 105 (2001): 37–44

Maurice Blanchot, *The Space of Literature* [1955], trans. Ann Smock (Lincoln and London: University of Nebraska Press, 1982)

——, *The Infinite Conversation* [1969], trans. Susan Hanson (Minneapolis: University of Minnesota Press, 1993)

John Brannigan, Ruth Robbins and Julian Wolfreys, eds, *Applying: To Derrida* (London: Macmillan, 1996)

Douglas Burnham, *An Introduction to Kant's Critique of Judgement* (Edinburgh: Edinburgh University Press, 2000)

Christopher Bush, 'Deaths of a Discipline', *Comparative Literature*, 57 (3) (summer 2005): 207–13

Judith Butler, *Gender Trouble: Feminism and the Subversion of Identity*, (London: Routledge, 1990)

——, *Bodies that Matter: On the Discursive Limits of 'Sex'* (London: Routledge, 1993)

John D. Caputo, *The Prayers and Tears of Jacques Derrida: Religion without Religion* (Bloomington: Indiana University Press, 1997)

Howard Caygill, *Art of Judgement* (Oxford: Blackwell, 1989)

Dipesh Chakrabarty, *Rethinking Working-Class History: Bengal 1890–1940* (Princeton, NJ: Princeton University Press, 1989)

——, *Provincializing Europe: Postcolonial Thought and Historical Difference* (Princeton, NJ: Princeton University Press, 2000)

——, *Habitations of Modernity: Essays in the Wake of Subaltern Studies* (Chicago: Chicago University Press, 2002)

Roland A. Champagne, '*Of Grammatology*', *The French Review*, 51 (5) (April 1978): 741–2

Partha Chatterjee and Gyanendra Pandey, eds, *Subaltern Studies VII* (New Delhi: Oxford University Press, 1992)

Rey Chow, *Ethics after Idealism: Theory-Culture-Ethnicity-Reading* (Bloomington and Indianapolis: Indiana University Press, 1998)

J. M. Coetzee, *Foe* (London: Martin Secker & Warburg, 1986)

G. A. Cohen, *Karl Marx's Theory of History: A Defence* (Oxford: Clarendon Press, 1978)

Miriam Cooke, *Women Claim Islam: Creating Islamic Feminism through Literature* (London: Routledge, 2001)

Harold Coward and Toby Forshay, eds, *Derrida and Negative Theology* (Albany: SUNY Press, 1992)

Simon Critchley, 'Das Ding: Lacan and Levinas', in *Ethics, Politics, Subjectivity* (London: Verso, 1999), 198–216

Hugh M. Davidson, 'Review of *Of Grammatology*', *Comparative Literature* 31 (2) (spring 1979): 167–9

Gilles Deleuze, *The Logic of Sense* [1969], ed. Constantin V. Boundas, trans. Mark Lester with Charles Stivale (New York: Columbia University Press, 1990)

Gilles Deleuze and Felix Guattari, *Anti-Oedipus: Capitalism and Schizophrenia* [1972], trans. Robert Hurley (London: Athlone, 1984)

Jacques Derrida, *Of Grammatology*, [1967], trans. Gayatri Chakravorty Spivak (Baltimore: Johns Hopkins, 1976)

——, *Positions* [1972], trans. Alan Bass (London: Athlone, 1981)

——, *Margins of Philosophy* [1967], trans. Alan Bass (London: Harvester Wheatsheaf, 1982) [incl. 'Différance', 1–28]

——, *Limited Inc.*, ed. Gerald Graff (Evanston, IL: Northwestern University Press, 1988) [incl. 'Signature Event Context', 1–24]

——, *Of Spirit: Heidegger and the Question* [1987], trans. Geoffrey Bennington and Rachel Bowlby (Chicago: Chicago University Press, 1989)

——, *Writing and Difference*, trans. Alan Bass (London: Routledge, 1990) [incl. 'Violence and Metaphysics', 79–153, and 'Freud and the Scene of Writing', 196–231]

——, *Spectres of Marx* [1993], trans. Peggy Kamuf (London: Routledge, 1994)

——, *A Derrida Reader*, ed. Peggy Kamuf (Hemel Hempstead: Harvester Wheatsheaf, 1991) [incl. 'Letter to a Japanese Friend', 270–6]

——, 'As *if* I were Dead: An Interview with Jacques Derrida', in *Applying to Derrida*, ed. John Brannigan, Ruth Robbins and Julian Wolfreys (London: Macmillan, 1996), 212–26.

——, *The Politics of Friendship* [1994], trans. George Collins (London: Verso, 1997)

——, 'Marx & Sons', in *Ghostly Demarcations: A Symposium on Jacques Derrida's 'Spectres of Marx'*, ed. Michael Sprinker (London: Verso, 1999), 213–69

Vijay Devedas and Brett Nicholls, 'Postcolonial Interventions: Gayatri Spivak, Three Wise Men and the Native Informant', *Critical Horizons* 3 (1) (2002): 73–101

Mahasweta Devi, *Imaginary Maps: Three Stories*, trans. Gayatri Chakravorty Spivak (New York and London: Routledge, 1995)

Arif Dirlik, 'The Postcolonial Aura: Third World Criticism in the Age of Multinational Capitalism', *Critical Inquiry*, 20 (winter 1994): 328–56

Assia Djebar, *Fantasia: An Algerian Calvacade* [1985], trans. Dorothy S. Blair (Portsmouth, NH: Heinemann, 1993)

Denis Donoghue, 'Review of *Of Grammatology*', *New Republic* 176 (16) (16 April 1977): 32–4

Stephen Dunn, *The Fall and Rise of the Asiatic Mode of Production* (London: Routledge and Kegan Paul, 1982)

Terry Eagleton, *Literary Theory: An Introduction* (Oxford: Blackwell, 1983)

——, 'In the Gaudy Supermarket', *London Review of Books*, 21 (10) (1999): 3, 5–6

Jon Elster, *An Introduction to Karl Marx* (Cambridge: Cambridge University Press, 1990)

Mary Lou Emery, *Jean Rhys at World's End* (Austin: University of Texas Press, 1990)

Rayah Feldman, 'Reply to Gayatri Chakravorty Spivak', *Women against Fundamentalisms*, 7 (1995): 3–4; see http://waf.gn.apc.org/journal7p3.htm

Michel Foucault, *Society Must Be Defended* [1997], trans. David Macey (London: Allen Lane, 2003)

Sigmund Freud, *The Interpretation of Dreams* [1900], in SE, vol. V (London: Hogarth Press, 1955)

——, 'On the Universal Tendency to Debasement in the Sphere of Love Contribution to the Psychology of Love II' [1912], in SE, vol. XI (London, Hogarth Press, 1953), 125–46

——, ' "A Child is being Beaten": A Contribution to the Study of the Origin of Sexual Perversions' [1919], in SE, vol. XVII (London: Hogarth Press, 1955), 175–204

Rodolphe Gasché, *The Tain of the Mirror: Derrida and the Philosophy of Reflection* (Cambridge, Mass.: Harvard University Press, 1986)

——, *Inventions of Difference: On Jacques Derrida* (Harvard: Harvard University Press, 1994) [incl. 'God, for Example', 150–70]

——, *The Wild Card of Reading: On Paul de Man* (Cambridge, Mass.: Harvard University Press, 1998)

Jeremy Gilbert, 'A Class Performance: Why the Class Struggle was a Really Good Idea', Paper presented at the Translating Class, Altering Hospitality Conference, Centre for Cultural Analysis, Theory and History, University of Leeds, June 2002

Antonio Gramsci, *Selections from Prison Notebooks* [1929–35], trans. and ed. Quintin Hoare and Geoffrey Nowell Smith (London: Lawrence and Wishart, 1971) [incl. 'Notes on Italian History', 44–120]

——, *Selections from the Political Writings (1921–1926)*, trans. and ed. Quintin Hoare (Lawrence and Wishart, 1978) [incl. 'Some Aspects of the Southern Question', 441–62]

Ranajit Guha, ed., *Subaltern Studies: Writings on South Asian History and Society, I–VI* (Delhi: Oxford University Press, 1982–9) [incl. Guha, 'On Some Aspects of the Historiography of Colonial India', vol. I, 1–8]

——, *Elementary Aspects of Peasant Insurgency in Colonial India* (Durham and London: Duke University Press, 1999)

Peter Hallward, *Absolutely Postcolonial: Between the Singular and the Specific* (Manchester: Manchester University Press, 2002)

——, *Alain Badiou: A Subject to Truth* (Minneapolis and London: University of Minnesota Press, 2003)

Michael Hardt and Antonio Negri, *Empire* (Cambridge, Mass.: Harvard University Press, 2000)

Barbara Harlow, *Resistance Literature* (New York: Methuen, 1987)

Irene E. Harvey, *Derrida and the Economy of Différance* (Bloomington: Indiana University Press, 1986)

Eric Haynot, ' "The Slightness of my Endeavour": An Interview with Gayatri Spivak', *Comparative Literature*, 57 (3) (summer 2005): 219–26

Marie-Aimée Hélie-Lucas, 'Bound and Gagged by the Family Code', in *Third World, Second Sex*, ed. Miranda Davies, vol. II (London: Zed Books, 1987), 3–15

Leslie Hill, *Blanchot: Extreme Contemporary* (London: Routledge, 1997)

Barry Hindess and Paul Q. Hirst, *Pre-Capitalist Modes of Production* (London: Routledge and Kegan Paul, 1975)

David Huddart, 'The Foreignness of Autobiography: Inventing Postcolonial Beginnings', PhD dissertation, University of Sussex, 2001

——, 'Making an Example out of Spivak', *Angelaki: Journal of the Theoretical Humanities*, 6 (2001): 35–46

Peter Hulme, 'The Locked Heart: The Creole Family Romance of *Wide Sargasso Sea*', in *Colonial Discourse/Postcolonial Theory*, ed. Francis Barker, Peter Hulme and Margaret Iversen (Manchester and New York: Manchester University Press, 1994), 72–88

Immanuel Kant, *A Critique of Pure Reason* [1781, 2/1787], trans. Norman Kemp Smith (London: Macmillan, 1929)

——, *Critique of Judgement* [1790], trans. Werner S. Pluhar (Indianapolis: Hackett Publishing, 1987) [Part II: 'Critique of Teleological Judgement', 1790]

——, 'Religion within the Boundaries of Mere Reason' [1793], in *The Cambridge Edition of the Works of Immanuel Kant*, ed. Allen W. Wood and George Di Giovanni (Cambridge: Cambridge University Press, 1996)

Thomas Keenan, *Fables of Responsibility: Aberrations and Predicaments in Ethics and Politics* (Stanford: Stanford University Press, 1997)

Thomas Kemple, *Reading Marx Writing: Melodrama, the Market and the 'Grundrisse'* (Stanford: Stanford University Press, 1995)

Naomi Klein, *No Logo* (London: Flamingo, 2000)

Sarah Kofman, *The Enigma of Woman* [1980], trans. Catherine Porter (Ithaca, NY: Cornell University Press, 1985)

Jacques Lacan, 'A Love Letter' [1975], in *Feminine Sexuality*, ed. Juliet Mitchell and Jacqueline Rose (Basingstoke: Macmillan, 1982), 137–61

——, *The Seminar of Jacques Lacan, Book I: Freud's Papers on Technique*, trans. John Forrester (New York and London: Norton, 1988)

Ernesto Laclau and Chantal Mouffe, *Hegemony and Socialist Strategy* (London: Verso, 1985)

Neil Larsen, *Determinations: Essays on Theory, Narrative and Nation in the Americas* (London and New York: Verso, 2001)

Marnia Lazreg, *The Eloquence of Silence: Algerian Women in Question* (London: Routledge, 1994)

Jerry D. Leonard, 'Reducing Spivak: Marxism, Deconstruction and the Post-Theoretical Mystique', PhD dissertation, University of Wisconsin-Milwaukee, 1996

——, 'Chapter 1: Whose Imprimatur?', *Cultural Logic* (2005); see http://eserver.org/clogic/leonard.html

Philip Leonard, *Nationality between Poststructuralism and Postcolonial Theory: A New Cosmopolitanism* (Basingstoke: Palgrave Macmillan, 2005)

Emmanuel Levinas, *Totality and Infinity: An Essay on Exteriority* [1961], trans. Alphonso Lingis (Pittsburgh: Duquesne University Press, 1969)

——, *Otherwise than Being, or Beyond Essence* [1974], trans. Alphonso Lingis (The Hague: Martinus Nijhoff, 1981)

John Llewellyn, *Derrida on the Threshold of Sense* (London: Macmillan, 1986)

Lisa Lowe, *Critical Terrains* (Ithaca, NY: Cornell University Press, 2001)

Laura E. Lyons and Cynthia Franklin, ' "On the Cusp of the Personal and the Impersonal": An Interview with Gayatri Chakravarty Spivak', *Biography: An Interdisciplinary Quarterly*, 27 (1) (winter 2004): 203–21

Jean François Lyotard, *The Différend: Phrases in Dispute* [1983], trans. Georges Van den Abbeele (Manchester: Manchester University Press, 1988)

Thomas Babington Macaulay, *Speeches by Lord Macaulay, with his Minute on Indian Education*, selected, with an introduction and notes, by G. M. Young (London: World's Classics, 1935)

Martin McQuillan, *Paul de Man* (London: Routledge, 2001)

Paul de Man, *Allegories of Reading: Figural Language in Rousseau, Nietzsche, Rilke, and Proust* (New Haven and London: Yale University Press, 1979)

——, *Blindness and Insight: Essays in the Rhetoric of Contemporary Criticism* [1977] (London: Methuen, 1983)

——, *The Resistance to Theory* (Minneapolis: University of Minnesota Press, 1986)

——, *Aesthetic Ideology* (Minneapolis: University of Minnesota Press, 1996)

Lata Mani, *Contentious Traditions: The Debate on Sati in Colonial India* (Berkeley: University of California Press, 1998)

Karl Marx, *Grundrisse* [1941], trans. Martin Nicholaus (Harmondsworth: Penguin, 1973)

——, *Surveys from Exile*, trans. and ed. David Fernbach (Harmondsworth: Pelican, 1973)

——, *Early Writings*, trans. Rodney Livingstone and Gregor Benton (Harmondsworth: Penguin, 1975)

——, *Capital*, 3 vols [1867–94; vols II and III ed. Friedrich Engels]: vol. I, trans. David Fernbach (Harmondsworth: Pelican, 1976); vol. II, trans. David Fernbach (Harmondsworth: Pelican, 1972) vol. III, trans. Ben Fowkes (London: Pelican, 1981)

——, *Selected Writings*, ed. David McLellan (Oxford: Oxford University Press, 1977)

——, 'The British Rule in India', in *Archives of Empire* vol. I, ed. Barbara Harlow and Mia Carter (Durham, NC: Duke University Press, 2003), 117–23

Karl Marx and Friedrich Engels *Marx-Engels-Werke*, Band 3 (Berlin: Dietz Verlag, 1962)

——, '"Indian Ink": Colonialism and the Figurative Strategy of *Jane Eyre*', in *Imperialism at Home: Race and Victorian Women's Fiction* (Ithaca, NY: Cornell University Press, 1996), 60–95

Chandra Talpade Mohanty, *Feminism without Borders: Decolonizing Theory, Practicing Solidarity* (London and Durham: Duke University Press, 2003) [incl. 'Women Workers and the Politics of Solidarity', 139–68]

Bart Moore-Gilbert, *Postcolonial Theory: Contexts, Practices, Politics* (London: Verso, 1997)

Stephen Morton, *Gayatri Chakravorty Spivak* (London: Routledge, 2002)

John Mowitt, *Text: Genealogy of an Antidisciplinary Object* (Durham, NC: Duke University Press, 1992)

Anuradha Dingwaney Needham, '"The Small Voice of History" in Arundahti Roy's *The God of Small Things*', *Interventions* 7 (3) (2005): 369–91

Benita Parry, 'Problems in Current Theories of Colonial Discourse', *Oxford Literary Review*, 9 (1987): 27–58

Carl Pletsch, 'The Three Worlds, or the Division of Social Scientific Labor 1950–1975', *Comparative Studies in Society and History*, 23 (4) (October 1981): 565–90

Pseudo-Dionysius, 'The Divine Names', in *The Complete Works*, trans. Colm Luibheid (London: SPCK, 1987), 47–132

Forest Pyle, '"By a Certain Subreption": Gayatri Spivak and the Lever of the Aesthetic', *Interventions*, 4 (2) (2002): 186–90

Bruce Robbins, 'The Sweatshop Sublime', *Publications of the Modern Language Association of America*, 117 (2002): 84–97

Caroline Rooney, *African Literature, Animism and Politics* (London: Routledge, 2000)

Arundahti Roy, *The God of Small Things* (New York: Random House, 1997)

Santi Rozario, 'The Feminist Debate on Reproductive Rights and Issues of Contraception in Bangladesh', *re/productions* Issue 1, 1997; see http://www.hsph.harvard.edu/Organizations/healthnet/Sasia/repro/rozario1.html

Edward Said, *Orientalism: Western Conceptions of the Orient* (London: Routledge Kegan Paul, 1978)

Mark Sanders, 'Postcolonial Reading', *Postmodern Culture*, 10 (1) (1999); see http://muse.jhu.edu/journals/pmc/v010/10.1.r_sanders.html

——, 'Representation: Reading Otherwise', *Interventions: An International Journal of Postcolonial Studies*, 4 (2) (2002): 198–204

——, *Complicities: The Intellectual and Apartheid* (Durham, NC: Duke University Press, 2002)

Sumit Sarkar, 'The Conditions and Nature of Subaltern Militancy: Bengal from Swadeshi to Non-Co-operation, *c*. 1905–22', in *Subaltern Studies III*, ed. Ranajit Guha (New Delhi: Oxford University Press, 1984), 271–320

——, *Writing Social History* (Delhi, Oxford University Press, 2000)

Saskia Sassen, *Globalization and its Discontents* (New York: The New Press, 1998)

Ferdinand de Saussure, *Course in General Linguistics* [1922], trans. Roy Harris (London: Duckworth, 1998)

Haun Saussy, 'Chiasmus', *Comparative Literature*, 57 (3) (summer 2005): 233–8

Corinne Scheiner, '*Teleiopoesis, Telepoesis*, and the Practice of Comparative Literature', *Comparative Literature*, 57 (3) (summer 2005): 239–45

Alfred Schmitt, *The Concept of Nature in Marx* [1962], trans. Ben Fowkes (London: New Left Books, 1971)

Vikram Seth, *Beastly Tales from Here and There* [1991] (London: Phoenix, 1993)

Sandhya Shetty, '(Dis)figuring the Nation: Mother, Metaphor, Metonymy', *differences* 7 (3) (1995): 50–79

Sandyha Shetty and Elisabeth Jane Bellamy, 'Postcolonialism's Archive Fever (Derrida, Spivak)', *Diacritics: a Review of Contemporary Criticism*, 30 (2000): 25–48

Tobin Siebers, 'Ethics in the Age of Rousseau: From Lévi-Strauss to Derrida', *Modern Language Notes*, 100 (4) (1985): 758–79

Simon Swift, ' "Can the Subaltern Speak?": A Critique of Rhetoric and Politics in the Work of Gayatri Spivak', masters dissertation, University of Leeds, 1998

——, 'Kant, Herder, and the Question of Philosophical Anthropology', *Textual Practice*, 19 (2) (2005): 219–38

——, *Romanticism, Literature and Philosophy: Expressive Rationality in Rousseau, Kant, Wollstonecraft and Contemporary Theory* (London and New York: Continuum, 2006)

Michael Taussig, *The Devil and Commodity Fetishism* (Chapel Hill, NC: University of North Carolina Press, 1980)

Gauri Viswanathan, *Masks of Conquest: Literary Study and British Rule in India* (London: Faber, 1990)

Merold Westphal, *Transcendence and Self-Transcendence: On God and Soul* (Bloomington and Indianapolis: Indiana University Press, 2004)

Karl A. Wittfogel, *Oriental Despotism: A Comparative Study of Power* (New Haven: Yale University Press, 1957)

Allen W. Wood, *Kant's Ethical Thought* (Cambridge: Cambridge University Press, 1999)

Meyda Yegenoglu and Mahmut Mutman, 'Mapping the Present: Interview with Gayatri Spivak', *New Formations*, 45 (2002): 9–23

Robert J. C. Young, *Postcolonialism: An Historical Introduction* (Oxford: Blackwell, 2001)

Index